OF HE[illegible]Z AS WRITTEN BY HIMSELF IN HIS LETTERS AND MEMOIRS

HECTOR BERLIOZ

ZINC READ

Published by
This edition copyright © 2024 by Zinc Read
Design and setting By Zinc Read
Email- zincread@gmail.com
ISBN-978-93-6360-858-0

CONTENTS

INTRODUCTION

AUTOBIOGRAPHY is open to the charge of egoism; somewhat unjustly since, in writing of oneself, the personal note must predominate and, in the case of a genius--sure of his goal and of his power to reach it--faith in himself amounts to what, in a smaller man, would be mere conceit.

This must be condoned and discounted for the sake of the priceless gift of insight into a personality of exceptional interest.

Berlioz' Memoir, graphic as it is, cannot be called satisfactory as a character-study. He says plainly that he is not writing confessions, but is simply giving a correct account of his life to silence the many false versions current at the time. Therefore, while describing almost too minutely some of his difficulties and most of his conflicts--whereby he gives the impression of living in uncomfortably hot water--his very real heroism comes out only in his Letters, and then quite unconsciously.

The Memoir and Letters combined, however, make up an interesting and fascinating picture of the heights, depths, limitations and curious inconsistencies of this weird and restless human being.

The music-ridden, brutal, undisciplined creature of the Autobiography--more a blind, unreasoning force of Nature than an ordinary being, subject to the restrictions of common humanity--could not possibly be the man who was rich in the unswerving affection of such widely different characters as Heine, Liszt, Ernst, Alexandre, Heller, Hiller, Jules Janin, Dumas and Bertin; there must be something unchronicled to account for their loyalty and patience. This something is revealed in the Letters.

There stands the real Berlioz--musician and poet; eager to drain life to the dregs, be they sweet or bitter, to taste the fulness of being. There we find a faithful record of thoughts, feelings, aspirations, and a reflection of every passing mood. With one notable exception: even to Ferrand he never admitted that the poor reception of *The Trojans* (for it met with but a *succes d'estime*) broke his heart.

* * * * *

As a record of events the Autobiography is deficient, and after 1848 becomes a mere sketch. Thus, while writing pages of description of orchestral players and musical institutions in German and Austrian cities--quite suitable to his newspaper articles, but wearisome in their iteration, and throwing no light upon himself--he is almost entirely silent on his later trips to London. And the visits to Baden--brightest days of his later years--are dismissed in a footnote.

He lingers pathetically over young days, and hurries through the dreary time close at hand. So, for a record of the daily conflict with physical pain; of the overshadowed domestic life--none the easier to bear in that it was partly his own fault; of the grinding, ever-present shortness of money; of his wild and beautiful dreams; and of the large place that Ferrand, Morel, Massart, Damcke and Lwoff (many of whom are not named in the memoir) held in his heart--we turn to the Letters.

The fearless, unbroken affection for his Jonathan--Humbert Ferrand; the passionate love for his only son, mingled with impatience at Louis' youthful instability; the whole-hearted ungrudging appreciation he extended to young and honest musicians--particularly to Camille Saint-Saens--are a grateful contrast to the gloomy defiance, tornado-like fury, and eternal jeremiads over the hypocrisy and hollowness of Paris that mar the Memoir.

* * * * *

Of his ill-starred first marriage he says but little, either in Memoir or Letters.

He and Miss Smithson were far too highly-strung for peaceful life to be possible, even without the added friction of ill-health, want of money (which, however, he says never daunted her), and the probable misunderstandings so likely to arise from their different nationalities.

It may be due to his special form of artistic temperament--that well-worn apology for everything *deregle*--that he could find room in his heart, or head, for more than one love at a time, and could even analyse and classify each.

Within a month he bounds from the nethermost despair over the uncertainties of his English divinity to the highest rapture over his Camille, his Ariel, as he calls Marie Pleyel.

Later on, when Marie is safely disposed of and Henriette is again in the ascendant, while she vacillates between family and lover, he seriously contemplates running off to Berlin with a poor girl whom he has befriended, and whom, when Henriette finally relents, he calmly hands over to Jules Janin to provide for.

Of his second wife we hear but little, except that even affection did not blind him to the defects in her musical gifts. For, on his first German tour, he wrote to Morel:

"Pity me! Marie wished to sing at Stuttgart, Mannheim Hechingen. The two first were bearable, but the last!... Yet she would not hear of my engaging another singer."

Then he incidentally and whimsically mentions an innocent embryo love-affair in Russia, and, in 1863, makes such tragic and mysterious reference to an impossible love, that Ferrand, seriously alarmed, thinks that Louis must have become more than usually troublesome.

The influence of Estelle Fournier, which pervaded his whole life, comes under a different category. He was without religion; she supplied its place. She was his dream-lady, the Beatrice to his Dante, that necessary worship which no great soul can forego. The proof of this is that, when he met her again--old, sweet, dignified and still beautiful to him--his allegiance never wavered; she was still the Mountain Star of his childhood's days.

If his capacity for love was unlimited, it was not so with his sense of humour, which was curiously circumscribed. Occasionally he rivals Heine in power of seeing the odd side of his own divagations; his account of his headlong flight from Rome to murder the whole erring Moke family is inimitable. Yet he never discovers--as a man with a true sense of humour would have done--that, in sharpening his rapier on Wagner and the Music of the Future, he is meting out to a struggling composer precisely the same measure that the Parisians had meted out to himself. It speaks volumes for the strength of his friendship with Liszt that even Wagnerism could not divide them.

* * * * *

La Cote Saint-Andre is a large village some thirty odd miles from Grenoble; here, in a handsome house in the Rue de la Republique, Louis Hector Berlioz was born. His home education and seclusion from healthy school-life and the society of other children of his age ill-fitted him for the battle of life, which began with his medical student career in Paris.

He describes the quarrels with his parents and stoppage of his allowance in 1826, but passes lightly over the privations and semi-starvation that undoubtedly laid the foundations of that internal disease which embittered his latter years. His graphic account of those early Parisian days is one of the most interesting parts of the Memoir. He declared that his time in Italy, after gaining the Prix de Rome, was musically barren. Yet this must be a mistake, since, to the memory of his mountain wanderings he owed the inspiration of *Harold*. And even if he apparently gained nothing in music, the experience of what to avoid and the influence of beautiful scenery--to which he was always peculiarly sensitive--counted for much in his general development.

With his return to Paris his character took form, and he began his life-long warfare against shams and empiricism. Newspaper work, hated as it was, had a great share in moulding him. Each year he grew more autocratic, and each year more hated for his uncompromising sledge-hammer speech. But Ferrand was correct in saying that he could write. His style is clear, incisive, perfect and even elegant French, although, naturally, owing to the exigencies of its production, it is often unequal. The first years of his marriage were ideal in spite of their penury. The young couple had a coterie of choice friends, amongst whom Liszt took a foremost place, but gradually the clouds gathered, the rift within the lute widened, until a separation became inevitable; even then Berlioz does not attempt--as so many men of his impatient spirit might have done--to shirk responsibility and throw upon others the burden of his hostage to fortune--an unsympathetic invalid--but works the harder at his literary tread-mill to provide her indispensable comforts. Poor Henriette's side of the story is untold, and one can but say:

"The pity of it!"

His troubles in Paris and the triumphs abroad that were their antidote made up the rest of his stormy, restless pilgrimage; yet even in ungrateful Paris he was not entirely neglected.

He received the Legion of Honour, and although professing to despise it, he always wore the ribbon. He was also chosen one of the Immortals, apropos of which M. Alexandre tells a funny story.

Alexandre was canvassing for him and found great difficulty in managing Adolph Adam, who was from Berlioz as the poles asunder.

First he went to Berlioz, who had flatly refused to make the slightest concession to Adam's prejudices.

"Come," said he, "do at least be amiable to Adam; you cannot deny that he is a musician, at any rate."

"I don't say he is not; but, being a great musician, how can he lower himself to comic-opera? If he chose he could *write such music as I do*."

Undismayed, Alexandre went to Adam.

"You will give your vote to Berlioz, will you not, dear friend? Although you cannot appreciate each other, you will own that he is a thorough musician."

"Certainly, he is a great musician, a really great one, but his music is awfully tiresome. Why!"--and little Adam straightened his spectacles--

"why, if he chose he could compose ... as well as I do. But, seriously, he is a man of some importance, and I promise that, after Clapisson, who already has our votes, Berlioz shall have the next vacancy."

By a strange coincidence, the next *fauteuil* was Adam's own, to which Berlioz was elected by nineteen votes.

In his weak state of health, Berlioz was quite unfit to face the innumerable worries incidental to the production of *The Trojans*. For seven years it had been his chief object in life, and if, as he said, he could have had everything requisite at his command, with unlimited capital to draw upon--as Wagner had with Louis of Bavaria--all might have been well. But to fight, contrive, temporise and propitiate all at once was more than his enfeebled frame and irascible spirit could stand.

Hence his great injustice to Carvalho, who, for Art's sake, sacrificed money, time and reputation to an extent that crippled him for many years.

Embittered by the failure of his opera, which ran for about twenty-five nights, he shut himself up in his rooms with Madame Recio, his devoted mother-in-law, and an old servant, and from that time visited only a few intimate friends.

One last shock Fate held in store. Louis died of fever abroad, and for his lonely father life had no more savour--he simply existed, with, however, two last flashes of the old bright flame. One when, at Herbeck's desire, he went to Vienna to conduct the *Damnation de Faust*, and the other when the Grand Duchess Helen prevailed on him to visit St Petersburg again.

That was the real end.

On leaving Russia he wandered drearily to Nice--a ghost revisiting its old-time haunts--then made one last appearance at Grenoble, and so the flame went out. He who had never peace in life was at rest at last.

* * * * *

Of his music this is not the place to speak. He has fully described his own ideas, others have analysed them, and we are now concerned with the man himself.

To this is due the somewhat disjointed form of the translation--the mixture of Memoir and Letters. It seemed the only possible way of showing Berlioz in all his aspects and of keeping the record chronologically correct.

Yet we could wish that he, who had so much affinity with England and its literature, could meet with due appreciation here.

He has founded no school (in spite of Krebs' prophecy), unless the "programme music" now so much in vogue can be traced back to him, but, beginning with Wagner, every orchestral composer since his day owes him a debt of gratitude for his discoveries--his daring and original combinations of instruments, and his magnificent grouping and handling of vast bodies of executants.

I

LA COTE SAINT-ANDRE

DECIDEDLY ours is a prosaic century. On no other grounds can my wounded vanity account for the humiliating fact that no auspicious omens, no mighty portents--such as heralded the birth of the great men of the golden age of poetry--gave notice of my coming. It is strange, but true, that I was born, quite unobtrusively, at La Cote Saint-Andre, between Vienne and Grenoble, on the 11th December 1803.

As its name implies, La Cote Saint-Andre lies on a hillside overlooking a plain--wide, green, and golden--of which the dreamy majesty is accentuated by the mountain belt that bounds it on the southeast, being in turn crowned by the mystic glory of distant Alpine glaciers and snowy peaks.

Needless to say, I was brought up in the Catholic faith. This--of all religions the most charming, since it gave up burning people--was for seven years the joy of my life, and although we have since fallen out, I still retain my tender memories of it.

Indeed, so greatly am I in sympathy with its creed that, had I had the misfortune to be born in the clutches of one of the dreary schisms hatched by Luther and Calvin, I should certainly, at the first awakening of my poetic instinct, have thrown off its benumbing grasp and have flung myself into the arms of the fair Roman.

My sweet remembrance of my first communion is probably due to my having made it with my elder sister at the Ursuline convent, where she was a boarder.

At early morn, accompanied by the almoner, I made my way to that holy house. The soft spring sunlight, the murmuring poplars swaying in the whispering breeze, the dainty fragrance of the morning air, all worked upon my sensitive mind, until, as I knelt among those fair white maidens, and heard their fresh young voices raised in the eucharistic hymn, my whole soul was filled with mystic passion. Heaven opened before me--a heaven of love and pure delight, a thousand times more glorious than tongue has told--and thus I gave myself to God.

Such is the marvellous power of genuine melody, of heart-felt expression! Ten years later I recognised that air--so innocently adapted to a religious ceremony--as "When my beloved shall return," from d'Aleyrac's opera *Nina*.

Dear, dead d'Aleyrac! Even your name is forgotten now!

This was my musical awakening.

Thus abruptly I became a saint, and such a desperate saint! Every day I went to mass, every Sunday I took the communion, every week I went to confession in order to say to my director:

"Father, I have done nothing."

"Well, my son," would the worthy man reply, "continue."

I followed his advice strictly for many years.

Louis Berlioz, my father, was a doctor. It is not my place to sing his praises. I need, therefore, only say that he was looked upon as an honoured friend, not only in our little town, but throughout the whole country side. Feeling acutely his responsibility as the steward of a difficult and dangerous profession, every minute he could spare from his sick people was given to arduous study, and never did the thought of gain turn him aside from his disinterested service to the poor and needy.

In 1810, the medical society of Montpellier offered a prize for the best treatise on a new and important point in medicine, which was gained by my father's monograph on Chronic Diseases. It was printed in Paris, and many of its theories adopted by physicians, who had not the common honesty to acknowledge their source. This somewhat surprised my dear, unsophisticated father, but he only said, "If truth prevails, nothing else matters."

Now (I write in 1848) he has long since ceased to practise, and spends his time in reading and peaceful thought.

Of the highest type of liberal mind, he is entirely without social, political, or religious prejudices; for instance, having promised my mother to leave my faith undisturbed, I have known him carry his tolerance so far as to hear me my catechism. This is considerably more, I must own, than I could do were my own son in question.

For many years my father has suffered from an incurable disease of the stomach. He scarcely eats at all, and nothing but constant and increasing doses of opium keep him alive. He has told me that, years ago, worn out by the prolonged agony, he took thirty-two grains at once.

"It was not as a cure that I took it," he said, significantly.

But, strange to say, this terrific dose of poison, instead of killing him, gave him for some time a respite from his sufferings.

When I was ten years old he sent me to a priest's school in the town to learn Latin, but the result not proving satisfactory he resolved to teach me himself.

And with the most untiring patience, the most intense care, my father became my instructor in history, literature, languages, geography--even in music.

Yet I must own that I do not think a solitary education like mine half as good for a boy as ordinary school life. Children brought up among relations, servants, and specially chosen friends only, do not get accustomed to the rough-and-tumble that best fits them to face the world. Real life is to them a dosed book, their angles are not rubbed off, and I know that, in my own case, at twenty-five I was still nothing but an awkward, ignorant child.

Indulgent as my father was over my work, yet, for a long while, he was unable to make me love the classics. It seemed impossible to me to concentrate my thoughts long enough to learn by heart a few lines of Horace and Virgil; impatient of the beaten track my wayward mind flew off to the entrancing unknown world of the atlas, roving gaily through the labyrinth of islands, capes, and straits of the Pacific and the Indian Archipelago. This was the origin of my love for travel and adventure.

My father truly said of me:

"He knows every isle of the South Seas, but cannot tell me how many departments there are in France!"

Every book of travel in the library was pressed into my service, and I should most certainly have run away to sea if we had lived in a seaport. My son inherits my taste. He chose the navy for his profession long ere he saw the sea. May he do honour to his choice!

However, in the end the love of poetry and appreciation of its beauty awoke in me. The first spark of passion that fired my heart and imagination was kindled by Virgil's magnificent epic, and I well remember how my voice broke as I tried to construe aloud the fourth book of the AEneid. One day, stumbling along, I came to the passage where Dido--the presents of AEneas heaped around her--gives up her life upon the funeral pyre; the agony of the dying queen, the cries of her sister, her nurse, her women; the horror of that scene that struck pity even to the hearts of the Immortals, all rose so vividly before me that my lips trembled, my words came more and more indistinctly, and at the line--

"Quaesivit coelo lucem ingemuitque reperta,"

I stopped dead.

Then my dear father's delicate tact stepped in. Apparently noticing nothing, he said, gently:

"That will do for to-day, my boy; I am tired."

And I tore away to give vent to my Virgilian misery unmolested.

II

ESTELLE

WILL it be credited that when I was only twelve years old, and even before I fell under the spell of music, I became the victim of that cruel passion so well described by the Mantuan?

My mother's father, who bore a name immortalised by Scott--Marmion--lived at Meylan, about seven miles from Grenoble. This district, with its scattered hamlets, the valley of the winding Isere, the Dauphiny mountains that here join a spur of the Alps, is one of the most romantic spots I know. Here my mother, my sisters, and I usually passed three weeks towards the end of summer.

Now and then my uncle, Felix Marmion, who followed the fiery track of the great Emperor, would pay a flying visit during our stay, wreathed with cannon smoke and ornamented with a fine sabre cut across the face. He was then only adjutant-major in the Lancers; but young, gallant, ready to lay down his life for one look from his leader, he believed the throne of Napoleon as stable as Mont Blanc. His taste for music made him a great addition to our gay little circle, for he both sang and played the violin well.

High over Meylan, niched in a crevice of the mountain, stands a small white house, half-hidden amidst its vineyards and gardens, behind which rise the woods, the barren hills, a ruined tower, and St Eynard--a frowning mass of rock.

This sweet secluded spot, evidently predestined to romance, was the home of Madame Gautier, who lived there with two nieces, of whom the younger was called Estelle. Her name at once caught my attention from its being that of the heroine of Florian's pastoral *Estelle and Nemorin*, which I had filched from my father's library, and read a dozen times in secret.

Estelle was just eighteen--tall, graceful, with large, grave, questioning eyes that yet could smile, hair worthy to ornament the helmet of Achilles, and feet--I will not say Andalusian, but pure Parisian, and on those little feet she wore ... pink slippers!

Never before had I seen pink slippers. Do not smile; I have forgotten the colour of her hair (I fancy it was black), yet, never do I recall Estelle but, in company with the flash of her large eyes, comes the twinkle of her dainty pink shoes. I had been struck by lightning. To say I loved her comprises everything. I hoped for, expected, knew nothing but that I was wretched, dumb, despairing. By night I suffered agonies, by day I wandered alone through the fields of Indian corn, or sought, like a wounded bird, the deepest recesses of my grandfather's orchard.

Jealousy--dread comrade of love--seized me at the least word spoken by a man to my divinity; even now I shudder at the clank of a spur, remembering the noise of my uncle's while dancing with her.

Every one in the neighbourhood laughed at the piteously precocious child, torn by his obsession. Perhaps Estelle laughed too, for she soon guessed all.

One evening, I remember, there was a party at Madame Gautier's, and we played prisoner's base. The men were bidden choose their partners, and I was purposely told to choose first. But I dared not, my heart-beats choked me; I lowered my eyes unable to speak. They were beginning to tease me when Estelle, smiling down from her beauteous height, caught my hand, saying:

"Come! I will begin; I choose Monsieur Hector."

But ah! she laughed!

Does time heal all wounds; do other loves efface the first? Alas, no! With me time is powerless. Nothing wipes out the memory of my first love.

I was thirteen when we parted. I was thirty when, returning from Italy, I passed near St Eynard again. My eyes filled with tears at the sight of the little white house--the ruined tower. I loved her still!

On reaching home I heard that she was married; but even that could not cure me. A few days later my mother said:

"Hector, will you take this letter to the coach-office. It is for a lady who will be in the Vienne diligence. While they change horses ask the guard for Madame F., give her this letter, and look carefully at her. You may recognise her, although you have not met for seventeen years."

Without suspicion I went on my errand and asked for Madame F. "I am she, Monsieur," said a voice that thrilled my heart. "It is Estelle," said my heart. Estelle! still lovely, still the nymph, the hamadryad of Meylan's green slopes. Still lovely with her proud carriage, her glorious hair, her dazzling smile. But ah! where were the little pink shoes? She took the letter. Did she know me? I could not tell, but I returned home quite upset by the meeting. My mother smiled at me.

"So Nemorin has not forgotten his Estelle," she said. *His* Estelle! Mother! mother! was that trick quite fair?

* * * * *

With love came music; when I say music I mean composition, for of course I had long since been able to sing at sight and to play two instruments, thanks, needless to say, to my father's teaching.

Rummaging one day in a drawer, I unearthed a flageolet, on which I at once tried to pick out "Malbrook." Driven nearly mad by my squeaks, my father begged me to leave him in peace until he had time to teach me the proper fingering of the melodious instrument, and the right notes of the martial song I had pitched on. At the end of two days I was able to regale the family with my noble tune.

Now, how strikingly this shows my marvellous aptitude for wind instruments. What a fruitful subject for a born biographer!

My father next taught me to read music, explaining the signs thoroughly, and soon after he gave me a flute. At this I worked so hard that in seven or eight months I could play quite fairly.

Wishing to encourage my talent, he persuaded several well-to-do families of La Cote to join together and engage a music-master from Lyons. He was successful in getting a second violin, named Imbert, to leave the Theatre des Celestins and settle in our outlandish little town to try and musicalise the inhabitants, on condition that we guaranteed a certain number of pupils and a fixed salary for conducting the band of the National Guard.

I improved fast, for I had two lessons a day; having also a pretty soprano voice I soon developed into a pleasant singer, a bold reader, and was able to play Drouet's most intricate flute concertos. My master had a son a few years older than myself, a clever horn-player, with whom I became great friends. One day, as I was leaving for Meylan, he came to see me.

"Were you going without saying good-bye?" he asked. "You may never see me again."

His gravity struck me at the moment, but the joy of seeing Meylan and my glorious *Stella montis* quite put him out of my head. But on my return home my friend was gone; he had hanged himself the very day I left, and no one has ever been able to discover why. It was a sad home-coming for me!

Among some old books I found d'Alembert's edition of Rameau's *Harmony*, and how many weary hours did I not spend over those laboured theories, trying vainly to evolve some sense out of the disconnected ideas. Small wonder that I did not succeed, seeing that one needs to be a past master of counterpoint and acoustics before one can possibly grasp the author's meaning. It is a treatise on harmony for the use of those only who know all about it already.

However, I thought I could compose, and began by trying arrangements of trios and quartettes that were simply chaos, without form, cohesion, or common sense. Then, quite undaunted, I listened carefully to the quartettes by Pleyel, that our music-lovers performed on Sundays, and studied Catel's *Harmony*, which I managed to buy. Suddenly I rent asunder the veil of the inmost temple, and the mystery of form and of the sequence of chords stood revealed. I hurriedly wrote a pot-pourri in six parts on Italian airs, and, as the harmony seemed tolerable, I was emboldened to compose a quintette for flute, two violins, viola, and 'cello, which was played by three amateurs, my master, and myself.

This was indeed a triumph though, unfortunately, my father did not seem as pleased as my other friends. Two months later another quintette was ready, of which he wished to hear the flute part before we performed it in public. Like most provincial amateurs, he thought he could judge the whole by a first-violin part, and at one passage he cried:

"Come now! That is something like music."

But alas! this elaborate effusion was too much for our performers--particularly the viola and 'cello--they meandered off at their own sweet will. Result--confusion. As this happened when I was twelve and a half, the writers who say I did not know my notes at twenty are just a little out. Later on I burnt[1] the two quintettes, but it is strange that, long afterwards in Paris, I used the very *motif* that my father liked for my first orchestral piece. It is the air in A flat for the first violin in the allegro of my overture to the *Francs-Juges*.

III

MUSIC AND ANATOMY

AFTER the death of his son, poor Imbert went back to Lyons; his place was taken by Dorant, a man of far higher standing. He was an Alsacian, and played almost every instrument, but he excelled in clarinet, 'cello, violin, and guitar. My elder sister--who had not a scrap of musical instinct, and could never read the simplest song, although she had a charming voice and was fond of music--learnt the guitar with Dorant and, of course, I must needs share her lessons. But ere long our master, who was both honest and original, said bluntly to my father:

"Monsieur, I must stop your son's guitar lessons."

"But why? Is he rude to you or so lazy that you can do nothing with him?"

"Certainly not. Only it is simply absurd for me to pretend to teach anyone who knows as much as I do myself."

So behold me! Past master of those three noble instruments--flageolet, flute, and guitar!

Can anyone doubt my heaven-sent genius or that I should be capable of writing the most majestic orchestral works, worthy of a musical Michael Angelo! Flute, guitar, flageolet!!! I never was any good at other instruments. Oh yes! I am wrong, I am not at all bad at the side-drums.

My father would never let me learn the piano--if he had, no doubt I should have joined the noble army of piano thumpers, just like forty thousand others. Not wishing me to be a musician, he, I believe, feared the effect of such an expressive instrument on my sensitive nature. Sometimes I regret my ignorance, yet, when I think of the ghastly heap of platitudes for which that unfortunate piano is made the daily excuse--insipid, shameless productions, that would be impossible if their perpetrators had to rely, as they ought, on pencil and paper alone--then I thank the fates for having forced me to compose silently and freely by saving me from the tyranny of finger-work--that grave of original thought.

As with most young folks, my early work was downright gloomy, it simply grovelled in melancholy. Minor keys were rampant. I knew it was a mistake, but it seemed impossible to escape from the black crape folds that had enshrouded my soul ever since the Meylan affair.

The natural result of constantly reading Florian's *Estelle* was that I ended by setting parts of that mawky pastoral to music.

The faded old-time poetry comes back to me as I write here in London, in the pale spring sunshine. Torn as I am by anxiety, worried by sordid, petty obstacles, by stupid opposition to my plans, it is strange to recall the sickly-sentimental words of a song I wrote in despair at leaving the Meylan woods, which were "lighted by the eyes"--and, may I add, by the little pink slippers of my cruel lady love.

"I am going to leave forever

This dear land and my sweet love,

So alas! must fond hearts sever,

As my tears and grief do prove!

River, that has served so gaily

To reflect her lovely face,

Stop your course to tell her, daily,

I no more shall see this place!"

Although it joined the quintettes in the fire before I went to Paris, yet in 1829, when I planned my *Symphonie Fantastique,* this little melody crept humbly back into my mind; it seemed to me to voice so perfectly the crushing weight of young and hopeless love that I welcomed it home and enshrined it, without any alteration, for the first violins in the largo of the opening movement--*Reveries.*

But the fatal hour of choosing a profession drew rapidly nearer. My father made no secret of his intention that I should follow in his footsteps and become a doctor, since this he considered the finest career in the world; I, on the other hand, made no secret of my opinion that it was, to me, the most repulsive.

Without knowing exactly what I did want, I was absolutely certain that I did *not* want to be tied to the bedsides of sick people, to pass my days in hospitals and operating theatres, and I determined that no power on earth should turn me into a doctor.

My resolve was intensified by the lives of Gluck and Haydn that I read about this time in the "Biographie Universelle." "How glorious," I cried, "to live for Art, to spend one's life in her beautiful service!" and then came a mere trifle which threw open the gates of that paradise for which I had been so blindly groping.

As yet I had never seen a full score; all I knew of printed music was a few scraps of solfeggi with figured bass or bits of operas with a piano accompaniment. But one day I stumbled across a piece of paper ruled with twenty-four staves, and, in a flash, I saw the splendid scope this would give for all kinds of combinations.

"What orchestration I might get with that!" I said, and from that minute my music-love became a madness equalled only in force by my aversion to medicine.

As I dared not tell my parents, it happened that by means of this very passion for music, my father tried decisive measures to cure me of what he called my "babyish antipathy" to his loved profession.

Calling me into his study where Munro's *Anatomy*, with its life-size pictures of the human framework, lay open on the table, he said:

"See, my boy, I want you to work hard at this. I cannot believe that you will let unreasoning prejudice stand in the way of my wishes. If you will do your best, I will order you the very finest flute to be got in Lyons, with all the new keys."

What could I say? My father's gravity, my love and respect for him, the temptation of the long-coveted flute, were altogether too much for me. Muttering a strangled "Yes," I rushed away to throw myself on my bed in the depths of misery.

Be a doctor! Learn to dissect! Help in horrible operations! Bury myself in the hideous realities of hospitals, wounds, and death, when I might tread the clouds with the immortals!--when music and poetry wooed me with open arms and divine songs.

No, no, no! Such a tragedy *could* not happen!

Yet it did.

My cousin, A. Robert--now one of the first doctors in Paris--was to share my father's lessons. Unluckily he played the violin well, being a member of my quintette party, and, of course, we spent more time over music than over osteology. Still he worked so hard at home that he was always ready with his demonstrations, and I was not. Hence frequent scoldings and the vials of my father's wrath poured out on my poor head. Nevertheless, by hook or by crook, I managed to learn all that my father could teach me without dissections, and when I was nineteen, I consented to go with Robert to Paris to embark on a medical career.

* * * * *

Before beginning to tell of the deadly conflict that, almost immediately on my arrival in Paris, I began with ideas, people and things generally, and which has continued unremittingly up to this day, I must have a short breathing space.

Moreover, to-day--the 10th April 1848--has been chosen for the great Chartist demonstration. Perhaps, in a few hours, these two hundred thousand men will have upset England, as the revolutionists have upset the rest of Europe, and this last refuge will have failed me. I shall know soon.

8 P.M.--Chartists are rather a decent sort of revolutionists. Those powerful orators--big guns--took the chair, and their mere presence was so convincing that speech was superfluous. The Chartists quite understood that the moment was not propitious for a revolution, and they dispersed quietly and in order. My good folks, you know as much about organising an insurrection as the Italians do about composing symphonies.

12th July.--No possibility of writing for the last three months, and now I am going back to my poor France--mine own country, after all! I am going to see whether an artist can live there, or how long it will take him to die amid those ruins beneath which Art lies--crushed, bleeding, dead!

Farewell, England!

France, 16th July.--Home once more. Paris has buried her dead. The paving-stones, torn up for barricades, are replaced; but for how long?

The Faubourg Saint-Antoine is one mass of desolation and ruin; even the Goddess of Liberty on the Bastille column has a bullet through her. Trees, maimed and uprooted; houses tottering to a fall; squares, streets, quays, still palpitating from the riot--all bear witness to the horrors they have suffered.

Who could think of Art at such a time! Theatres are closed, artists undone, professors idle, pupils fled, pianists become street musicians, painters sweep the gutters, and architects mix mortar in the national work-sheds.

Although the National Assembly has voted a subsidy to the theatres, and some help to the poorest of the artists, what is that among so many?

Take a first violin of the opera, for instance; his pay is nine hundred francs a year, which is eked out by private lessons. What chance has he of saving? Transportation would be a boon to him and his colleagues, for they might earn a living in America, Sydney, or the Indies. But even this is denied them. They fought *for* the Government and against the insurgents, and being only deserving poor instead of malefactors, they cannot even claim this last favour--it is reserved for criminals.

Surely this way--in this awful, hideous confusion of just and unjust, of good and evil, of truth and untruth--this way doth madness lie!

I must write on and try to forget.

IV

PARIS

WHEN Robert and I got to Paris in 1822, I loyally kept my promise to my father by studying nothing but medicine. My first trial came when my cousin, telling me that he had bought a *subject*, took me to the hospital dissecting room.

But the foul air, the grinning heads, the scattered limbs, the bloody cloaca in which we waded, the swarms of ravenous rats and sparrows fighting for the debris of poor humanity, overwhelmed me with such a paroxysm of wild terror that, at one bound, I was through the nearest window, and tearing home as if Death and the Devil were at my heels.

The following night and day were indescribable. Hell seemed let loose upon me, and I felt that no power on earth should drag me back to that Gehenna. The wildest schemes for evading my horrible fate--each madder than the last--chased each other through my burning brain; but finally, worn out and despairing, I yielded to Robert's persuasion, and went back to the charnel house.

Strange to say, this time I felt nothing but cold, impersonal disgust, worthy of an old soldier in his fiftieth battle. I actually got to the point of ferretting in some poor dead creature's chest for scraps of lung to feed the sparrow-ghouls of this unsavoury den, and when Robert said, laughing:

"Hallo! you are getting quite civilised. Giving the birds their meat in due season!"

I retorted: "And filling all things living with plenteousness," as I threw a blade-bone to a wretched famished rat that sat up watching me with anxious eyes.

Life, however, had some compensations.

Some secret affinity drew me to my anatomy demonstrator, Professor Amussat, probably because he, like myself, was a man of one idea, and was as passionately devoted to his science--medicine--as I to my beloved art, music. His marvellous discoveries have brought him world-wide fame, but, insatiable searcher after truth as he is, he takes no rest. He is a genius, and I am honoured in being allowed to call him friend.

I also enjoyed the chemistry lectures of Gay-Lussac, of Thenard (physics) and, above all, the literature course of Andrieux, whose quiet humour was my delight.

Drifting on in this sort of dumb quiescence, I should probably have gone to swell the disastrous list of commonplace doctors, had I not, one night, gone to the Opera. It was Salieri's *Danaides*.

The magnificent setting, the blended harmonies of orchestra and chorus, the sympathetic and beautiful voice of Madame Branchu, the rugged force of Derivis, Hypermnestra's air--which so vividly recalled Gluck's style, made familiar to me by the scraps of *Orpheus* I had found in my father's library--all this, intensified by the sad and voluptuous dance-music of Spontini, sent me up to fever-pitch of excitement and enthusiasm.

I was like a young man, who, never having seen any boat but the cockle-shells on the mountain tarns of his homeland, is suddenly put on board a great three-decker in the open ocean. I could not sleep, of course, and consequently my next day's anatomy lesson suffered, and to Robert's frenzied expostulations I responded with airs from the *Danaides*, humming lustily as I dissected.

Next week I went to hear Mehul's *Stratonice* with Persuis' ballet *Nina*. I did not think much of the music, with the exception of the overture, but I was greatly affected by hearing Vogt play on the *cor anglais* the very air sung, years before, by my sister's friends at my first communion in the Ursuline chapel. A man sitting near told me that it was taken from d'Aleyrac's opera *Nina*.

In spite of this double life of mine and the hours spent in brooding over my hard fate, I stuck doggedly to my promise for some time longer. But, hearing that the Conservatoire library, with its wealth of scores, was open to the public, I could not resist the temptation to go and learn more of my adored Gluck. This gave the death-blow to my promise; music claimed me for her own.

I read and re-read, I copied, I learnt Gluck's scores by heart, I forgot to eat, drink, or sleep, and when at last I managed to hear *Iphigenia in Tauris*, I swore that, despite father, mother, relations and friends, a musician I would be and nothing else.

Without waiting till my courage oozed away, I wrote to my father telling him of my decision, and begging him not to oppose me. At first he replied kindly, hoping that I should see the error of my ways; but, as time went on, he realised that I was not to be persuaded, and our letters grew more and more acrimonious, until they ended in a perfect bombardment of mutual passion and recrimination.

In the midst of the storm I started composing, and wrote, amongst other things, an orchestral cantata on Millevoye's poem *The Arab Horse*.

I also, in the Conservatoire library, made friends with Gerono, a pupil of Lesueur, and, to my great joy, he offered to introduce me to his master, in the hope that I might be allowed to join his harmony class. Armed with my cantata, and with a three-part canon as a sort of aide-de-camp, I appeared before him. Lesueur most kindly read through the cantata carefully, and said: "You have plenty of dramatic force, plenty of feeling, but you do not know how to write yet. The whole thing is so crammed with mistakes that it would be simply waste of time for me to point them out. Get Gerono to teach you harmony--just enough to make my lectures intelligible--then I will gladly take you as a pupil."

Gerono readily agreed, and, in a few weeks, I had mastered Lesueur's theory, based on Rameau's chimera--the resonance of the lower chords, or what he was pleased to call the bass figure--as if thick strings were the only vibrating bodies in the world, or rather as if their vibrations could be taken as the fundamental basis of vibration for all sonorous bodies!

However, I saw from Gerono's manner of laying down the law that I must swallow it whole, since it was religion and must be blindly followed, or else say good-bye to my chance of joining Lesueur's class. And such is the force of example that I ended by believing in it so thoroughly and honestly that Lesueur considered me one of his most promising and fervent disciples.

Do not think me ungrateful for his kindliness and for the affection he shewed me up to his last hour, but, oh! the precious time wasted in learning and unlearning his mouldy, antediluvian theories.

At one time I really did admire his little oratories, and it grieved me sorely to find my admiration fading, slowly and surely. Now I can hardly bear to look at one of his scores; it is to me as the portrait of a dear friend, long loved, lost and lamented.

When I compare to-day with that far-off time when, regularly each Sunday, I went to the Tuileries chapel to hear them, how old, how tired, how bereft of illusions I feel. That was the day of great enthusiasms, of rich musical passions, of beautiful dreams, of ineffable, infinite joys.

As I usually arrived early at the Chapel Royal, my master would spend the time before service began in explaining the meaning of his composition. It was as well, for the music had no earthly connection with the words of the mass!

Lesueur inclined mostly to the sweet pastorals of the Old Testament--idylls of Naomi, Ruth, Rachel--and I shared his taste. The calm of the unchanging East, the mysterious grandeur of its ruins, its majestic history, its legends--these were the magnetic pole of my imagination. He often allowed me to join him in his walks, telling me of his early struggles, his triumphs and the favour of Napoleon. He even let me, up to a certain point, discuss his theories, but we usually ended on our common meeting-ground of Gluck, Virgil and Napoleon. After these long talks along the edge of the Seine or under the leafy shade of the Tuileries gardens, I would leave him to take the solitary walks which had become to him a necessity of daily life.

Some months after I had become his pupil, but before my admission to the Conservatoire, I took it into my head to write an opera, and nothing would do but that I must get my witty literary master, Andrieux, to write me a libretto. I cannot remember what I wrote to him, but he replied:

"MONSIEUR,--Your letter interests me greatly. You cannot but succeed in the glorious art you have chosen, and it would afford me the greatest pleasure to be your collaborateur. But, alas! I am too old, my studies and thoughts are turned in quite other directions. You would call me an outer barbarian if I told you how long it is since I set foot in the Opera. At sixty-four I can hardly be expected to write love songs, a requiem would be more appropriate. If only you had come into the world thirty years earlier, or I thirty years later, we might have worked together. With heartiest good wishes,

"ANDRIEUX."

"17th June 1823."

M. Andrieux kindly brought his own letter, and stayed a long time chatting. As he was leaving he said:

"Ah! I, too, was an ardent lover of Gluck ... and of Piccini,[2] too!!"

This failure discouraged me, so I turned to Gerono, who was something of a poetaster, and asked him (innocent that I was) to dramatise *Estelle* for me. Luckily no one ever heard this lucubration, for my ditties were a fair match for his words.

This pink-and-white namby-pamby effusion was followed by a dark and dismal thing called *The Gamester*. I was really quite enamoured of this sepulchral dirge, which was for a bass voice with orchestral accompaniment, and I set my heart on getting Derivis to sing it.

Just then the Theatre-Francais advertised a benefit for Talma--*Athalie*, with Gossec's choruses. "With a chorus," said I, "they must have an orchestra. My scena is not difficult, and if only I can persuade Talma to put it on the programme Derivis will certainly not refuse to sing it."

Off I posted to Talma, my heart beating to suffocation--unlucky omen! At the door I began to tremble, and desperate misgivings seized me. Dared I beard Nero in his own palace? Twice my hand went up to the bell, twice it dropped, then I turned and fled up the street as hard as I could pelt.

I was but a half-tamed young savage even then!

V

CHERUBINI

A SHORT time after this M. Masson, choirmaster of St Roch, suggested that I should write a mass for Innocents' Day.

He promised me a month's practice, a hundred picked musicians, and a still larger chorus. The choir boys of St Roch should copy the parts carefully, so that that would cost me nothing.

I started gaily. Of course the whole thing was nothing but a milk-and-water copy of Lesueur, and--equally of course--when I showed it to him he gave most praise to those parts wherein my imitation was the closest.

Masson swore by all his gods that the execution should be unrivalled, the one thing needful being a good conductor, since neither he nor I was used to handling such *vast masses of sound*. However, Lesueur most kindly induced Valentino, conductor of the opera, to take the post, dubious though he was of our vocal and instrumental legions.

The day of the general rehearsal came, and with it our *vast masses*--twenty choristers (fifteen tenors and five basses), twelve children, nine violins, one viola, one oboe, one horn, one bassoon.

My rage and despair at this treatment of Valentino--one of the first conductors in the world--may be imagined.

"It's all right," quoth Master Masson, "they will all turn up on the day."

Valentino shrugged his shoulders resignedly, raised his baton, and they started.

In two seconds all was confusion; the parts were one mass of mistakes, sharps and flats left out, ten-bar pauses omitted, a little further on thirty bars clean gone.

It was the most appalling muddle ever heard, and I simply writhed in torment. There was nothing for it but to give up utterly my fond dream of a grand orchestral performance.

Still, it was not lost time as far as I was concerned, for, in spite of the shocking execution, I saw where my worst faults lay, and, by Valentino's advice, I rewrote the whole mass--he generously promising to help me when I should be ready for my revenge.

But alas! while I worked my parents heard of the fiasco, and made another determined onslaught by ridiculing my chosen vocation, and laughing my hopes to scorn. Those were the bitter dregs of my cup of shame; I swallowed them and silently persevered.

Unable, for lack of money, to employ professional copyists, and being justly afraid of amateurs, when my score was finished I wrote out every part myself. It took me three months. Then, like Robinson Crusoe with the boat he could not launch, I was at a stand-still. How should I get it performed? Trust to M. Masson's musical phalanx? That would be too idiotic. Appeal to musicians myself? I knew none. Ask the help of the Chapel Royal? My master had distinctly told me that was impossible, no doubt because, had he allowed me such a privilege, he would have been bombarded with similar requests from my fellow-students.

My friend, Humbert Ferrand, came to the rescue with a bold proposal. Why not ask M. de Chateaubriand to lend me twelve thousand francs? I believe that, on the principle of it being as well to be hanged for a sheep as a lamb, I also asked for his influence with the Ministry. Here is his reply:

"PARIS, *31st Dec. 1824*.

"MONSIEUR,--If I had twelve thousand francs you should have them. Neither have I any influence with the ministers. I am indeed sorry for your difficulties, for I love art and artists. However, it is through trial that success comes, and the day of triumph is a thorough compensation for past sufferings. With most sincere regret,

"CHATEAUBRIAND."

Thus I was completely disheartened, and had no plausible answer to make when my parents wrote threatening to stop the modest sum that alone made life in Paris possible.

Fortunately I met, at the opera, a young and clever music-lover, Augustin de Pons, belonging to a Faubourg St Germain family, who, stamping with impotent rage, had witnessed my disaster at St Roch. He was fairly well off then, but, in defiance of his mother, he later on married a second-rate singer, who left him after long wanderings through France and Italy.

Entirely ruined he returned to Paris to vegetate by giving singing lessons. I was able to be of some use to him when I was on the staff of the *Journal des Debats*, and I greatly wish I could have done more, for his generous and unasked help was the turning-point of my career, and I shall never forget it.

Even last year he found life very hard; I tremble to think what may have become of him since the February revolution took away his pupils.

Seeing me one day in the foyer, he shouted:

"I say, what about your mass? When shall we have another go at it?"

"It is done," I answered, "but what chance have I of getting it performed?"

"Chance? Why, confound it all, you have only got to pay the performers. How much do you want? Twelve or fifteen hundred francs? Two thousand?"

"Hu-s-s-sh, don't roar so, for heaven's sake! If you really mean it I shall be most grateful for twelve hundred francs."

"All right. Hunt me up to-morrow and we'll engage the opera chorus and a real good orchestra. We must give Valentino a good innings this time."

And we did. The mass was grandly performed at St Roch, and was well spoken of by the papers. Thus, thanks to that blessed de Pons, I got my first hearing and my foot in the stirrup--as it were--of all things most difficult and most important in Paris.

I boldly undertook to conduct the rehearsals of chorus and orchestra myself, and, with the exception of a slip or two, due to excitement, I did not do so badly. But alas! how far I was from being an accomplished conductor, and how much labour and pains it has cost me to become even what I am.

After the performance, seeing exactly how little my mass was worth, I took out the Resurrexit--which seemed fairly good--and held an *auto-da-fe* of the rest, together with the *Gamester*, *Estelle*, and the *Passage of the Red Sea*. A calm inquisitorial survey convinced me of the justice of their fate.

* * * * *

Mournful coincidence! After writing these lines I met a friend at the Opera Comique, who asked:

"When did you come back?"

"Some weeks ago."

"Then you know about de Pons? No? He poisoned himself last week. He said he was tired of living, but I am afraid that, really, he was unable to live since the Revolution scattered his pupils."

Horrible! horrible! most horrible!

I must rush out and work off this horror in the fresh air.

* * * * *

Lesueur, seeing how well I got on, thought it best for me to become a regular Conservatoire student and, with the consent of Cherubini, the director, I was enrolled.

It was a mercy I had not to appear before the formidable author of *Medea*, for the year before I had put him into one of his white rages by thwarting him.

Now the Conservatoire had not been run on precisely Puritanic lines, so, when Cherubini succeeded Perne as director, he thought proper to begin by making all sorts of vexatious rules. For instance, men must use only the door into the Faubourg Poissoniere and women that into the Rue Bergere--which were at opposite ends of the building.

One day, knowing nothing of the new rule, I went in by the feminine door, but was stopped by a porter in the middle of the courtyard and told to go back and all round the streets to the masculine door. I told the man I would be hanged if I did, and calmly marched on.

I had been buried in *Alcestis* for a quarter of an hour, when in burst Cherubini, looking more wicked and cadaverous and dishevelled even than usual. With my enemy, the porter, at his heels, he jerked round the tables, narrowly eyeing each student, and coming at last to a dead stop in front of me.

"That's him," said the porter.

Cherubini was so furious that, for a time, he could not speak, and, when he did, his Italian accent made the whole thing more comical than ever--if possible.

"Eh! Eh! Eh!" he stuttered, "so it is you vill come by ze door I vill not 'ave you?"

"Monsieur, I did not know of the new rule; next time----"

"Next time? Vhat of zis next time? Vhat is it zat you come to do 'ere?"

"To study Gluck, Monsieur, as you see."

"Gluck! and vhat is it to you ze scores of Gluck? Vhere get you permission for enter ze library?"

"Monsieur" (I was beginning to lose my temper too), "the scores of Gluck are the most magnificent dramatic works I know, and I need no permission to use the library since, from ten to three, it is open to all."

"Zen I forbid zat you return."

"Excuse me, I shall return whenever I choose."

That made him worse.

"Vha-Vha-Vhat is your name?" he stammered.

"My name, Monsieur, you shall hear some day, but not now."

"Hotin," to the porter, "catch 'im and make 'im put in ze prison."

So off we went, the two--master and servant--hot foot after me round the tables. We knocked over desks and stools in our headlong flight, to the amazement of the quiet onlookers, but I dodged them successfully, crying mockingly as I reached the door:

"You shan't have either me or my name, and I shall soon be back here studying Gluck."

That was my first meeting with Cherubini, and I rather wondered whether he would remember it when I met him next in a less irregular manner. It is odd that, twelve years later, in spite of him, I should have been appointed first curator, then librarian of that very library. As for Hotin, he is now my devoted slave and a rabid admirer of my music. I have many other Cherubini stories to tell. Any way, if he chastised me with whips, I certainly returned the compliment with scorpions.

VI

MY FATHER'S DECISION

THE hostility of my people had somewhat died down, thanks to the success of my mass, but, naturally another reverse started it with renewed fury.

In the 1826 preliminary examination of candidates for admission to the Institute I was hopelessly plucked. Of course my father heard of it, and promptly wrote that, if I persisted in staying on in Paris, my allowance would stop.

My dear master kindly wrote asking him to reconsider his letter, saying that my eventual success was certain, since I *oozed music at every pore*. But, by ill luck, he brought in religious arguments--about the worst thing he could have done with my free-thinking father, whose blunt--almost rude--answer could not but wound Lesueur on his most susceptible side. From the beginning:

"Monsieur, I am an atheist," the rest may be guessed. The forlorn hope of gaining my end by personal pleading sent me back to La Cote, where I was received frostily and left to my own reflections for some days, during which I wrote to Ferrand:

"No sooner away from the capital than I want to talk to you. My journey was tiresome as far as Tarare, where I began a conversation with two young men, whom I had, so far, avoided, thinking they looked *dilettanti*. They told me they were artists, pupils of Guerin and Gros, so I told them I was a pupil of Lesueur. They said all sorts of nice things of him, and one of them began humming a chorus from the *Danaides*.

"The *Danaides*!" I cried, "then you are not a mere trifler?"

"Not I," he answered; "have I not heard Derivis and Madame Branchu thirty-four times as Danaus and Hypermnestra?"

"O-o-oh!" and we fell upon each other's neck.

"I know Derivis," said the other man.

"And I Madame Branchu."

"Lucky fellows!" I said. "But how is it that, since you are not professional musicians, you have not caught Rossini fever and turned your backs on nature and common sense?"

"Well, I suppose it is because, being used to seeking all that is grandest and best in nature for our pictures, we recognise the same spirit in Gluck and Salieri, and so turn our backs on fashionable music."

"Blessed people! Such as they are alone worthy of being allowed to listen to *Iphigenia*!"

* * * * *

Again my parents returned to the charge, telling me to choose my profession, since I refused to be a doctor. Again I replied that I could and would only be a musician and must return to Paris to study.

"Never," said my father, "you may give up that idea at once."

I was crushed; with paralysed brain I sank into a torpor from which nothing roused me. I neither ate nor spoke nor answered when spoken to, but spent part of the day wandering in the woods and fields and the rest shut up in my own room. I was mentally and morally dying for want of air. Early one morning my father came to my bedside:

"Get up and come to my study," he said, "I want to talk to you." He was grave and sad, not angry.

"I have decided, after many sleepless nights, that you shall go back to Paris, but only for a time. If you should fail on further trial, I think you will do me the justice to own that I have done all that can be expected, and will consent to try some other career. You know my opinion of second-rate poets--every sort of mediocrity is contemptible--and it would be a deadly humiliation to feel that you were numbered among the failures of the world."

Without waiting to hear more, I promised all he wished. "But," he continued, "since your mother's point of view is diametrically opposed to mine, I desire, in order to avoid trouble, that you do not mention this, and that you start for Paris secretly."

But it was impossible to hide this sudden bound from utter despair to delirious joy and Nanci, my sister, with many promises not to tell, wormed my secret out of me. Of course she kept it as well as I did, and by nightfall, everyone, including my mother, knew my plans.

Now it will hardly be believed that there are still people in France who look upon anyone connected with theatres or theatrical art as doomed to everlasting perdition, and since, according to French ideas, music hardly exists outside a theatre, it, too, shares the same fate.

Apropos of this I nearly made Lesueur die of laughing over a reply of one of my aunts.

We were arguing on this very point, and I said at last:

"Come, Auntie, I believe you would object to have even Racine a member of your family!"

"Well, Hector," she said seriously, "we *must* be respectable before everything."

Lesueur insisted that such sentiments could only emanate from an elderly maiden aunt, in spite of my asseverations that she was young and as pretty as a flower.

Needless to say, my mother believed I was setting my feet in the broad road that led not only to destruction in the next world, but to social ruin in this. I quickly saw by her wrathful face that she knew all, and did my best to slink out of her way, but it was useless. Trembling with rage and using "you" instead of the old familiar "thou," she said:

"Hector, since your father countenances your folly I must speak and save you from this mortal sin. You shall not go; I forbid it. See, here I--your mother--kneel at your feet to beg you humbly to give up this mad design and----"

"Mother! mother!" I interrupted, "I cannot bear it! For pity's sake don't kneel to me."

But she knelt on, looking up at me as I stood in miserable silence, and finally she said:

"You refuse, wretched boy? Then go! Drag our honoured name through the fetid mud of Paris; kill your parents with shame and disgrace. Curses on you! You are no more my son, and never again will I look upon your face."

Could narrow-mindedness towards Art and provincial prejudice go farther? I truly believe that my hatred of these mediaeval doctrines dates from that horrible day.

But that was not the end of the trial.

My mother hurried off to our little country house, Le Chuzeau, and when the time of my departure came my father begged me to make one final effort at reconciliation. We all went to Le Chuzeau, where we found her reading in the orchard. As we drew near she fled. We waited, we hunted, my father called her, my sisters and I cried bitterly, but all in vain. Without a kind word or look from my mother, with her curse upon my head, I started on my life's career.

VII

PRIVATION

ONCE back in Paris, and fairly started in Lesueur's class, I began to worry about my debt to de Pons.

It would certainly never be paid off out of my monthly allowance of a hundred and twenty francs. I therefore got some pupils for singing, flute and guitar, and, by dint of strict economy, in a few months I scraped together six hundred francs, with which I hurried off to my kind creditor.

How could I save out of such a sum? Well, I had a tiny fifth-floor room at the corner of the Rue de Harley and the Quai des Orfevres, I gave up restaurant dinners and contented myself with a meal of dry bread with prunes, raisins or dates, which cost about fourpence.

As it was summer time I took my dainties, bought at the nearest grocer's, and ate them on that little terrace on the Pont Neuf at the foot of Henry IV.'s statue; watching the while the sun set behind Mont Valerien, with its exquisite reflections in the murmuring river below, and pondering over Thomas Moore's poems, of which I had lately found a translation.

But de Pons, troubled at my privations--which, since we often met, I could not hide from him--brought fresh disaster upon me by a piece of well-meant but fatal interference. He wrote to my father, telling him everything, and asking for the balance of his debt. Now my father already repented bitterly his leniency towards me; here had I been five months in Paris without in the least bettering my position. No doubt he thought that I had nothing to do but present myself at the Institute to carry all before me: win the Prix de Rome, write a successful opera, get the Legion of Honour, and a Government pension, etc., *etc.*

Instead of this came news of an unpaid debt. It was a blow and naturally reacted on me.

He sent de Pons his six hundred francs, and told me that, if I refused to give up my musical wild-goose chase, I must depend on myself alone, for he would help me no more.

As de Pons was paid, and I had my pupils, I decided to stay in Paris-- my life would be no more frugal than heretofore. I was really working very steadily at music. Cherubini, of the orderly mind, knowing I had not gone through the regular Conservatoire mill to get into Lesueur's class, said I must go into Reicha's counterpoint class, since that should have preceded the former. This, of course, meant double work.

I had also, most happily, made friends some time before with a young man named Humbert Ferrand--still one of my closest friends--who had written the *Francs-Juges* libretto for me, and in hot haste I was writing the music.

Both poem and music were refused by the Opera committee and were shelved, with the exception of the overture; I, however, used up the best *motifs* in other ways. Ferrand also wrote a poem on the Greek Revolution, which at that time fired all our enthusiasm; this too I arranged. It was influenced entirely by Spontini, and was the means of giving my innocence its first shock at contact with the world, and of awakening me rudely to the egotism of even great artists.

Rudolph Kreutzer was then director of the Opera House, where, during Holy Week, some sacred concerts were to be given. Armed with a letter of introduction from Monsieur de Larochefoucauld, Minister of Fine Arts, and with Lesueur's warm commendations, I hoped to induce Kreutzer to give my scena.

Alas for youthful illusions!

This great artist--author of the *Death of Abel*, on which I had written him heaven only knows what nonsense some months before--received me most rudely.

"My good friend" (he did not know me in the least), he said shortly, turning his back on me, "we can't try new things at sacred concerts--no time to work at them. Lesueur knows that perfectly well."

With a swelling heart I went away.

The following Sunday Lesueur had it out with him in the Chapel Royal, where he was first violin. Turning on my master in a temper, he said:

"Confound it all! If we let in all these young folks, what is to become of us?"

He was at least plain spoken!

Winter came on apace. In working at my opera I had rather neglected my pupils, and my Pont Neuf dining-room, growing cold and damp, was no longer suitable for my feasts of Lucullus.

How should I get warm clothes and firewood? Hardly from my lessons at a franc a piece, since they might stop any day.

Should I write to my father and acknowledge myself beaten, or die of hunger in Paris? Go back to La Cote to vegetate? Never. The mere idea filled me with maddening energy, and I resolved to go abroad to join some orchestra in New York or Mexico, to turn sailor, buccaneer, savage, anything, rather than give in.

I can't help my nature. It is about as wise to sit on a gunpowder barrel to prevent it exploding as it is to cross my will.

I was nearly at my wits' end when I heard that the Theatre des Nouveautes was being opened for vaudeville and comic opera. I tore off to the manager to ask for a flautist's place in the orchestra. All filled! A chorus singer's? None left, confound it all! However the manager took my address and promised to let me know if, by any possibility there should be a vacancy. Some days later came a letter saying that I might go and be examined at the Freemason's Hall, Rue de Grenelle. There I found five or six poor wights in like case with myself, waiting in sickening anxiety--a weaver, a blacksmith, an out-of-work actor and a chorister. The management wanted basses, my voice was nothing but a second-rate baritone; how I prayed that the examiner might have a deaf ear.

The manager appeared with a musician named Michel, who still belongs to the Vaudeville orchestra. His fiddle was to be our only accompaniment.

We began. My rivals sang, in grand style, carefully prepared songs, then came my turn. Our huge manager (appropriately blessed with the name of St Leger) asked what I had brought.

"I? Why nothing."

"Then what do you mean to sing?"

"Whatever you like. Haven't you a score, some singing exercise, anything?"

"No. And besides"--with resigned contempt--"I don't suppose you could sing at sight if we had."

"Excuse me, I will sing at sight anything you give me."

"Well, since we have no music, do you know anything by heart?"

"Yes. I know the *Danaides*, *Stratonice*, the *Vestal*, *OEdipus*, the two *Iphigenias*, *Orpheus*, *Armida*----"

"There, that will do! That will do! what a devil of a memory you must have! Since you are such a prodigy, give us "*Elle m'a prodigue*" from Sacchini's *OEdipus*. Can you accompany him, Michel?"

"Certainly. In what key?"

"E flat. Do you want the recitative too?"

"Yes. Let's have it all."

And the glorious melody:

"Antigone alone is left me,"

rolled forth, while the poor listeners, with pitifully down-cast faces, glanced at each other recognising that, though I might be bad, they were infinitely worse.

The following day I was engaged at a salary of fifty francs a month.

And this was the result of my parents' efforts to save me from the bottomless pit! Instead of a cursed dramatic composer I had become a damned theatre chorus-singer, excommunicated with bell, book and candle. Surely my last state was worse than my first!

One success brought others. The smiling skies rained down two new pupils and a fellow-provincial, Antoine Charbonnel, whom I met when he came up to study as an apothecary. Neither of us having any money, we--like Walter in the *Gambler*--cried out together:

"What! no money either? My dear fellow, let's go into partnership."

We rented two small rooms in the Rue de la Harpe and, since Antoine was used to the management of retorts and crucibles, we made him cook. Every morning we went marketing and I, to his intense disgust, would insist on bringing back our purchases under my arm without trying to hide them. Oh, pharmaceutical gentility! it nearly landed us in a quarrel.

We lived like princes--exiled ones--on thirty francs a month each. Never before in Paris had I been so comfortable. I began to develop extravagant ideas, bought a piano--*such* a thing! it cost a hundred and ten francs. I knew I could not play it, but I like trying chords now and then. Besides, I love to be surrounded by musical instruments and, were I only rich enough, would work in company with a grand piano, two or three Erard harps, some wind instruments and a whole crowd of Stradivarius violins and 'cellos.

I decorated my room with framed portraits of my musical gods, and Antoine, who was as clever as a monkey with his fingers (not a very good simile, by-the-way, since monkeys only destroy) made endless little useful things--amongst others a net with which, in spring-time, he caught quails at Montrouge, to vary our Spartan fare.

But the humour of the whole situation lay in the fact that, although I was out every evening at the theatre, Antoine never guessed--during the whole time we lived together--that I had the ill-luck to *tread the boards* and, not being exactly proud of my position, I did not see the force of enlightening him. He supposed I was giving lessons at the other end of Paris.

It seems as if his silly pride and mine were about on a par. Yet no; mine was not all foolish vanity. In spite of my parents' harshness, for nothing in the world would I have given them the intense pain of knowing how I gained my living. So I held my tongue and they only heard of my theatrical career--as did Antoine Charbonnel--some seven or eight years after it ended, through biographical notices in some of the papers.

VIII

FAILURE

IT was at this time that I wrote the *Francs-Juges* and, after it, *Waverley*. Even then, I was so ignorant of the scope of certain instruments that, having written a solo in D flat for the trombones in the introduction to the *Francs-Juges,* I got into a sudden panic lest it should be unplayable.

However one of the trombone players at the opera, to whom I showed it, set my mind at rest.

"On the contrary," said he, "D flat is a capital key for the trombone; that passage ought to be most effective."

Overjoyed, I went home with my head so high in the air that I could not look after my feet, whereby I sprained my ankle. I never hear that thing now without feeling my foot ache; probably other people get the ache in their heads.

Neither of my masters could help me in the least in orchestration--it was not in their line. Reicha did certainly know the capacity of most wind instruments, but I do not think he knew anything of the effect of grouping them in different ways; besides it had nothing to do with his department, which was counterpoint and fugue. Even now it is not taught at the Conservatoire.

However, before being engaged at the Nouveautes I had made the acquaintance of a friend of Gardel, the well-known ballet-master, and he often gave me pit tickets for the opera, so that I could go regularly.

I always took the score and read it carefully during the performance, so that, in time, I got to know the sound--the voice, as it were--of each instrument and the part it filled; although, of course, I learnt nothing of either its mechanism or compass.

Listening so closely, I also found out for myself the intangible bond between each instrument and true musical expression.

The study of Beethoven, Weber and Spontini and their systems; searching enquiry into the gifts of each instrument; careful investigation of rare or unused combinations; the society of *virtuosi* who kindly explained to me the powers of their several instruments, and a certain amount of instinct have done the rest for me.

Reicha's lectures were wonderfully helpful, his demonstrations being absolutely clear because he invariably gave the reason for each rule. A thoroughly open-minded man, he believed in progress, thereby coming into frequent collision with Cherubini, whose respect for the masters of harmony was simply slavish.

Still, in composition Reicha kept strictly to rule. Once I asked his candid opinion on those figures, written entirely on *Amen* or *Kyrie eleison*, with which the Requiems of the old masters bristle.

"They are utterly barbarous!" he cried hotly.

"Then, Monsieur, why do you write them?"

"Oh, confound it all! because everyone else does."

Miseria!

Now Lesueur was more consistent. He considered these monstrosities more like the vociferations of a horde of drunkards than a sacred chorus, and he took good care to avoid them. The few found in his works have not the slightest resemblance to them, and indeed his

"Quis enarrabit coelorum gloriam"

is a masterpiece of form, style and dignity.

Those composers who, by writing such abominations, have truckled to custom, have prostituted their intelligence and unpardonably insulted their divine muse.

Before coming to France Reicha had been in Bonn with Beethoven, but I do not think they had much in common. He set great value on his mathematical studies.

"Thanks to them," he used to say, "I am master of my mind. To them I owe it that my vivid imagination has been tamed and brought within bounds, thereby doubling its power."

I am not at all sure that his theory was correct. It is quite possible that his love for intricate and thorny musical problems made him lose sight of the real aim of music, and that what the eye gained by his curious and ingenious solution of difficulties the ear did not lose in melody and true musical expression.

For praise or blame he cared nothing; he lived only to forward his pupils, on whom he lavished his utmost care and attention.

At first I could see that he found my everlasting questions a perfect nuisance, but in time he got to like me. His wind instrumental quintettes were fashionable for a time in Paris; they are interesting but cold. On the other hand, I remember hearing a magnificent duet, from his opera *Sappho*, full of fire and passion.

* * * * *

When the Conservatoire examinations of 1827 came on I went up again, and fortunately passed the preliminary, thereby becoming eligible for the general competition.

The subject set was Orpheus torn by the Bacchantes. I think my version was fair, but the incompetent pianist who was supposed to do duty for an orchestra (such is the incredible arrangement at these contests) not being able to make head or tail of my score, the powers that were--to wit, Cherubini, Paer, Lesueur, Berton, Boieldieu and Catel, the musical section of the Institute--decided that my music was impracticable, and I was put out of court.

So, after my Kreutzer experience of selfish jealousy, I now had a sample of wooden-headed sticking to the letter of the law. In thus taking away my modest chance of distinction did none of them think of the consequences of driving me to despair like this?

I had got a fortnight's leave from the Nouveautes for the competition; when it was over I should have again to take up my burden. But just as the time expired I fell ill with a quinsy that nearly made an end of me.

Antoine was always trotting after grisettes and left me almost entirely alone. I believe I should have died without help had I not one night, in a fit of desperation, stuck a pen-knife into the abscess that choked me. This somewhat unscientific operation saved me, and I was beginning to mend when my father--no doubt touched by my steady patience and perhaps anxious as to my means of livelihood--wrote and restored me my allowance.

Thanks to this unhoped-for kindness, I gave up chorus-singing--no small relief, since, apart from the actual bodily fatigue, the idiotic music I had to suffer from would soon have either given me cholera or turned me into a drivelling lunatic.

Free from my dreary trade I gave myself up, with redoubled zest, to my Opera evenings and to the study of dramatic music. I never thought of instrumental, since the only concerts I had heard were the cold and mean Opera performances, of which I was not greatly enamoured. Haydn and Mozart, played by an insufficient orchestra in too large a building, made about as much effect as if they had been given on the *plaine de Grenelle*. Beethoven, two of whose symphonies I had read, seemed a sun indeed, but a sun obscured by heavy clouds. Weber's name was unknown to me, while as for Rossini----

The very mention of him and of the fanaticism of fashionable Paris for him put me in a rage that is not lessened by the obvious fact that he is the antithesis of Gluck and Spontini. Believing these great masters perfect, how could I tolerate his puerilities, his unmerciful big drum, his constant repetition of one form of cadence, his contempt for great traditions? My prejudice blinded me even to this exquisite instrumentation of the *Barbiere* (without the big drum too!) and I longed to blow up the *Theatre Italien* with all its Rossinian audience and so put an end to it at one fell swoop. When I met one of the tribe I eyed him with a Shylockian scowl.

"Miscreant!" I growled between my teeth, "would that I might impale thee on a red-hot iron."

Time has not changed my opinion, and though I think I can refrain from blowing up a theatre and impaling people on hot irons, I quite agree with our great painter, Ingres, who, speaking of some of Rossini's work, said:

"It is the music of a vulgar-minded man."

IX

A NIGHT AT THE OPERA

HERE is a picture of one of my opera evenings.

It was a serious business for which I prepared by reading over and studying whatever was to be given.

My faithful pit friends and I had but one religion, with one god, Gluck, and I was his high priest. Our fanaticism for our favourites was only equalled by our frantic hatred of all composers whom we judged to be without the pale.

Did one of my fellow-worshippers tremble or waver in his faith, promptly would I drag him off to the opera to retract--even going so far sometimes as to pay for his ticket. On one special seat would I place my victim, saying, "Now for pity's sake don't move. Nowhere else can you hear so well--I know because I have tried the right place for every opera."

Then I would begin to expound, reading and explaining obscure passages as I went along; we were always in very good time, first to get the places we wanted; next, so as not to miss the opening notes of the overture; lastly, in order to taste to the uttermost the exciting, thrilling expectation of a great pleasure of which one knows the realisation will exceed one's hopes. The gradual filling of the orchestra--at first as dreary as a stringless harp; the distribution of the parts--an anxious moment this, for the opera might have been changed; the joy of reading the hoped-for title on the desks of the double-basses, which were nearest to us; or the horror of seeing it was replaced by some wretched little drivel like Rousseau's *Devin du Village*--when we would rush out in a body, swearing at all and sundry.

Poor Rousseau! What would he have said if he could have heard our curses? He, who thought more of his feeble little opera than of all the masterpieces through which his name lives. How could he foresee that it would some day be extinguished for ever by a huge powdered periwig, thrown at the heroine's feet by some irreverent scoffer. As it happened, I was present that very night and, naturally, kind friends credited me with this little unrehearsed effect. I am really quite innocent, I even remember being quite as angry about it as I was amused--so I do not think I should or could have done such a thing. Since that night of joyous memory the poor *Devin* has appeared no more.

But to go back to my story.

Reassured on the subject of the performance, I continued my preachment, singing the leading motifs, explaining the orchestration and doing my best to work my little gang up to a pitch of enthusiasm, to the great wonderment of our neighbours who--mostly simple country folks--were so wrought upon by my speeches that they quite expected to be carried away by their emotions, wherein they were usually grievously disappointed.

I also named each member of the orchestra as he came in and gave a dissertation on his playing until I was stopped short by the three knocks behind the scenes. Then we sat with beating hearts awaiting the signal from Kreutzer or Valentino's raised baton. After that, no humming, no beating time on the part of our neighbours. Our rule was Draconian.

Knowing every note of the score, I would have let myself be chopped in pieces rather than let the conductor take liberties with it. Wait quietly and write my expostulations? Not exactly! No half-measures for me!

There and then I would publicly denounce the sinners and my remarks went straight home.

For instance, I noticed one day that in *Iphigenia in Tauris* cymbals had been added to the Scythian dance, whereas Gluck had only employed strings, and in the Orestes recitative, the trombones, that come in so perfectly appropriately, were left out altogether.

I decided that if these barbarisms were repeated I would let them know it and I lay in wait for my cymbals.

They appeared.

I waited, although boiling over with rage, until the end of the movement, then, in the moment's silence that followed, I yelled:

"Who dares play tricks with Gluck and put cymbals where there are none?"

The murmuring around may be imagined. The public, not being particularly critical, could not conceive why that young idiot in the pit should get so excited over so little. But it was worse when the absence of the trombones made itself evident in the recitative.

Again that fatal voice was heard:

"Where are those trombones? This is simply outrageous!"

The astonishment of audience and orchestra were fairly matched by Valentino's very natural anger. I heard afterwards that the unlucky trombones were only obeying orders; their parts were quite correctly written.

After that night the proper readings were restored, the cymbals were silent, the trombones spoke; I was serene.

De Pons, who was just as crazy as I on this point, helped me to put several other points straight but once we went too far and dragged in the public at our heels.

A violin solo advertised for Baillot was left out. We clamoured for it furiously, the pit fired up, then the whole house rose and howled for Baillot. The curtain fell on the confusion, the musicians fled precipitately, the audience dashed into the orchestra smashing everything they could lay hands on and only stopping when there was nothing left to smash.

In vain did I cry:

"Messieurs, messieurs! what are you doing? To break the instruments is too barbarous. That's Father Chenie's glorious double-bass with its diabolic tone."

But they were too far gone to listen, and the havoc was complete.

This was the bad side of our unofficial criticism; the good side was our wild enthusiasm when all went well. How we applauded anything superlative that no one noticed, such as a fine bass, a happy modulation, a telling note of the oboe! The public took us for embryo *claqueurs*, the *claque* leader, who knew better and whose little plans were upset, tried to wither us with thunderbolt glances, but we were bomb-proof.

There is no such enthusiasm in France nowadays, not even in the Conservatoire, its last remaining stronghold.

Here is the funniest scene I ever remember at the opera. I had swept off Leon de Boissieux, an unwilling proselyte, to hear *OEdipus*; however, nothing but billiards appealed to him, and, finding him utterly impervious to the woes of Antigone and her father, I stepped over into a seat in front, giving him up in despair.

But he had a music-loving neighbour and this is what I heard, while my young man was peeling an orange and casting apprehensive glances at the other man, who was evidently in a state of wild excitement.

"Sir, for pity's sake, do try to be calm."

"Impossible! It's killing me! It is so terrible, so overwhelming!"

"My good man, you will be ill if you go on like this. You really shouldn't."

"Oh! oh! Leave me alone! Oh!"

"Come! come! Do cheer up a bit. Remember it is nothing but a play. Here, take a piece of my orange."

"It's sublime----"

"Yes, it's Maltese----"

"What glorious art!"

"Don't say 'No.'"

"Oh, sir! what music!"

"Yes, it's not bad."

By this time the opera had got to the lovely trio, "Sweet Moments," and the exquisite delicacy of the simple air overcame me too. I hid my face in my hands, and tears trickled between my fingers. I might have been plunged in the depths of woe.

As the trio ended two strong arms lifted me off my seat, nearly crushing my breast-bone in; the enthusiast, recognising one fellow-worshipper amongst the cold-blooded lot around, hugged me furiously, crying:

"B-b-b-by Jove, sir! isn't it beautiful?"

"Are you a musician?"

"No, but I am as fond of it as if I were."

Then, regardless of surrounding giggles and of my orange-devouring neophyte, we exchanged names and addresses in a whisper.

He was an engineer, a mathematician! Where, the devil, will true musical perception next find a lodging, I wonder? His name was Le Tessier, but we never met again.

X

WEBER

INTO the midst of this stormy student life of mine came the revelation of Weber, by means of a miserable, distorted version of *Der Freyschutz,* called *Robin des Bois,* which was performed at the Odeon. The orchestra was good, the chorus fair, the soloists simply appalling.

One wretched woman alone, Madame Pouilley, by the imperturbably wooden way in which she went through her part--even that glorious air in the second act--would have been enough to wreck the whole opera. Small wonder that it took me a long while to unearth all the beauty of its hidden treasures.

The first night it was received with hisses and laughter, the next the audience began to see something in the Huntsmen's Chorus, and they let the rest pass. Then they rather fancied the Bridesmaid's Chorus and Agatha's Prayer, half of which was cut out. A glimmering notion that Max's great aria was fairly dramatic followed; finally it burst upon them that the Wolf's Glen scene was really quite comic; so all Paris rushed to see this misshapen horror, the Odeon got rich, and Castilblaze netted a hundred thousand francs for destroying a masterpiece.

Now I must own frankly that I was getting rather tired of high tragedy, in spite of my conservatism, and, chopped about as it was, the sweet wild savour of this woodland pastoral, its dainty grace and tender melancholy opened to me a new world of music.

I deserted the opera in favour of the Odeon, where I had the *entree* to the orchestra, and soon knew *Der Freyschutz* (according to Castilblaze) by heart.

More than twenty years have passed since Weber himself passed through Paris for the first and last time. He was on his way to his London death-bed, and breathlessly I followed in his track, hoping and longing to meet him face to face.

One morning Lesueur said:

"Why were you not here five minutes sooner? Weber has been playing our French scores by heart to me."

A few hours later in a music shop--

"Whom do you think we had here just now? Why, Weber!"

At the Odeon people were saying:

"Weber has just gone by. He is up in one of the boxes."

It was maddening--I, alone, never saw him. Unlike Shakespeare's apparitions, he was visible to all but one.

Too obscure to dare to write, without a friend who could introduce me, he passed out of my world.

Ah, why do not the thrice-gifted ones of this world know of the passionate love and devotion their works inspire! If they could but divine the suppressed admiration of a few faithful hearts! Would they not gladly gather these chosen disciples about them to become a bulwark against the shafts of envy, hatred, malice, and luke-warm tolerance of which a thoughtless world makes them the target!

Weber was justly angry when he found out how Castilblaze--veterinary surgeon of music--had butchered his beautiful work, and he published a complaint before leaving Paris. Castilblaze actually had the audacity to play the injured innocent, and to say that it was entirely owing to his adaptation that *Freyschutz* had succeeded at all!

The wretch!----yet a poor sailor gets fifty lashes for the slightest insubordination.

Exactly the same thing had been done a few years earlier with Mozart's *Magic Flute*. It had been botched into a ghastly *pot-pourri* by Lachnith--whom I hereby pillory with Castilblaze--and given as the *Mysteries of Isis*.

Thus mocked, travestied, deprived of a limb here, an eye there--twisted and maimed--these two men of genius were introduced to the French public.

How is it that they put up with these atrocities?

Mozart assassinated by Lachnith.

Weber by Castilblaze--who did the same for Gluck, Mozart, Rossini, and Beethoven.

Beethoven's symphonies "corrected" by Fetis, by Kreutzer, and by Habeneck (of this I have more to say).

Moliere and Corneille chopped up by Theatre Francais demons.

Shakespeare "arranged" for performance in England by Colley Cibber! The list is endless.

No, a thousand times no! No man living has a right to try and destroy the individuality of another, to force him to adopt a style not his own, and to give up his natural point of view. If a man be commonplace, let him remain so; if he be great--a choice spirit set above his fellows--then, in the name of all the gods, bow humbly before him, and let him stand erect and alone in his glory.

I know that Garrick improved *Romeo and Juliet* by putting his exquisite, pathetic ending in the place of Shakespeare's; but who are the miscreants who doctored *King Lear, Hamlet, The Tempest, Richard the Third*?

That all comes from Garrick's example. Every mean scribbler thinks he can give points to Shakespeare.

But to go back to music. At the last sacred concerts, after Kreutzer had experimentalised by making cuts in one Beethoven symphony, did not Habeneck follow suit by dropping out several instruments in another, and M. Costa, in London, try all sorts of weird conclusions with big drums, ophicleides, and trombones in *Don Giovanni* and *Figaro*? Well! if conductors lead the way, who can blame the small fry for following after?

But is not this the ruin of Art? Ought not we, who love and honour her, who are jealous for the prescriptive rights of human intellect, to hound down and annihilate the transgressor; to cry aloud:

"Thy crime is ridiculous. Thy stupidity beneath contempt. Despair and die! Be thou contemned, be thou derided, be thou accursed! Despair and die!!!"

* * * * *

My devotion to Gluck and Spontini at first somewhat blinded me to the glories of Mozart. Not only had I a prejudice against Italian, both language and singers, but in *Don Giovanni* the composer has written a passage that I call simply criminal. Dona Anna bewails her fate in a passage of heart-rending beauty and sorrow, then, right in the middle, after *Forse un giorno* comes an impossible piece of buffoonery that I would give my blood to wipe out.

This and other similar passages that I found in his compositions sent my admiration for Mozart down below zero. I felt I could not trust his dramatic instinct, and it was not until years later, when I found the original score of the *Magic Flute* instead of its travesty, the *Mysteries of Isis*, and made acquaintance with the marvellous beauty of his quartettes and quintettes, and some of his sonatas, that this Angelic Doctor took his due place in my mind.

XI

HENRIETTE

I CANNOT go minutely into all the sorrowful details of the great drama of my life, upon which the curtain rose about this time (1827).

An English company had come over to Paris to play Shakespeare, and at their first performance--*Hamlet*--I saw in Ophelia the Henriette Smithson who, five years later, became my wife. The impression made upon my heart and mind by her marvellous genius was only equalled by the agitation into which I was plunged by the poetry she so nobly interpreted.

Shakespeare, coming upon me unawares, struck me down as with a thunderbolt. His lightning spirit, descending upon me with transcendent power from the starry heights, opened to me the highest heaven of Art, lit up its deepest depths, and revealed the best and grandest and truest that earth can shew.

I realised the paltry meanness of our French view of that mighty brain. The scales fell from my eyes, I saw, felt, understood, lived; I arose and walked!

But the shock was overwhelming, and it was long ere I recovered. Intense, profound melancholy, combined with extreme nerve-exhaustion, reduced me to a pitiable state of mind and body that only a great physiologist could diagnose.

A martyr to insomnia, I lost all elasticity of brain, all concentration, all taste for my best loved studies, and I wandered aimlessly about the Paris streets and through the country round.[3]

By dint of overtiring my body, I managed, during this wretched time, to get four spells of death-like sleep or torpor, and four only; one night in a field near Ville-Juif, one day near Sceaux; a third in the snow by the frozen Seine near Neuilly, and the last on a table in the Cafe Cardinal, where I slept five hours, to the great fright of the waiters, who dared not touch me lest I should be dead.

Returning one day from this dreary wandering in search of my lost soul, I noticed Moore's *Irish Melodies* open on the table at

"When he who adores thee,"

and, catching up a pen, I wrote the music to that heart-rending farewell straight off. It is the *Elegie* at the end of my set of songs called *Ireland*. This is the only time I can remember being able to depict a sentiment while actively under its influence, and seldom have I gone so direct to the heart of it.

It is a most difficult song both to sing and to accompany. To do it justice the singer must create his own atmosphere, so must the pianist and only the most sensitive and artistic souls should attempt it.

For this reason, during all the twenty odd years since it was written, I have never asked anyone to try it; but one day Alizard picked it up and began trying it without the piano. Even that upset me so terribly that I had to beg him to stop. He understood. I know he would have interpreted it perfectly, and it was more than I could bear. I did begin to set it to an orchestral accompaniment, but I thought:

"No, this is not for the general public. I could not stand their calm indifference," and I burnt the score.

Yet some day it may chance, in England or Germany, to find a niche in some wounded breast, some quivering soul--in France and Italy it is a hopeless alien.

Coming away from *Hamlet*, I vowed that never more would I expose myself to Shakespearian temptation, never more singe my scorched wings in his flame.

Next morning *Romeo and Juliet* was placarded. In terror lest the free list of the Odeon should be suspended by the new management, I tore round to the box-office and bought a stall. I was done for!

Ah! what a change from the dull grey skies and icy winds of Denmark to the burning sun, the perfumed nights of Italy! From the melancholy, the cruel irony, the tears, the mourning, the lowering destiny of Hamlet, what a transition to the impetuous youthful love, the long-drawn kisses, the vengeance, the despairing fatal conflict of love and death in those hapless lovers!

By the third act, half suffocated by my emotion, with the grip of an iron hand upon my heart, I cried to myself: "I am lost--am lost!"

Knowing no English I could but grope mistily through the fog of a translation, could only see Shakespeare as in a glass--darkly. The poetic weft that winds its golden thread in network through those marvellous creations was invisible to me then; yet, as it was, how much I learnt!

An English critic has stated in the *Illustrated London News* that, on seeing Miss Smithson that night, I said:

"I will marry Juliet and will write my greatest symphony on the play."

I did both, but I never said anything of the kind. I was in far too much perturbation to entertain such ambitious dreams. Only through much tribulation were both ends gained.

After seeing these two plays I had no more difficulty in keeping away from the theatre. I shuddered at the bare idea of renewing such awful suffering, and shrank as if from excruciating physical pain.

Months passed in this state of numb despair, my only lucid moments being dreams of Shakespeare and of Miss Smithson--now the darling of Paris--and dreary comparisons between her brilliant triumphs and my sad obscurity.

As I gradually awoke to life again, a plan began to take shape in my mind. She should hear of me; she should know that I also was an artist; I would do what, so far, no French artist had ever done--give a concert entirely of my own works. For this three things were needed--copies, hall, and performers.

Therefore (this was early in the spring of 1828) I set to work, and, writing sixteen hours out of twenty-four, I copied every single part of the pieces I had chosen, which were the overtures to *Waverley* and the *Francs-Juges*, an aria and trio from the latter, the scena *Heroic Greek*, and the cantata on the *Death of Orpheus*, that the Conservatoire committee had judged unplayable.

While copying furiously I saved furiously too, and added some hundreds of francs to my store, wherewith to pay the chorus; for orchestra I knew I might count on the friendly help of the staff of the Odeon, with a sprinkling of assistants from the Opera and the Nouveautes.

My chief difficulty was the hall; it always is in Paris. For the only suitable one--the Conservatoire--I must have a permit from M. de Larochefoucauld and also the consent of Cherubini.

The first was easily obtained; not so the second.

At the first mention of my design Cherubini flew in a rage.

"Vant to gif a conchert?" he said, with his usual suavity.

"Yes, monsieur."

"Must 'ave permission of Fine Arts Director first."

"I have it."

"M. de Larossefoucauld, 'e consent?"

"Yes, monsieur."

"But me, I not consent. I vill oppose zat you get ze 'all."

"But, monsieur, you can have no reasonable objection, since the hall is not engaged for the next fortnight."

"But I tell to you zat I vill not 'ave zat you gif zis conchert. Everyone is avay and no profit vill be to you."

"I expect none. I merely wish to become known."

"Zere is no necessity zat you become known. And zen for expense you vill want monee. Vhat 'ave you of monee?"

"Sufficient, monsieur."

"A-a-ah! But vhat vill you make 'ear at zis conchert?"

"Two overtures, some excerpts from an opera and the *Death of Orpheus*."

"Zat competition cantata? I vill not 'ave zat! She is bad--bad; she is impossible to play."

"You say so, monsieur; I judge differently. That a bad pianist could not play it is no reason that a good orchestra should not."

"Zen it is for insult of ze Academie zat you play zis?"

"No, monsieur; it is simply as an experiment. If, as is possible, the Academy was right in saying my score could not be played, then certainly the orchestra will not play it. If the Academy was wrong, people will only say that I made good use of its judgment and have corrected my score."

"You can only 'ave your conchert on ze Sunday."

"Very well, I will take Sunday."

"But zose poor *employes*--ze doorkeepers--zey 'ave but ze Sunday for repose zem. Vould you take zeir only rest-day? Zey vill die--zose poor folks--zey vill die of fatigue."

"On the contrary, monsieur. These poor folks are delighted at the chance of earning a few extra francs, and they will not thank you for depriving them of it."

"I vill not 'ave it; I vill not! And I write to ze Director zat he vizdraw permission."

"Most hearty thanks, monsieur, but M. de Larochefoucauld never breaks his word. I also shall write and retail our conversation exactly. Then he will be able to weigh the arguments on both sides."

I did so, and was afterwards told by one of his secretaries that my dialogue-letter made the Director laugh till he cried. He was, above all, touched at Cherubini's tender consideration for those poor devils of *employes* whom I was going to kill with fatigue.

He replied, as any man blessed with commonsense would, repeating his authorisation and adding:

"You will kindly show this letter to M. Cherubini, who has already received the necessary *orders*."

Of course I posted off to the Conservatoire and handed in my letter; Cherubini read it, turned pale, then yellow, and finally green, then handed it back without a word.

This was my first Roland for the Oliver he gave me in turning me out of the library. It was not to be my last.

XII

MY FIRST CONCERT

HAVING secured orchestra, hall, chorus and parts, I only wanted soloists and a conductor. Bloc, of the Odeon, kindly accepted the latter post, and Alexis Dupont, although very unwell, took under his wing my *Orpheus*, which he had promised to sing before the jury of the Institute, had it been passed.

But unluckily his hoarseness got so much worse that, when the day came, he was unable to sing at all, so I was deprived of the wicked joy of putting on the programme, "*Death of Orpheus*; lyric poem, judged impossible of execution by the Academie des Beaux Arts, performed May 1828."

A concert at which most of the executants helped for love and not for money naturally came off poorly in rehearsals; still, at the final rehearsal the overtures went fairly well, the *Francs-Juges* calling forth warm applause from the orchestra; the finale of the cantata being even more successful.

In this, after the *Bacchanal*, I made the wind carry on the motif of Orpheus' love-song to a strange rushing undertone accompaniment by the rest of the players, while the dying wail of a far-off voice cries:

"Eurydice! Eurydice! hapless Eurydice!"

The wild sadness of my music-picture affected the whole orchestra, and they hailed it with wild enthusiasm. I am sorry now that I burnt it, it was worth keeping for those last pages alone.

With the exception of the *Bacchanal*--the famous piece in which the Conservatoire pianist got hung up--which was given with magnificent verve, nothing else in the cantata went very well and, thanks to Dupont's illness, it was withdrawn. No doubt Cherubini preferred to say that it was because the orchestra could not play it.

In this cantata I first noticed how impossible conductors, unused to grand opera, find it to give way to the capricious and varied time of the recitative. Bloc, only accustomed to songs interspersed with spoken dialogue, was quite confused and, in some places, never got right at all, which made a learned periwigged amateur, who was at rehearsal, say, as he shook his head at me:

"Give me good old Italian cantatas! Now that's the music that never bothers a conductor. It plays itself, it runs alone."

"Yes," I said dryly, "just as old donkeys plod round and round their treadmill."

That is how I set about making friends.

Much against the grain I replaced *Orpheus* by the *Resurrexit* from my mass, and finally the concert came off.

Duprez, with his sweet, weak voice, did well in the aria; the overtures and *Resurrexit* were also a success, but the trio with chorus was a regular failure.

Not only was the trio miserably sung, but the chorus missed its entry and never came in at all!

I need hardly say that, after paying expenses, including the chorus that held its tongue in such a masterly manner, I was completely cleaned out.

However, the concert was a most useful lesson to me.

Not only did I become known to artists and public, which (*pace* Cherubini!) was a necessity, but, by doggedly facing the innumerable difficulties of a composer, I gained most valuable experience.

Several of the papers praised me, and even Fetis--Fetis, who afterwards[4] ... spoke of me, in a drawing-room, as a coming man.

But what of Miss Smithson?

Alas! I found out that, absorbed in her own engrossing work, of me and my concert she never heard a whisper!

To HUMBERT FERRAND.

"*6th June 1828.*--Are you parched with anxiety to know the result of my concert? I have only waited in order to send you the papers too. Triumphant success! After the applause at the general rehearsals of Friday and Saturday I had no more misgivings.

"Our beloved *Pastoral* was ruined by the chorus that only found out it had not come in just as the whole thing finished. But oh, the *Resurrexit*! and oh, the applause! As soon as one round finished another began until, being unable to stand it all, I doubled up on the kettle-drum and cried hard.

"Why were you not there, dear friend, faithful champion? I thought of and longed for you.

"At that wild trombone and ophicleide solo in the *Francs-Juges*, one of the first violins shouted:

"'The rainbow is the bow of your violin, the winds play your organ and the seasons beat time!'

"Whereupon the whole orchestra started applauding a thought of which they could not possibly grasp the extent. The drummer by my side seized my arm, ejaculating, 'Superb--sublime,' while I tore my hair and longed to shriek:

"'Monstrous! Gigantic! Horrible!'

"All the opera people were present, and there was no end to the congratulations. The most pleased were Habeneck, Derivis, Dupont, Mademoiselle Mori, Herold, *etc*. Nothing was lacking to my success--not even the criticisms of Panseron and Brugnieres, who say my style is new and bad, and that such writing is not to be encouraged.

"My dear, dear fellow! in pity send me an opera. How can I write without a book? For heaven's sake finish something!"

"*June*.--All day long I have been tearing about the country, leagues upon leagues, and I still live. I feel so lonely! Send me something to work at, some bone to gnaw! The country was lovely; the people all looked happy. In the flooding light the trees rustled softly; but, oh! I was alone--all alone in that wide plain. Space, time, oblivion, pain and rage held me in their terrific grasp. Struggle wildly as I might, life seemed to escape me; I held but a few pitiful fragments in my trembling hands.

"Oh! the horror, at my age and with my temperament, to have these harrowing delusions, and, with them, the miserable persecutions of my family! My father has again stopped my allowance; my sister writes to-day that he is immovable. Oh, for money! money! Money *does* bring happiness.

"Still ... my heart beats as if with joy, the blood courses through my veins.

"Bah! I am all right. Joy, hang it! I will have joy!"

"*Sunday morning.*

"DEAR FRIEND,--Do not worry over my aberrations--the crisis is past. I cannot explain in a letter, which might go astray; but I beg you will not breathe a word of my state of mind to anyone, it might get round to my father and distress him. All that I can do is suffer in silence until time changes my fate.

"Yesterday's wild excursion did for me entirely. I can hardly move.--*Adieu*."

In an artist's life sometimes wild tempests succeed each other with bewildering rapidity, and so it was with me about this time.

Hardly had I recovered from the successive shocks of Weber and Shakespeare, when above my horizon burst the sun of glorious

Beethoven to melt for me that misty inmost veil of the holiest shrine in music, as Shakespeare had lifted that of poetry.

To Habeneck, with all his shortcomings, is due the credit of introducing the master he adored to Paris. In order to found the Conservatoire concerts, now of world-wide fame, he had to face opposition, abuse and irony, and to inspire with his own ardour a set of men who, not being Beethoven enthusiasts, did not see the force of slaving for poor pay at music that, to them, appeared simply eccentric.

Oh! the nonsense I have heard them airing on those miracles of inspiration and learning--the symphonies!

Even Lesueur--honest, but devoted to antiquated dogmas--stood aside with Cherubini, Paer, Kreutzer and Catel, until, one day, I swept him off to hear the great C minor symphony.

I told him it was his duty to know and appreciate personally such a notable fact as this revelation of a new and glorious style to us, the children of the old classicism.

Conscientiously anxious to judge fairly, he would not have me by to distract him, but shut himself up with strangers at the back of a box.

The symphony over, I hurried round to hear his verdict, and found him, with flushed face, striding up and down a passage.

"Ouf!" he cried, "let me get out; I must have air! It's incredible! Marvellous! It has so upset and bewildered me, that when I wanted to put on my hat I *couldn't find my head*. Let me go by myself. I will see you to-morrow."

I felt triumphant, and took care to go round next day. We spoke of nothing but the masterpiece we had heard; yet he seemed to reply to my ravings rather constrainedly. Still I persevered, until, after dragging out of him another acknowledgment of his heart-felt appreciation, he ended, with a curious smile:

"Yes, it's all very well; but such music ought not to be written."

"No fear, dear master," I retorted; "there will never be too much of it!"

Poor human nature! Poor master! How much regret, envy, narrow-mindedness; what a dread of the unknown and confession of incapacity lay beneath your words! "Such music should not be written," because the speaker knows instinctively that he himself could never write it.

Thus do all great men suffer from their contemporaries.

Haydn said much the same of Beethoven, whom he called a *great pianist*.

Gretry of Mozart, who, he said, had put the statue in the orchestra and the pedestal on the stage.

Handel, who said his cook was more of a musician than Gluck.

Rossini, who vowed that Weber's music gave him a stomach-ache.

But the antipathy of the two latter to Gluck and Weber I believe to be due to quite another reason--a natural inability in these two comfortable portly gentlemen to understand the point of view of the two men of heart and sensibility.

This deliberately obstinate attitude of Lesueur towards Beethoven opened my eyes to the utter worthlessness of his conservative tenets, and from that moment I left the broad, smooth road wherein he had guided my footsteps, for a hard and thorny way over hedges and ditches, hills and valleys. But I could not hurt the old man by my apostasy, so did my best to dissimulate my change of mind, and he only found it out long after, on hearing a composition I had never shewn him.

It was just at this time that I set out on my treadmill round as critic for the papers.

Ferrand, Cazales and de Carne--well-known political names--agreed to start a periodical to air their views, which they called *Revue Europeenne,* and Ferrand suggested that I should undertake the musical correspondence.

"But I can't write," I objected; "my prose is simply detestable. And, besides----"

"No, it is not," said Ferrand; "have I not got your letters? You will soon be knocked into shape. Besides, we shall revise what you write before it is printed. Come along to de Carne and hear all about it."

What a weapon this writing for the press would be wherewith to defend truth and beauty in art! So, ignorant of the web of fate I was throwing around my own shoulders, I smiled innocently and walked straight into the meshes.

I was likely to be diffident of my writing powers, for, once before, being furious at the attacks made upon Gluck by the Rossini faction, I asked M. Michaud, of the *Quotidienne,* to let me reply. He consented, and I said to myself, gaily:

"Now, you brutes, I have got you; I'll smite you hip and thigh!"

But I smote no one and nothing.

My utter ignorance of journalism, of the ways of the world, of press etiquette and my untamed musical passions, landed me in a regular bog. My article went far beyond the bounds of newspaper warfare, and M. Michaud's hair stood on end.

"But, my dear fellow, you know, I cannot possibly publish a thing like that. You are pulling people's houses down about their ears. Take it back and whittle it down a bit."

But I was too lazy and too disgusted, so there it ended.

This laziness of mine does not apply to composition, which comes naturally to me. Hour after hour I labour at a score, sometimes for eight hours at a time; no work is too minute, no pains too great.

Prose, however, is always a burden. Sometimes I go back eight or ten times to an article for the *Journal des Debats*; even a subject I like takes me at least two days. And what blots, what scrawls, what erasures! My first copy is a sight to behold.

Propped up by Ferrand, I wrote for the *Revue Europeenne* appreciative articles on Beethoven, Gluck and Spontini that made a certain mark, and thus began my apprenticeship to the difficult and dangerous work that has taken such a fatal hold on my life.

Never since have I shaken myself free, and strangely diversified have been its influences on my career both in France and abroad.

XIII

AN ACADEMY EXAMINATION

TORN by my Shakespearian love, which seemed intensified instead of diverted by the influence of Beethoven; dreamy, unsociable, taciturn to the verge of moroseness, untidy in dress, unbearable alike to myself and my friends, I dragged on until June 1828 when, for the third time, I tempted fate at the Institute and won a second prize.

This was a gold medal of small value, but it carried with it a free pass to all the lyric theatres, and a fair prospect of the first prize the following year.

The Prix de Rome was much better worth having. It insured three thousand francs a year for five years, of which the two first must be spent in Italy, and the third in Germany. The remaining two might be passed in Paris, after which the winner was left to sink or swim at his own sweet will.

This is how the affair was worked until 1865, when the Emperor revised the statutes. I shall hardly be believed, but, since I won both prizes, I only state what I know to be absolutely true.

The competition was open to any Frenchman under thirty, who must go through the preliminary examination, which weeded out all but the most promising half dozen.

The subject set is always a lyric scena, and by way of finding out whether the candidates have melody, dramatic force, instrumentation, and other knowledge necessary for writing such a scena, they are set down to compose a *vocal fugue*! *Each fugue must be signed.*

Next day the musical section of the Academy sits in judgment on the fugues, and, since some of the signatures are those of the Academicians' pupils, this performance is not entirely free from the charge of partiality.

The successful competitors then have dictated to them the classical poem on which they are to work. It always begins this way:

"And now the rosy-fingered dawn;"

or,

"And now with lustre soft the horizon glows;"

or,

"And now fair Phoebus' shining car draws near;"

or,

"And now with purple pomp the mountains decked."

Armed with this inspiring effusion the young people are locked up in their little cells with pens, paper, and piano until their work is done.

Twice a day they are let out to feed, but they may not leave the Institute building. Everything brought in for their use is carefully searched lest outside help should be given, yet every day, from six to eight, they may have visitors and invite their friends to jovial dinners, at which any amount of assistance--verbal or written--might be given.

This lasts for twenty-two days, but anyone who has finished sooner is at liberty to go, leaving his manuscript--*signed as before*--with the secretary.

Then the grave and reverend signors of the jury assemble, having added to their number two members of any other section of the Institute--either engravers, painters, sculptors or architects--anything, in short, but musicians.

You see, they are so thoroughly competent to judge an art of which they know nothing.

There they sit and solemnly listen to these scenas boiled down on a piano. How *could* anyone profess to judge an orchestral work like that? It might do for simple old-fashioned music, but nothing modern--that is, if the composer knows how to marshal the forces at his command--could by any possibility be rendered on the piano.

Try the Communion March from Cherubini's great Mass. What becomes of those long-drawn, mystical wind-notes that fill one's soul with religious ecstasy; of those exquisitely interwoven flutes and clarinets to which the whole effect is due?

They have completely vanished, since the piano can neither hold nor inflate a sound.

Does it not follow, then, that the piano, by reducing every tone-character to one dead level, becomes a guillotine whereby the noblest heads are laid low and mediocrity alone survives?

Well! After this precious performance the prize is awarded, and you conclude that this is the end of it all?

Not a bit! A week later the whole thirty-five Academicians, painters and architects and sculptors and engravers on copper and engravers of medals all turn up to give the final verdict.

They do not shut out the six musicians, although they are going to judge music.

Again the pianists and the singers go through the compositions, then round goes the fatal urn, in order that the judgment of the previous week may be confirmed, modified, or reversed.

Justice compels me to add that the musicians return the compliment by going to judge the other arts, of which they are as blindly ignorant as are their colleagues of music.

On the day of the distribution of prizes the chosen cantata is performed by a full orchestra. It seems just a little late; it might have been more serviceable to get the orchestra before judgment--seeing that after this there is no repeal--but the Academy is inquisitive; it really does wish to know something about the work it has crowned. Laudable curiosity!

* * * * *

In my time there was an old doorkeeper at the Institute whose indignation at all this procedure was most amusing. It was his duty to lock us up and let us out, and, being also usher to the Academicians, he was on the inside track and made some very odd notes.

He had been a cabin boy, which at once enlisted my sympathies; for I always loved sailors, and can listen imperturbably to their long-winded yarns; no matter how far they wander from the point I am always ready with a word to set them right again.

We were the best of friends, Pingard and I. One day, talking of Syria, he mentioned Volney.

"M. le Comte," he said, "was so good and easy-going that he always wore blue woollen stockings."

But his respect for me became unbounded enthusiasm when I asked whether he knew Levaillant.

"M. Levaillant!" he cried, "Rather! One day at the Cape I was sauntering along, whistling, when a big sun-burnt man with a beard turned round on me. I suppose he guessed I was French from my whistle. Of course I whistle in French, monsieur.

"'I say, you young rogue, you're French?'

"'I should say I was. Givet is my part of the country.'

"'Oh, you *are* French?'

"'Yes.'

"And he turned his back and strode off. You see I did know M. Levaillant!"

The good old boy made such a friend of me that he told me a lot he would not have dared to repeat to anyone else.

I remember a lively conversation with him the day I got the second prize.

We had a piece of Tasso set that year, towards the end of which the Queen of Antioch invokes the god of the Christians she has contemned. I had the impudence to think that, although the last section was marked *agitato,* this ought to be a prayer, and I wrote it *andante.* I was rather pleased with it on the whole.

When I got to the Institute to hear whether the painters and sculptors, and architects, and engravers of medals, and line-engravers had settled whether I were a good or bad musician, I ran against Pingard on the stairs.

"Well?" I asked, "what have they decided?"

"Oh, hallo, Berlioz! I am glad you have come. I was hunting for you."

"What have I got? Do hurry up! First? Second? Nothing?"

"Oh, do wait; I'm all of a tremble. Will you believe you were only two votes short of the first prize?"

"The first I've heard of it."

"It's true, though. The second is all very well, but I call it beastly that you missed the first by two votes. I am neither a painter, nor a sculptor, nor an architect, so of course I know nothing about music, but I'll be hanged if that *God of the Christians* of yours didn't set my heart gurgling and rumbling to such a tune that if I had met you that minute I should have--have--stood you a drink!"

"Thanks awfully, Pingard. I admire your taste. But, I say--you have been on the Coromandel coast?"

"Yes, of course. Why?"

"To Java?"

"Yes, but----"

"Sumatra?"

"Yes."

"Borneo?"

"Yes."

"You are a friend of Levaillant?"

"I should think so. Hand in glove with him."

"You know Volney?"

"The good Count with the blue woollen stockings? Certainly."

"Very well, then, you *must* be a splendid judge of music."

"But--why? How?"

"Well, I don't know exactly how or why. But it seems to me that your title is just as good as that of the gentlemen who do judge. Tell me, though, what happened."

"Oh, my goodness! It's always the same old game. If I had thirty children, devil take me if one of them should be an artist of any sort. You see, I am on the inside track, and know how they sell their votes. It's nothing but a blessed old shop. See here! Once I heard M. Lethiere asking M. Cherubini for his vote for a pupil."

"Don't refuse, my dear fellow," he said, "we are such old friends, and my pupil really has talent."

"No, he shall not have my vote," Cherubini answered. "He promised my wife an album of drawings that she wanted badly. He hasn't even done her a single tree!"

"That's rather too bad of you," said M. Lethiere. "I vote for your people, and you might vote for mine. Look here! I'll do you the album myself. I can't say more than that."

"Ah, that's another pair of boots. What is your pupil's name and picture? I must not get muddled. Pingard, a pencil and paper!"

"They went off into the window corner and wrote something, then I heard the musician say--

"All right, I will vote for him."

"Now, isn't that disgusting? If I had had a son in the competition and they had played him a trick like that, wouldn't it have been enough to make me chuck myself out of window?"

"Come, Pingard, calm down a bit and tell me about to-day."

"Well, when M. Dupont had finished singing your cantata they began writing their verdicts, and I brought the hurn" (Pingard always would stick in that "h"). "There was a musician close by whispering to an architect, 'Don't give him your vote; he's no good at all, and never will be. He is gone on that eccentric creature Beethoven, and we shall never get him right again.' 'Really!' said the architect. 'Yet--' 'Well, ask Cherubini. You will take his word, won't you? He will tell you that

Beethoven has turned the fellow's head--' I beg pardon," said Pingard, breaking off his story, "but who is this M. Beethoven? He doesn't belong to the Academy, and yet everyone seems to be talking of him."

"No, no! He's a German. Go on."

"There isn't much more. When I passed the hurn to the architect I saw that he gave his vote to No. 4 instead of to you. Suddenly one of the musicians said, 'Gentlemen, I think you ought to know that, in the second part of the score we have just heard, there is an exceedingly clever and effective piece of orchestration to which the piano cannot do justice. This ought to be taken into consideration.' 'Don't tell us a cock-and-bull story like that,' cried another musician. 'Your pupil has broken the rules and written two quick arias instead of one, and he has put in an extra prayer. We cannot allow rules to be set at nought like this; it would be establishing a precedent.' 'Oh, this is too ridiculous! What says the secretary?' 'I think that we might pardon a *certain* amount of licence, and that the jury should distinctly understand that passage that you say cannot be properly given by the piano.' 'No, no!' cried Cherubini, 'it's all nonsense. There is no such clever piece of work. It is a regular jumble, and would be abominable for the orchestra.'

"Then on all sides rose the architects, painters, sculptors, etc., saying, 'Gentlemen, for pity's sake agree somehow! We can only judge by what we hear, and if you will not agree--' And all began to talk at once, and it became distinctly a bore, so M. Regnault and two others marched out without voting. They counted the votes. You only got second prize."

"Thanks, Pingard, but, I say--they manage things better at the Cape Academy, don't they?"

"The Cape? Why, you know they have not got one. Fancy a Hottentot Academy!"

"Well then, Coromandel?"

"None there."

"Java?"

"None either."

"What, no Academy at all in the East? Poor Orientals!"

"They manage to get along pretty well without."

"What outer barbarians!"

I bade the old usher good-bye, thinking what a blessing it would be if I could send the Academy to civilise Borneo.

Two years later the Prix de Rome was mine, but poor old Pingard was dead. It was a pity.

If he had heard my "Burning of the Palace of Sardanapalus" he might have stood me ... two drinks!

XIV

FAUST--CLEOPATRA

AGAIN I relapsed into my habitual gloom and indolence. Like a dead invisible planet I circled round that radiant sun that alas! was doomed so soon to fade into mournful oblivion.

Estelle, star of my dawn, was eclipsed and lost in the noontide brilliance of her mighty rival--my overwhelming and glorious love.

Although I took care never to pass the theatre, never willingly to look at Othelia's portraits in the shop windows, yet still I wrote--receiving never a sign in reply. My first letters frightened her, and she bade her maid take her no more.

The company was going to Holland, and its last nights were advertised. Still I kept away; to see her again was more than I could bear.

However, hearing that she was to act two scenes from *Romeo and Juliet* with Abbott, for the benefit of Huet, the actor, I had a sudden fancy to see my own name on a placard beside that of the great actress.

I *might* be successful under her very eyes!

Full of this childish notion I got permission from the manager and conductor of the Opera Comique to add an overture of my own to the programme.

On going to rehearsal I found the English company just finishing; broken-hearted Romeo held Juliet in his arms. At sight of the group I gave a hoarse, despairing cry and wringing my hands wildly, I fled from the theatre. Juliet saw and heard me; terror-stricken she pointed me out to those around, begging them to *beware of the gentleman with the wild eyes*.

An hour later I went back to an empty theatre. The orchestra assembled and my overture was run through--like a sleep walker I listened, hearing nothing--when the performers applauded me I wondered vaguely whether Miss Smithson would like it too! Fool that I was!!

It seems impossible that I could, even then, have been so ignorant of the world as not to know that, be the overture what it may, at a benefit, no one in the audience listens. Still less the actors, who only arrive in time for their turns and trouble themselves not at all about the music.

My overture was well played, fairly received--but not encored--Miss Smithson heard nothing of it and left next day for Holland.

By a strange chance (I could never get her to believe it *was* chance) I had taken lodgings at 96 Rue de Richelieu, opposite her house. Worn out, half dead, I lay upon my bed until three the next afternoon; then, rising, I crawled wearily to the window.

Cruel Fate! At that very minute she came out and stepped into her carriage *en route* for Amsterdam.

Was ever misery like mine?

Oh God! my deadly, awful loneliness; my bleeding heart! Could I bear that leaden weight of anguish, that empty world; that hatred of life; that shuddering shrinking from impossible death?

Even Shakespeare has not described it; he simply counts it, in *Hamlet*, the cruellest burden left in life.

Could I bear more?

I ceased to write; my brain grew numb as my suffering increased. One power alone was left me--to suffer.

To HUMBERT FERRAND.

"GRENOBLE, *Sept. 1828*.

"DEAR FRIEND,--I cannot go to you; come to me at La Cote! We will read *Hamlet* and *Faust* together, Shakespeare and Goethe! Silent friends who know all my misery, who alone can fathom my strange wild life. Come, do come! No one here understands the passion of genius. The sun blinds them, they think it mere extravagance. I have just written a ballad on the King of Thule, you shall have it to put in your *Faust*--if you have one.

"'Horatio, thou art e'en as just a man

As e'er my conversation cop'd withal.'

"I am wretched. Do not be so cruel as not to come!"

"PARIS, *November 1828*.[5]

"Forgive me for not writing sooner; I was so ill, so stupid, it was better to wait.

"La Fontaine might well say: 'Absence is the greatest of ills.' She is gone; this time to Bordeaux and I live no more; or rather I live too acutely, for I suffer, hourly, the agonies of death. I can hardly drag through my work.

"You know that I am appointed Superintendent of the Gymnase-Lyrique and have to choose or replace the players and to take care of instruments, parts and scores.

"Subscribers are coming in; so are malicious anonymous letters. Cherubini sits on the fence wondering whether to help or to hinder us, and we go calmly on.

"I have not seen Chateaubriand; he is in the country, but I will speak of your piece directly I do."

"End of 1828.

"Do you know M. d'Eckstein, and can you give me an introduction to him? I hear that he is connected with a new and powerful paper,[6] in which Art is to be given prominence. If I am considered good enough, I should like to be musical correspondent. Help me if you can."

Another landmark in my life was the reading of Goethe's *Faust*; I could not lay it down, but read and read and read--at table, in the streets, in the theatres.

Although a prose translation, songs and rhymed pieces were scattered throughout, and these I set to music, then, without having heard a note of them, was crazy enough to have them engraved. A few copies, under the title of *Eight Scenes from Faust* were sold in Paris, and one fell into the hands of M. Marx, the great Berlin critic, who wrote most kindly to me about it. This unexpected encouragement from such a source gave me real pleasure, particularly as the writer did not dwell too much on my many and great faults. I know some of the ideas were good, since I afterwards used them for the *Damnation de Faust,* but I know, also, how hopelessly crude and badly written they were. As soon as I realised this, I collected and burnt all the copies I could lay hands on.

Under Goethe's influence I wrote my *Symphonie Fantastique*--very slowly and laboriously in some parts, incredibly quickly and easily in others. The *Scene aux Champs* worried me for three weeks, over and over again I gave it up, but the *Marche au Supplice* was dashed off in a single night. Of course they were afterwards touched and retouched.

Bloc, being anxious that my new symphony should be heard, suggested that I should be allowed to give a concert at the Theatre des Nouveautes.

The directors, attracted by the eccentricity of my work, agreed, and I invited eighty performers to help, in addition to Bloc's orchestra. On my making enquiries about accommodation for such an army of executants the manager replied, with the calm assurance of ignorance:

"Oh, that's all right. Our property man knows his business." The day of rehearsal arrived, and so did my hundred and thirty musicians--with nowhere to put them!

I just managed to squeeze the violins into the orchestra, and then arose an uproar that would have driven a calmer man than myself out of his senses. Cries for chairs, desks, candles, strings, room for the drums, etc., *etc.* Scene shifters tore up and down improvising desks and seats, Bloc and I worked like sixty--but it was all useless; a regular rout; a passage of the Beresina.

However Bloc insisted on trying two movements to give the directors some idea of the whole. So, all in a muddle, we struggled through the *Ball Scene* and the *Marche au Supplice,* the latter calling forth frantic applause.

But my concert never came off. The directors said that "they had no idea so many arrangements were necessary for a symphony." Thus my hopes were dashed, and all for want of a few desks. Since then I always look into the smallest details for myself.

Wishing to console me for this disappointment, Girard, conductor of the Theatre Italien, asked me to write something shorter than my unlucky symphony, that he could have carefully performed at his theatre.

I therefore wrote a dramatic fantasia with choruses on the *Tempest,* but no sooner did he see it than he said:

"This is too big for us; it must go to the opera."

Without loss of time I interviewed M. Lubbert, director of the Royal Academy. To my relief and delight, he at once agreed to have it played at a concert for the Artists' Benevolent Fund that was to take place shortly. My name was known to him through my Conservatoire concert, and he had seen notices of me in the papers. He, therefore, believed in me, put me through no humiliating examination, gave me his word, and kept it religiously.

"He was a man, Horatio."

All went splendidly at rehearsal; Fetis did his best for me, and everything seemed to smile, when, with my usual luck, an hour before the concert there broke over Paris the worst storm that had been known for fifty years. The streets were flooded and practically impassable, and during the first half of the concert, when my *Tempest*--damned tempest!--

was being played, there were not more than three hundred people in the place.

Extracts from Letters to H. FERRAND.

"*April 1829.*--Here is *Faust*, dear friend. Could you, without stinting yourself, lend me another hundred francs to pay the printer? I would rather borrow from you than from anyone else; yet had you not offered, I should not have dared to ask. Your opera (*Franc-Juges*) is splendid. You are indeed a poet! That finale of the Bohemians at the end of the first act is a master stroke. I do not believe anything so original has ever been done in a libretto before. And I repeat, it is magnificent."

"*June.*--No word from you for three months. Why is it? Does your father suppress our letters, or can it be that you, at last, believe the slanders you hear of me?

"I got a pupil, so have managed to pay the printer.

"I am very happy, life is charming--no pain, no despair, plenty of day dreams; to crown all, the *Francs-Juges* has been refused by the Opera Committee! They find it long and obscure, only the Bohemian scene pleases them; but Duval thinks it remarkable and says there is a future for it.

"I am going to make an opera like *Freyschutz* of it, and if I win the prize perhaps Spohr (who is not jealous, but is most helpful to young musicians) will let me try it at Cassel.

"No word have I had from you since I spoke of my hopeless love. Nothing more has happened. This passion will be my death; how often one hears that hope alone keeps love alive--am I not a living proof of the contrary?

"All the English papers ring with her praises; I am unknown! When I have written something great, something stupendous, I must go to London to have it performed. Oh for success!--success under her very eyes.

"I am writing a life of Beethoven for the *Correspondant*, and cannot find a minute for composition--the rest of my time I copy out parts. What a life!"

Once more came June, and with it my third attempt on the Prix de Rome. This time I really did hope, for not only had I gained a second prize, but I heard that the musical judges thought well of me.

Being over-confident I reasoned (falsely, as it turned out), "Since they have decided to give me the prize, I need not bother to write exactly in the style that suits them; I will compose a really artistic cantata."

The subject was Cleopatra after Actium. Dying in convulsions, she invokes the spirits of the Pharaohs, demanding--criminal though she be--whether she dare claim a place beside them in their mighty tombs. It was a magnificent theme, and I had often pondered over Juliet's--

"But if when I am laid into the tomb,"

which is, at least in terror of approaching death, analogous to the appeal of the Egyptian Queen.

I was fool enough to head my score with those very words--the unpardonable sin to my Voltairean judges--and wrote what seemed to me a weird and dramatic piece, well suited to the words. I afterwards used it, unchanged, for the *Chorus of Shades* in *Lelio*; I think it deserved the prize. But it did not get it. None of the compositions did. Rather than give it to a "young composer of such revolutionary tendencies" they withheld it altogether.

Next day I met Boieldieu, who, on seeing me, said:

"My dear boy, what on earth possessed you? The prize was in your hand, and you simply threw it away."

"But, monsieur, I really did my best."

"That's just it! Your *best* is the opposite of your *good*. How could I possibly approve? I, who like nice gentle music--cradle-music, one might say."

"But, monsieur, could an Egyptian queen, passionate, remorseful, and despairing, die in mortal anguish of body and soul to the sound of cradle-music?"

"Oh, come! come! I know you have plenty of excuses, but they go for nothing. You might at least have written gracefully."

"Gladiators could die gracefully, but not Cleopatra. She had not to die in public."

"There! you *will* exaggerate so! No one expects her to dance a quadrille. Why need you introduce such odd, queer harmonies into that invocation? I am not well up in harmony, and I must own that those outlandish chords of yours are beyond me."

I bit my lip, not daring to make the obvious reply:

"Is it my fault that you know no harmony?"

"And then," he went on, "why do you introduce a totally new rhythm in your accompaniments? I never heard anything like it."

"I did not understand, monsieur, that we were not to try new modes if we were fortunate enough to find the right place for them."

"But, my dear good fellow, Madame Dabadie is a capital musician, yet one could see it took all her care and talent to get her through."

"Really, monsieur, I have yet to learn that music can be sung without either talent or care."

"Well, well! you will have the last word. But do be warned for next year. Come and see me and we will talk it over like *French gentlemen*."

And, chuckling over the point he had made (for his last words were a quotation from his own *Jean de Paris*), he walked off.

Yes, Boieldieu was right. The Parisians liked soothing music, even for the most dramatic and harrowing situations. Pretty, innocent, gentlemanly music, pleasant and making no demand upon one's deepest feelings.

Later on they wanted something different, and now they do not know what they want, or rather they want nothing at all. Ah me! what was the good God thinking of when He dropped me down in this pleasant land of France?

Yet I love her whenever I can forget her idiotic politics. How gay she is, how dainty in wit, how bright in retort--how she boasts and swaggers and humbugs, royally and republicanly! I am not sure, though, that this last *is* amusing.

XV

A NEW LOVE

To HUMBERT FERRAND.

"*July 1829.*--I am sorry I did not send your music before, but I may as well own that I am short of money. My father has taken another whim and sends me nothing, so I could not afford the thirty or forty francs for the copying. I could not do it myself, as I was shut up in the Institute. That abominable but necessary competition! My only chance of getting the filthy lucre, without which life is impossible.

'Auri sacra fames quid non mortalia pectora cogis!'

My father would not even pay my expenses in the Institute. M. Lesueur did so for me."

"*August.*--Forgive my negligence. My only excuses are the Academy competition and the new pangs of my despised love. My heart can be likened only to a virgin forest, struck and kindled by the thunderbolt; now and again the fire smoulders, then comes the whirlwind, and in a second the trees are a mass of living, hissing flame and all is death and desolation.

"I will spare you a description of the latest blows.

"That shameful competition!

"Boieldieu says I go further than Beethoven, and he cannot even understand Beethoven; and that, to write like that, *I must have the most hearty contempt for the Academicians!* Auber told me much the same thing, and added, 'You hate the commonplace, but you need never be afraid of writing platitudes. The best advice I can give you is to write as insipidly as you can, and when you have got something that sounds to you horribly flat, *you will have just what they want!*'

"That is all very well, but when I go writing for butchers and bakers and candlestick-makers I certainly shall not go to the passion-haunted, crime-stained Queen of Egypt for a text."

To FERDINAND HILLER.

"1829.--What is this overwhelming emotion, this intense power of suffering that is killing me? Ask your guardian angel, that bright spirit that has opened to you the gate of Heaven. Oh, my friend! can you believe that I have burnt the manuscript of my prose elegy? I have Ophelia ever before me; her tears, her tragic voice; the fire of her glorious eyes burns into my soul--I am so miserable, so inexpressibly unhappy, oh, my friend!

"I seem to see Beethoven looking down on me with calm severity; Spontini--safely cured of woes like mine--with his pitying indulgent smile; Weber from the Elysian Fields, whispers consoling words into my ear....

"Mad, mad, mad! is this sense for a student of the Institute; a domino-player of the Cafe de la Regence?

"Nay, I *will* live--live for music--the highest thing in life except true love! Both make me utterly miserable but at least I shall have lived! Lived, it is true, by suffering, by passion, by lamentation and by tears--yet I *shall* have lived! Dear Ferdinand! a year ago to-day I saw *her* for the last time. Is there for us a meeting in another world?

"Ah, me! miserable! Alone! cursed with imagination beyond my physical strength, torn by unbounded, unsatisfied love!--still, I have known the great ones of the heaven of music; I have laughed as I basked in the radiance of their glory! Immortals, stretch out your hands, raise me to the shelter of your golden clouds that I may be at rest!

"Voice of Reason:

"'Peace, fool! ere many years have passed your pain will be no more.'

Henriette Smithson and

Hector Berlioz

will rest in the oblivion of the grave and other unfortunates will also suffer and die!" ...

To H. FERRAND.

"*November 1829.*--Oh Ferrand! Ferrand! why were you not here for my concert? Yesterday I was so ill that I could not crawl; to-day the fire of hell that inspired my *Francs-Juges* overture, courses through my veins.

"All my heart, my passion, my love are in that overture.

"After the crowd had dispersed the performers waited for me in the courtyard and greeted me with wild applause. At the Opera in the evening it was the same thing--a regular ferment!

"My friend, my friend! Had you but been there!

"But it was more than I could stand, and now I am a prey to the most awful depression and despair; tears choke me, I long to die.

"After all, there will be a small profit--about a hundred and fifty francs, of which I must give two-thirds to Gounet, who so kindly lent it me--I think he is more in need than you. But my debt to you troubles me, and as soon as I can get together enough to be worth sending, you shall have it." ...

* * * * *

"*December.*--I am bored! wretched! That is nothing new, but I get more and more soul-weary, more utterly bored as time goes on. I devour time as ducks gobble water, in order to live and, like the ducks, I find nothing but a few scrubby insects for nourishment. What will become of me! What shall I do!"

To H. FERRAND.

"*January 1830.*--I do not know where to turn for money. I have only two pupils, they bring me in forty-four francs a month; I still owe you money besides the hundred francs to Gounet--this eternal penury, these constant debts, even to such old and tried friends as you, weigh on me terribly. Then again your father still nurses the mistaken idea that I am a gambler--I, who never touch a card and have never set foot in a gaming house--and the thought that he disapproves of our friendship nearly drives me mad. For pity's sake, write soon!"

* * * * *

"*February.*--Again, without warning and without reason, my ill-starred passion wakes. She is in London, yet I feel her presence ever with me. I listen to the beating of my heart, it is like a sledge-hammer, every nerve in my body quivers with pain.

"Woe upon her! Could she but dream of the poetry, the infinite bliss of such love as mine, she would fly to my arms, even though my embrace should be her death.

"I was just going to begin my great symphony (*Episode in an Artist's Life*) to depict the course of this infernal love of mine--but I can write nothing."

* * * * *

"*May.*--Your letter comforts me, dear friend, how good it is to be blessed with a friend such as you! A man of heart, of soul, of imagination! How rare that kindred spirits such as ours should meet and sympathise.

"Words fail to tell the joy your affection gives me. You need not fear for me with Henriette Smithson. I am no longer in danger in that quarter; I pity and despise her. She is nothing but a commonplace woman with an instinct for expressing the tortures of the soul that she has never felt;

she is quite incapable of appreciating the noble, all-devouring love with which I honoured her.

"The rehearsals of my symphony begin in three days; all the parts are copied--there are two thousand three hundred pages. I hope to goodness we shall have good receipts to pay for it all. The concert takes place on the 30th May. And you alone will not be there! Even my father wishes to come. Ah, my symphony!

"I wish the theatre people would somehow plot to get *her* there--that wretched woman! But she certainly would not go if she read my programme. She could not but recognise herself. What will people say? My story is so well known."

At this time a new influence came into my life which, for a time, eclipsed my Shakespearian passion.

Hiller, the German composer-pianist, whom I had known intimately ever since his arrival in Paris, fell violently in love with Marie Moke, a beautiful and talented girl, who, later on, became one of our greatest pianists.

Her interest in me was aroused by Hiller's account of my mental sufferings, and--so Fate willed--we were thrown much together at a boarding-school where we both gave lessons--she on the piano and I on--the guitar! Odd though it be, I still figure in the prospectus of Madame d'Aubre as professor of that noble instrument.

Meeting Mademoiselle Moke constantly, her dainty beauty and bewitching mockery of my high-tragedy airs and dismal visage soon turned my thoughts from my absorbing passion and won her a shrine in my heart. She was but eighteen!

Hiller, poor fellow, behaved admirably. He recognised that it was Fate, not treachery on my part and, heart-broken as he was, he wished me every happiness and left for Frankfort.

This is all I need say of this violent interlude that, by stirring my senses, turned me aside for a while from the mighty love that really held my heart. In my Italian journey I will tell of the dramatic sequel. Mademoiselle Moke nearly proved the proverb that it is not well to play with fire!

* * * * *

In 1830 the Competition took place later than usual--on the 15th July. For the fifth time I went up, firmly resolved, if I should fail, to go no more.

As I finished my cantata the Revolution broke out and the Institute was a curious sight. Grape shot rattled on the barred doors, cannon balls shook the facade, women screamed and, in the momentary pauses, the interrupted swallows took up their sweet, shrill cry. I hurried over the last pages of my cantata, and on the 29th was free to maraud about the streets, pistol in hand, with the "blessed riffraff" as Barbier said.

I shall never forget the look of Paris during those few days. The frantic bravery of the gutter-snipe, the enthusiasm of the men, the calm, sad resignation of the Swiss and Royal Guards, the odd pride of the mob in being "masters of Paris and looting nothing." One day, just after this harmonious revolution, I had a strange musical shock.

Going through the Palais Royal, I heard some young men singing a familiar air; it was my own:

"Forget not our wounded companions, who stood

In the day of distress by our side;

While the moss of the valley grew red with their blood

They stirred not, but conquered and died."[7]

Not used to such fame I, in great delight, asked the leader whether I might join in, and incontinently began a hot argument with him as to the time at which it should be taken. Of course I was not recognised.

As we sang, three of the National Guard handed round their shakos to collect money for the wounded and there was a welcome deluge of five franc pieces. The crowd increased and our breathing space became less and less; we should have ended in being smothered had not a kindly haberdasher asked us up to her first floor windows, that looked out upon the covered gallery, whence we could rain down our music upon the crowd below, as the Pope does his blessing from the balcony of St Peter's.

First we gave them the *Marseillaise*. At the opening bar the noisy crowd stood motionless; at the end of the second verse the same silence; even so with the third. Irate at their apparent coldness, I roared out--

"Confound it all! SING!"

And they sang.

Remember, those four or five thousand tightly packed people were--men, women and children--hot from the barricades, inflamed with lust for combat, and imagine how their

"Aux armes, citoyens!"

rolled out.

Aghast at the explosion we had provoked, our little band stood silent as birds after a thunder clap.

I, literally not metaphorically, sank on the floor.

Some time before this I had arranged the *Marseillaise* for full orchestra and double chorus and had dedicated it to Rouget de Lisle, who wrote inviting me to go and see him at Choisy, as he had several proposals to make to me.

Unfortunately I could not go then, as I was on the point of starting for Italy, and he died before I returned. I only heard much later that he had written many fine songs besides the *Marseillaise* and had also a libretto for *Othello* put aside; it is probably this that he wished to discuss with me.

As soon as peace was patched up and Louis Philippe introduced by Lafayette as "the best of republics" the Academy started work once more.

And as the judges, thanks to a piece which I have since burnt, believed me reclaimed from my heresies, they gave me the first prize. Although, in former years, I had been greatly disappointed at not getting it I was not in the least pleased when I did.

Of course I appreciated its advantages; my parents' pride, the kudos, the freedom for five years from money troubles--yet, knowing the system on which prizes were awarded, could I feel any proper pride in my success?

Two months after came the distribution of prizes and the performance of the successful work. It was all very hackneyed.

Every year the same musicians perform pieces turned out on the same pattern; the same prizes, awarded with the same discrimination, are handed over with the same ceremony. Every year on the same day, at the same time, standing on the same step of the same staircase, the same Academician repeats the same words to the winner.

Day, first Saturday in October; time, four in the afternoon; step, the third; the Academician--we all know who.

Then comes the performance with full orchestra (in my case it was not quite full, for there was only a clarinet and a half, the old boy who played the first--having only one tooth and being asthmatic besides--

being only able to squeeze out a note here and there). The conductor raises his baton----

The sun rises; 'cello solo, gentle crescendo.

The little birds wake; flute solo, violin tremolo.

The little rills gurgle; alto solo.

The little lambs bleat; oboe solo.

And as the crescendo goes on and the little birds and little brooks and little beasts finish their performance, one suddenly discovers that it is noon; then follow the successive airs up to the third, with which the hero usually expires and the audience once more breathes freely.

Then the secretary, holding in one hand the artificial laurel wreath and in the other the gold medal, worth enough to keep the recipient until he leaves for Rome (in point of fact, I have proved that it is worth exactly a hundred and sixty francs) pompously enunciates the name of the author.

The laureate rises,

"His smooth, chaste forehead, newly shorn,

is wreathed with modest blushes."

He embraces the secretary--faint applause. He embraces his master, seated close by--more applause. Next come his mother, his sisters, his cousins, and his aunts to the tune of more applause; then his fiancee, after which--treading on people's toes and tearing ladies' dresses in the blind confusion of his headlong career--he regains his seat, bathed in perspiration. Loud applause and laughter.

This is the crowning moment, and I know lots of people who go for nothing but the fun of it.

I do not say this in bitterness of spirit, although, when my turn came, neither father nor mother, nor fiancee[8] were there to congratulate me. My master was ill, my parents estranged, my mistress--ah!

So I only embraced the secretary, and I do not fancy that my "modest blushes" were noticed because, instead of being "newly shorn," my forehead was buried in a shock of long red hair, which, in conjunction with certain other points in my physiognomy certainly earned me a place in the owl tribe.

Besides, I was not in at all an embrace-inspiring humour that day. Truth obliges me to confess that I was in a howling, rampant rage.

I must go back a little and explain why.

The subject set was the *Last Night of Sardanapalus*, and it ended with his gathering his most beautiful slaves around him and, with them, mounting the funeral pyre.

I was just going to write a symphonic description of the scene--the cries of the unwilling victims; the king's proud defiance of the flames, the crash of the falling palace--when I suddenly bethought me that that way lay suicide--since the piano, as usual, would be the only means of interpretation.

I therefore waited and, as soon as the prize was awarded and I knew I could not be deprived of it, I wrote my CONFLAGRATION.

At the final orchestral rehearsal it made such a sensation that several of the Academicians came up and congratulated me most warmly, without a trace of pique at the trick I had played upon them. The rumour of it having gone abroad, the hall was packed--for I found I had already made a sort of bizarre reputation.

Not feeling particularly confident in the powers of Grasset, the conductor, I stood close beside him, manuscript in hand, while Madame Malibran, who had been unable to find a seat in the hall, sat on a stool at my elbow between two double-basses. That was the last time I ever saw her.

All went smoothly; Sardanapalus assembled his slaves, the fire was kindled, everyone listened intently, and those who had been at rehearsal whispered:

"Now it's coming. Just listen. It's simply wonderful!"

Curses and excommunications upon those musicians who do not count their rests!! That damned horn, that should have given the signal to the side-drums, never came in. The drums were afraid to begin, so gave no signal to the cymbals, nor the cymbals to the big-drum.

The violins went wobbling on with their futile tremolo and my fire went out without one crackle!

Only a composer who has been through a like experience can appreciate my fury.

Giving vent to a wild yell of rage, I flung my score smash into the middle of the band and knocked over two desks. Madame Malibran jumped as if she had been shot, and the whole place was in an uproar.

It was a regular catastrophe--worst and cruellest of all I had hitherto borne; but alas! by no means the last.

XVI

LISZT

To HUMBERT FERRAND.

"*24th July 1830.*

"DEAR FRIEND,--All that the most tender delicate love can give is mine. My exquisite sylph, my Ariel, loves me more than ever and her mother says that, had she read of love like mine, she could not have believed it.

"I am shut up in the Institute *for the last time*, for the prize *shall* be mine this year, our happiness hangs on it. Every other day Madame Moke sends her maid with messages. Can you credit it, Humbert? This angel, with the finest talent in Europe, is mine! I hear that M. de Noailles, in whom her mother believes greatly, has pleaded my cause, despite my want of money. If only you could hear my Camille *thinking aloud* in the divine works of Beethoven and Weber, you would lose your head as I do."

"*23rd August 1830.*

"I have gained the Prix de Rome. It was awarded unanimously--a thing that has never been known before. What a joy it is to be successful when it gives pleasure to those one adores!

"My sweet Ariel was dying of anxiety when I took her the news, her dainty wings were all ruffled until I smoothed them with a word. Even her mother, who does not look too favourably on our love, was touched to tears.

"On the 1st November there is to be a concert at the Theatre Italien. The new conductor, Girard, whom I know well, has asked me to write him an overture for it. I am going to take Shakespeare's *Tempest*; it will be quite a new style of thing.

"My great concert with the *Symphonie Fantastique* is to be on the 14th November, but I must have a *theatrical* success; Camilla's parents insist upon that as a condition of our marriage. I hope I shall succeed.

"I do not want to go to Italy. I shall go and ask the King to let me off. It is a ridiculous journey for me to take, and I might just as well be allowed my scholarship in Paris.

"As soon as I have collected the money you so kindly lent me, you shall have it. Good-bye, good-bye. I have just come from Madame Moke's, from touching the hand of my adored Camille, that is why mine trembles and my writing is so bad. Yet to-day she has not played me either Beethoven or Weber.

"*P.S.*--That wretched Smithson girl is still here. I have not seen her."

To HUMBERT FERRAND.

"*October 1830.*--You will be glad to hear that I am to be heard at the Opera. All thanks to Camille! In her slender form, witching grace, and musical genius I found Ariel personified. I have planned a tremendous overture, which I have submitted to the director. Ariel! Ariel! Camille! I bless, I adore, I love thee more than poor language can express. Give me a hundred musicians, a hundred and fifty voices, then can I tell thee all!

* * * * *

"That poor Ophelia comes again and again to my mind. She has lost more than six thousand francs in the Opera Comique venture. She is still here, and met me the other day quite calmly. I was utterly miserable the whole evening, and went and told Ariel, who laughed at me tenderly."

In spite of all my eloquence, I could not get out of that tiresome journey to Rome. But I would not leave Paris without having *Sardanapalus* performed properly, and for the third time my artist friends most generously offered me their aid, and Habeneck consented to conduct.

The day before the concert Liszt came to see me. We had not, so far, met. We began talking of *Faust*, which he had not read, but which he afterwards got to love as I did. We were so thoroughly sympathetic to each other that, from that day, our friendship neither faltered nor waned. At my concert everyone noticed his enthusiasm and vociferous applause.

As my work is exceedingly complicated, it is not surprising that the execution was by no means perfect; yet some parts of the Symphony made a sensation. The *Scene aux Champs* fell quite flat, and, on the advice of Ferdinand Hiller, I afterwards entirely rewrote it.

Sardanapalus was well done, and the *Conflagration* came off magnificently. It raised a conflagration in Paris too, in the shape of a war of musicians and critics.

Naturally the younger men--particularly those with that sixth sense, artistic instinct--were on my side, but Cherubini and his gang were wild with rage.

He happened to pass the concert-room doors as people were going in, and a friend stopped him, asking:

"Are you not coming to hear Berlioz's new thing?"

"I need not zat I go hear how sings should not be done," he replied.

He was much worse after the concert, and sent for me.

"You go soon," he said.

"Yes, monsieur."

"It vill be zat you are cross off ze register of Conservatoire, zat your studies are finish. But it seem to me zat you should make visit to me. One goes not out of Conservatoire like out of a stable."

I very nearly said:

"Why not, since we are treated like horses?" but luckily had the good sense merely to say that I had not the slightest intention of leaving Paris without saying farewell to him.

So to Rome, *nolens volens,* I had to go, useless as it seemed.

The Roman Academy may be of service to painters and sculptors, but, as far as music is concerned, it is lost time, considering the state of music in Italy. Neither is the life led by the students exactly conducive to study and progress.

Usually the five or six laureates arrange to travel in company, and share expenses. A coach-driver agrees, for a modest sum, to take charge of this cargo of great men, and dump it down in Italy. As he never changes horses it takes a long time, and must be rather amusing.

I did not try it, as I had to stay in Paris for various reasons till the middle of January and then wished to go round by La Cote Saint-Andre--where my laurel wreath earned me a warm welcome--after which, alone, and dreary, I turned my face towards Italy.

To HUMBERT FERRAND.

"*November 1830.*--Just a few lines in haste to tell you that I am giving a gigantic concert at the Conservatoire--the *Francs-Juges* overture, the *Sacred Song* and *Warrior's Song* from the Melodies, and *Sardanapalus* with one hundred performers for the CONFLAGRATION, and last of all, the *Symphonie Fantastique.*

"Come, oh, do come. It will be terrible. Habeneck conducts. The *Tempest* is to be played a second time at the Opera. It is new, fresh, strange, grand, sweet, tender, surprising. Fetis wrote two splendid articles on it for the *Revue Musicale.* Some one said to him the other day that I was possessed of a devil. 'The devil may possess his body, but, by Jove! a god possesses his head,' he retorted.

"*December.*--You really must come; I had a frantic success. They actually encored the *Marche au Supplice.* I am mad! mad! My marriage is fixed for Easter 1832, on condition that I do not lose my pension, and that I go to Italy for a year. My blessed symphony has done the deed, and won this concession from Camille's mother.

"My guardian angel! for months I shall not see her. Why cannot I--cradled by the wild north wind upon some desolate heath--fall into the eternal sleep with her arms around me!"

To FERDINAND HILLER.

"LA COTE SAINT-ANDRE, *January 1831*.--I am at home once more, deluged with compliments, caresses, and tender solicitude by my family, yet I am miserable; my heart barely beats, the oppression of my soul suffocates me. My parents understand and forgive.

"I have been to Grenoble, where I spent half my time in bed, the other half in calling upon people who bored me to extinction. On my return I found awaiting me my longed-for letter from Paris.

"Now comes yours, to spoil all! Devil take you! Was it necessary to tell me that I am luxuriating in despair, that *no one* cares twopence for me, least of all the people for whom I am pining?

* * * * *

"In the first place, I am not pining for *people*, but for one person; in the second, if you have your reasons for judging her severely I have mine for believing in her implicitly, and I understand her better than any one.

"How can you tell what she thinks? What she feels? Because you saw her gay, and apparently happy, at a concert why should you draw conclusions adverse to me? If it comes to that, you might have said the same of me if you had seen me at a family dinner at Grenoble, with a pretty young cousin on either side of me.

"My letter is brusque, my friend, but you have upset me terribly. Write by return and tell me what the world says of my marriage."

"*31st January 1831*.--Although my overpowering anxiety still endures, I can write more calmly to-day. I am still too ill to get up, and the cold is frightful here.

"Tell me what you mean by this sentence in your last letter: 'You wish to make a sacrifice; I fear me sadly that, ere long, you will be forced to make a most painful one.' For heaven's sake never use ambiguous words to me, above all in connection with *her*. It tortures me. Tell me frankly what you mean."

XVII

ITALY

A WILD INTERLUDE

THE weather was too severe to cross the Alps, I therefore determined to out-flank them and go by sea from Marseilles. It was the first time I had seen the sea and, as some days passed before I could hear of a boat, I spent most of my time wandering over the rocks near Notre Dame de la Garde.

After a while I heard of a Sardinian brig bound for Leghorn, and engaged a passage in her in company with some decent young fellows I had met in the Cannebiere.

The captain would not undertake to feed us, so, reckoning that we should make Leghorn in three or four days, we laid in provisions for a week.

In fine weather, few things are more delightful than a Mediterranean voyage--particularly one's first. Our first few days were glorious; all my companions were Italians, and had many stories to tell--some true, some not, but all interesting. One had fought in Greece with Canaris, another--a Venetian--had commanded Byron's yacht, and the tales he told accorded well with what one might expect of the author of *Lara*.

Time went on, but we got no nearer Leghorn. Each morning, going on deck, my first question was, "What town is that?" and the eternal answer was, "Nizza, signor, still Nizza." I began to think that the charming town of Nice had some sort of magnetic attraction for our boat.

I found out my mistake when a furious Alpine wind burst down upon us. The captain, to make up for lost time, crowded on all sail and the vessel heeled over and drove furiously before the gale. Towards evening we made the Gulf of Spezzia, and the tramontana increased to such a pitch that the sailors themselves trembled at the captain's foolhardiness. I stood by the Venetian, holding on to a bar and listening to his maledictions on the captain's madness, when suddenly a fresh gust of wind caught the boat and sent her over on her beam-ends, the captain rolling away into the scuppers.

In a flash the Venetian was at the tiller, shouting orders to the sailors, who were by this time calling on the Madonna:

"Don't bother about the Madonna now," he cried, "get in the sails."

The sails were reefed, the ship righted, and next day we reached Leghorn with only one sail, so strong was the wind.

A few hours after, our sailors came to the hotel in a body to congratulate us on our escape. And, though the poor devils hardly earned enough to keep body and soul together, nothing would induce them to take a farthing. It was only by great persuasion that we got them to share an impromptu meal. My friends had confided to me that they were on the way to join the insurrection in Modena; they had great hopes of raising Tuscany and then marching on Rome.

But alas for their young hopes! Two were arrested before reaching Florence and thrown into dungeons, where they may still lie rotting; the others, I heard later, did well in Modena, but finally shared the fate of gallant and ill-starred Menotti.

So ended their sweet dream of liberty.

I had great trouble in getting from Florence to Rome. Frenchmen were revolutionists and the Pope did not welcome them warmly. The Florentine authorities refused to *viser* my passport, and nothing but the energetic protests of Monsieur Horace Vernet, the director of the Roman Academy, prevailed on them to let me go.

Still alone, I made my way to Rome. My driver knew no French so I was reduced to reading the memoirs of the Empress Josephine, as we dawdled on our road. The country was not interesting; the inns were most uncomfortable; nothing gave me reason to reverse my decision that Italy was a horrid country and I most unlucky in being compelled to stay in it.

But one morning we reached a group of houses called La Storta and, as he poured out a glass of wine, my *vetturino* said casually, with a jerk of his head and thumb:

"There is Rome, signore."

Strange revulsion of feeling! As I gazed down on the far-off city, standing in purple majesty in the midst of its vast desolate plain, my heart swelled with awe and reverence, and suddenly I realised all the grandeur, all the poetry, all the might of that heart of the world.

I was still lost in dreams of the past when the carriage stopped in front of the Academy.

The Villa Medici, the home of the students and director of the *Academie de France*, was built in 1557 by Annibale Lippi, one wing being added by Michael Angelo. It stands on the side of the Pincian, overlooking the city; on one side of it is the Pincian Way, on the other the magnificent gardens designed in Lenotre's style, and opposite, in the midst of the waste fields of the Villa Borghese, stands Raphael's house.

Such are the royal quarters that France has munificently provided for her children. Yet the rooms of the pupils are mostly small, uncomfortable, and very badly furnished.

The studios of the painters and sculptors are scattered about the grounds as well as in the palace, and from a little balcony, looking over the Ursuline gardens, there is a glorious view of the Sabine range, Monte Cavo and Hannibal's Camp.

There is a fair library of standard classics, but no modern books whatever; studiously-minded people may go and kill time there up to three in the afternoon, for there is really nothing to do. The sole obligation of the students is, once a year, to send a sample of their work to the Academy in Paris; for the rest of the time they do exactly as they please.

The director simply has to see that rules are kept and the whole establishment well managed; with the inmates' work he has nothing to do whatever.

It would be hardly fair that he should; to overlook and advise twenty-two young men in five different branches of art would hardly be within one man's compass.

The Ave Maria was ringing as I entered the portals of the Villa and, as that was the dinner-hour, I went straight to the refectory. As soon as I appeared in the doorway there was a hurrah that raised the roof.

"Ho! ho! Berlioz! Oh that blessed head! that fiery mop! that dainty nose! I say, Jalay, his nose knocks spots out of yours; take a back-seat, my good man!"

"He can give *you* points in hair anyway."

"Ye gods, *what* a crop!"

"Heigh, Berlioz! how about those infernal side-drums that wouldn't start the *Fire*! By Jove! he was in a wax. Good reason, too! I say, have you forgotten me?"

"I know your face well enough, but your name----"

"He says 'you.' Don't give yourself airs, old boy, we are all 'thou' here."

"Well, what is *thy* name?"

"Signol."

"No, it isn't; it's *Ros*signol."[9]

"Lord, what a beastly bad pun!"

"Do let him sit down."

"Whom? The pun?"

"Get out! Berlioz, of course."

"I say, Fleury, bring us some punch--real good stuff. We'll stop this idiot's mouth."

"Now our musical section is complete."

"Montfort" (the laureate of the year before me), "embrace your comrade."

"No, he sha'n't!"

"Yes, he shall!" and they all yelled together.

"Look here; while you others are fighting, he's eating all the macaroni. Leave me a bit!"

"Well, embrace him all round and get it done with."

"Oh, bother! Now it's going to begin all over again."

"I say, I'm not going to drink wine when there's punch."

"Not much! Break the bottles. Look out, Fleury!"

"Gentlemen! Gentlemen! Don't break the glasses, please! You will want them for the punch. You would not like to drink punch out of little glasses."

"Perish the thought! You are a man of sense, Fleury. You were only just in time, though."

Fleury was the prop of the house; a thoroughly good fellow, who well deserved the trust of the Academy directors. Nothing ruffled him; he was so used to our scenes that he kept the aspect of a graven image, which made it all the funnier for us.

When I had got over my tempestuous reception, I looked round the hall. On one wall were about fifty portraits of former students, on the other a series of the most outrageous life-sized caricatures, also of inmates of the Academy. Unluckily, for want of wall-space, these soon came to an end.

That evening, after an interview with M. Vernet, I followed my comrades to the Cafe Greco--the dirtiest, darkest, dampest hole imaginable. How it justifies its existence as the artist's favourite cafe I cannot imagine. We smoked abominable cigars and drank coffee that was none the nicer for being served on dirty little wooden tables, as sticky and greasy as the walls.

Next day I made Mendelssohn's acquaintance; but more of this when I come to write of Germany.[10]

For a while I got on fairly well in this new life, then gradually my anxiety about my Paris letters, which were not forthcoming, increased to such an extent that, in defiance of the kindly expostulations of M. Horace Vernet, who tried to restrain me by saying that I must be struck off the list of *pensionnaires* if I broke the Academy's most stringent rule, I decided to return to Paris.

I started, but at Florence was kept in bed a week by quinsy, and so made the acquaintance of Schlick, the Danish sculptor, a thoroughly good fellow of much talent. During this week I rewrote the Ball Scene for my *Symphonie Fantastique*, and added the present Coda.

It was not quite finished when, the first time I was able to go out, I fetched my letters from the post. Among them was one of such unparalleled impudence that I fairly took leave of my senses. Needless to say, it was from Camilla's mother. In it, after accusing me of *bringing annoyance* into her household, she announced the marriage of my *fiancee* to M. Pleyel.

In two minutes my plans were laid. I must hurry to Paris to kill two guilty women and one innocent man; for, this act of justice done, I, too, must die!

They would expect me, therefore I must go disguised. I hurried to Schlick and showed him the letter.

"It is scandalous," he said. "What will you do?"

I thought it best to deceive him so as to be absolutely free.

"Do? Why, return to France. But I will go to my father's, not to Paris."

"Right!" he replied. "Your own home will best soothe your wounded heart. Keep up your spirits."

"I will; but I must go at once."

"You can easily go this evening. I know the official people here, and will get your passport and a seat for you in the mail. Go and pack."

Instead of packing, I went to a milliner in the Lung 'Arno.

"Madame," I said, "I want a lady's-maid's outfit by five o'clock--dress, hat, green veil, everything. Money is no object. Can you do it?"

She agreed, and leaving a deposit, I went back to the hotel. Taking the score of the Ball Scene, I wrote across it:

"I have not time to finish, but if the Concert Society will perform the piece in the absence of the composer, I beg that Habeneck will double the flute passage at the last entry of the theme, and will write the following chords for full orchestra. That will be sufficient finale," threw it into a valise with a few clothes, loaded my pistols, put into my pockets two little bottles, one of strychnine, the other of laudanum; then, conscience-clear with regard to my arsenal, spent the rest of the time raging up and down the streets of Florence like a mad dog.

At five, I went back to the shop to try on my clothes, which were satisfactory, and with the modiste's "good wishes for the success of my little comedy," I went back to say good-bye to Schlick, who looked upon me as a lost sheep returning to the fold!

A farewell glance at Cellini's *Perseus*, and we were off.

League after league went by and I sat with clenched teeth. I could neither eat nor speak. About midnight the driver and I exchanged a few words about my pistols, he remarking that, if brigands attacked us, we must on no account attempt to defend ourselves, proceeded to take off the caps and hide them under the cushions.

"As you like," I said, indifferently. "I have no wish to compromise you."

On our arrival at Genoa (I having tasted nothing but the juice of an orange, to the astonishment of the courier, who could not make out whether I belonged to this world or the next), I found that, in changing carriages at Pietra Santa, my finery had been left behind.

"Confound it all!" I thought; "this looks as if some cursed good angel stood in the way of my plan."

Again I hunted up a dressmaker, and after trying three, succeeded in getting a new outfit. Meanwhile, the Sardinian people, seeing me trotting after work-girls like this, took it into their sapient heads that I must be a conspirator, a *carbonero*, a liberator, and refused to *viser* my passport for Turin. I must go by Nice.

"Then, for heaven's sake, *viser* it for Nice. I don't care. I'll go *via* the infernal regions so long as I get through."

Which was the greater fool--the policeman, who saw in every Frenchman an emissary of the Revolution, or myself, who thought I could not set foot in Paris undisguised; forgetting that, by hiding for a day in a hotel, I could have found fifty women to rig me out perfectly?

Self-engrossed people are really delightful. They fancy everyone is thinking about them, and the deadly earnest with which they act up to the idea is simply delicious!

So, behold me on my way to Nice, going over and over my little Parisian drama.

Disguised as the Countess de M.'s lady's-maid, I would go to the house about nine o'clock with an important letter. While it was being read, I would pull out my double-barrelled pistols, kill number one and number two, seize number three by the hair and finish her off likewise; after which, if this vocal and instrumental concert had gathered an audience, I would turn the fourth barrel upon myself. Should it miss fire (such things happen occasionally), I had a final resource in my little bottles.

Grand climax! It seems rather a pity it never came off.

Now, despite my rage, I began to say:

"Yes, it will be most agreeable, but--to have to kill myself too, is distinctly annoying. To say farewell to earth, to art; to leave behind me only the reputation of a churl, who did not understand the gentle art of living; to leave my symphony unfinished, the scores unwritten--those glorious scores that float through my brain.... Ah!"

"But no; they shall, they must all die!"

Each minute I drew nearer to France.

That night, on the Cornice road, love of life and love of art whispered sweet promises of days to come, and I sat listening, vaguely, dreamily, when the driver stopped to put on the drag. Roused mentally by the thunder of the waves upon the iron cliffs below, the stupendous majesty of Nature burst upon me with greater force than ever before, and woke anew the tempest in my heart--the awful wrestling of Life and Death.

Holding with both hands on to my seat, I let out a wild "Ha!" so hoarse, so savage, so diabolic that the startled driver bounced aside as if he had indeed had a demon for his fellow-traveller.

In my first lucid moments I remember thinking, "If only I could find some solid point of rock to cling to before the next wave of fury and madness sweeps over my head, I might yet be saved!"

I found one. We stopped to change horses at a little Sardinian village--Ventimiglia, I believe[11]--and, begging five minutes from the guard, I hurried into a cafe, seized a scrap of paper, and wrote to M. Vernet, praying him to keep me on the roll of students, if I were not already crossed off, assuring him that I had not yet broken the rule, and promising not to cross the frontier until I received his answer at Nice, where I would await it.

Temporarily safeguarded by my word of honour, yet free to take up my Red Indian scheme of vengeance again, should I be excluded from the Academy, I got quietly into the carriage and suddenly discovered that ... I was hungry, having eaten nothing since leaving Florence.

Oh, good, gross Nature! I was positively reviving!

I got to Nice, still growling at intervals; but, after a few days came M. Vernet's answer--a friendly paternal letter that touched me deeply.

Though ignorant of the reason of my trouble, the great artist gave me the best advice, showing me that hard work and love of art were the sovereign remedies for a mind diseased; telling me that the Minister knew nothing of my escapade, and that I should be received with open arms in Rome.

"They are saved!" I sighed. "Suppose I live too?--live quietly, happily, musically? Why not? Let's try!"

So for a month I dwelt alone at Nice, writing the *King Lear* overture, bathing in the sea, wandering through orange groves, and sleeping on the healthy slopes of the Villefranche hills.

Thus passed the twenty happiest days of my life.

Oh, Nizza!

But the King of Sardinia's police put an end to this idyllic life. I had spoken to one or two officers of the garrison, and had even played billiards with them. This was sufficient to rouse the darkest suspicions.

"This musician cannot have come to hear *Mathilde de Sabran*" (the only opera given just then), "since he never goes near the theatre. He wanders alone on the hills, no doubt expecting a signal from some revolutionary vessel; he never dines at *table d'hote* in order to avoid spies; he is ingratiating himself with our officers in order to start negotiations with them in the name of Young Italy. It is a flagrant conspiracy!"

I was summoned to the police office.

"What are you doing here, sir?"

"Recruiting after a terrible illness. I compose, I dream, I thank God for the glorious sun, the sea, the flower-clothed hillsides----"

"You are not an artist?"

"No."

"Yet you wander about with a book in your hand. Are you making plans?"

"Yes, the plan of an overture to *King Lear*--at least the instrumentation is nearly finished, and I believe its reception will be tremendous."

"What do you mean by reception? Who is this King Lear?"

"Oh, a wretched old English king."

"English king?"

"Yes; according to Shakespeare he lived about eighteen hundred years ago, and was idiotic enough to divide his kingdom between two wicked daughters, who kicked him out when he had nothing more to give them. You see, there are few kings that----"

"Never mind kings now. What do you mean by instrumentation?"

"It is a musical term."

"Same excuse again! Sir, I know that you cannot possibly compose wandering about the beach with only a pencil and paper, and no piano, so tell me where you wish to go, and your passport shall be made out. You cannot remain here."

"Then I will go back to Rome, and, by your leave, continue to compose without a piano."

Next day I left Nice, greatly against the grain, but I was brisk and light-hearted, well and thoroughly cured. Thus once more loaded pistols missed fire.

Never mind. My little drama was interesting, and I cannot help regretting it--just a little!

To H. FERRAND.

"*11th May 1831.*--Well, Ferrand, I am getting on. Rage, threats of vengeance, grinding of teeth, tortures of hell--all over and done with!

"If your silence means laziness on your part, it is too bad of you. When one comes back to life, as I have done, one feels the need of a friendly arm, of an outstretched hand.

"Yes, Camille has married Pleyel, and I am glad of it. I see now the perils that I have escaped.

"What meanness! what shabbiness! what apathy! what infinite--almost sublime--villainy, if sublime can agree with ignobility (I have stolen that newly coined word from you).

"*P.S.*--I have just finished a new overture--to *King Lear*."

XVIII

ITALIAN MUSIC

I DID not hurry back to Rome, but spent some time in Genoa, where I heard Paer's *Agnese*, and where I could find no trace of bust or statue or tradition of Columbus. I also tried in vain to hear something of Paganini, who at that moment was electrifying Paris, while I--with my usual luck--was kicking my heels in his native town.

Thence I went back to Florence, which of all Italian cities appeals to me most. There the spleen that devours me in Rome and Naples takes flight. With barely a handful of francs--since my little excursion had made a big hole in my income, knowing no one and being consequently entirely free--I passed delicious days visiting odd corners, dreaming of Dante and Michael Angelo, and reading Shakespeare in the shady woods on the Arno bank.

Knowing, however, that the Tuscan capital could not compare with Naples and Milan in opera, I took no thought for music until I heard people at *table d'hote* talking of Bellini's *Montecchi*, which was soon to be given. Not only did they praise the music, but also the libretto. Italians, as a rule, care so little for the words of an opera that I was surprised, and thought:

"At last I shall hear an opera worthy of that glorious play. What a subject it is! Simply made for music. The ball at Capulet's house, where young Romeo first sees his dazzling love; the street fight whereat Tybalt presides--patron of anger and revenge; that indescribable night scene at Juliet's balcony; the witty sallies of Mercutio; the prattle of the nurse; the solemnity of the friar trying to soothe these conflicting elements; the awful catastrophe and the reconciliation of the rival families above the bodies of the ill-fated lovers."

I hurried to the Pergola Theatre.

What a disappointment! No ball, no Mercutio, no babbling nurse, no balcony scene, no Shakespeare!

And Romeo sung by a small thin *woman*, Juliet by a tall stout one. Why--in the name of all things musical--why?

Do they think that women's voices sound best together? Then why not do away with men's entirely?

Why should Juliet's lover be deprived of all virility? Could a woman or a child have slain Tybalt, having burst the gates of Juliet's tomb and stretched County Paris a corpse at his feet?

Surely Othello and Moses with high women's voices would not be more utterly incongruous.

In justice, I must say that Bellini has got a most beautiful effect in a really powerful incident. The lovers, dragged apart by angry parents, tear themselves free and rush into each other's arms, crying: "We meet again in heaven."

He has used a quick, impassioned *motif*, sung in unison, that expresses most eloquently the idea of perfect union.

I was unwontedly moved, and applauded heartily. Thinking that I had better know the worst that Italian opera could perpetrate, had better--as it were--drink the cup to the dregs, I went to hear Paccini's *Vestal*. Although I knew it had nothing in common with Spontini's opera, I little dreamed of the bitterness of the cup I had to face. Licinius, again, was a woman.... After a few minutes' painfully strained attention I cried, with Hamlet, "Wormwood! wormwood!" and fled, feeling I could swallow no more, and stamping so hard that my great toe was sore for three days after.

Poor Italy!

At least, thought I, it will be better in the churches. This was what I heard.

A funeral service for the elder son of Louis Bonaparte and Queen Hortense was being held.

What thoughts crowded into my mind as I stood amid the flaming torches in the crape-hung church! A Bonaparte! *His* nephew, almost his grandson, dead at twenty; his mother, with his only brother, an exile in England.

I thought of the gay creole child dancing on the deck of the ship that carried her to France, untitled daughter of Madame Beauharnais, adopted daughter of the master of Europe, Queen of Holland, exiled, forgotten, bereft, without a kingdom, without a home!

Oh, Beethoven! Great soul! Titan, who couldst conceive the *Eroica* and the *Funeral March*, is not this a meet subject for thy genius?...

The organist pulled out the small flute stops and fooled about over twittering little airs at the top of the key-board, exactly like wrens preening themselves on a sunny wall in winter!

Again, hearing great things of the Corpus Christi music in Rome, I hurried there in company with several Italians bent on the same errand.

They raved all the way of the wonders we should see, dangling before my eyes tiaras, mitres, chasubles, etc., *etc.*

"But the music?" I asked.

"Oh, signor, there will be an immense choir," then they went back to their crosses and incense, and bell-ringing and cannon.

"But the music?" I repeated.

"Oh, there will be a gigantic choir."

"Well, anyway," I thought, "things will be on a magnificent scale," and my vivid imagination raced off to the glories of Solomon's Temple and the colossal pageants of ancient Egypt. Cruel gift of Nature that clothes dull life in a golden veil! It simply made more appalling and impossible the shrill nasal voices of the singers, the quacking clarinets, the bellowing trombones, and the rampant vulgarity of the big drums. It was brutal unadulterated cacophony.

Rome calls this military music!

Then, behold me once more safe at the Villa Medici, welcomed by the director and my comrades, who most kindly and tactfully hid their curiosity concerning my crazy journey. I had gone off having good reason to go; I had come back--so much the better. No remarks, no questions.

To GOUNET, HILLER, *ETC.*

"*6th May 1831.*--I have made acquaintance with Mendelssohn; Monfort knew him before.

"He is a charming fellow; his execution is as perfect as his genius, and that is saying a good deal. All I have heard of his is splendid, and I believe him to be one of the great musicians of his time.

"He has been my cicerone. Every morning I hunt him up; he plays me Beethoven; we sing *Armida*; then he takes me to see ruins that, I must candidly own, do not impress me much. His is one of those clear pure souls one does not often come across; he believes firmly in his Lutheran creed, and I am afraid I shocked him terribly by laughing at the Bible.

"I have to thank him for the only pleasant moments I had during the anxious days of my first stay in Rome.

"You may imagine what I felt like when I received that astonishing letter from Madame Moke announcing her daughter's marriage. She calmly said that she never agreed to our engagement, and begs me, dear kind creature! not to kill myself.

"Hiller knows the whole story, and how I left Paris with her ring upon my finger, given in exchange for mine. However, I am quite recovered and can eat as usual. I am saved, they are saved! I threw myself into the arms of music, and felt how blessed it is to have friends.

"I am working hard at *King Lear*.

"Write to me, each of you, a particular and separate and individual letter."

To F. HILLER.

"Has Mendelssohn arrived yet? His talent is wonderful, extraordinary, sublime. You need not suspect me of partiality in saying this, for he frankly owns that he cannot in the least understand my

The Villa Medici, Rome

music. Greet him for me; he does not think so, but I truly like him thoroughly."

XIX

IN THE MOUNTAINS

I QUICKLY fell into the Academy routine. A bell called us to meals, and we went as we were--with straw hats, blouses plastered with clay, slippered feet, no ties--in fact, in studio undress.

After breakfast we lounged about the garden at quoits, tennis, target practice, shooting the misguided blackbirds who came within range, or trained our puppies; in all of which amusements M. Horace often joined us.

In the evening, at that everlasting Cafe Greco, we smoked the pipe of peace with the "men down below," as we dubbed artists not attached to the Academy. After which we dispersed; those who virtuously returned to the Academy barracks gathering in the garden portico, where my bad guitar and worse voice were in great request, and where we sang *Freyschutz*, *Oberon*, *Iphigenia* or *Don Giovanni*, for, to the credit of my messmates be it spoken, their musical taste was far from low.

On the other hand, we sometimes had what we called English concerts. We each chose a different song and sang it in a different key, beginning by signal one after another; as this concert in twenty-four keys went on crescendo, the frightened dogs in the Pincio kept up a howling obligato and the barbers on the Piazza di Spagna down below winked at each other, saying slyly, "French music!"

On Thursdays we went to Madame Vernet's receptions, where we met the best society in Rome; and on Sundays we usually went long excursions into the country. With the director's permission, longer journeys might be undertaken and usually several of our number were absent.

As for me, since Rome never appealed to me, I took refuge in the mountains; had I not done so, I doubt whether I could have lived through that time. It may seem strange that the mighty shade of old Rome should not impress me, but I had come from Paris, the centre of civilisation, and was at one blow severed from music, from theatres (they were only open for four months), from literature, since the Papal censor excluded almost everything that I cared to read, from excitements, from everything that, to me, meant real life.

Balls, evening parties, shooting days in the Campagna, and rides made up the inane mill-round in which I turned. Add to that the scirocco, the incessant yearning for my beloved art, my sorrowful memories, the misery of being for two years exiled from the musical world, and the utter impossibility of composing in that stagnating atmosphere, and it will hardly be wondered at that I was as savage as a trained bull-dog, and that the well-meant efforts of my friends to divert me only drove me to the verge of madness.

I remember in one of my Campagna rides with Mendelssohn expressing my surprise that no one had ever written a scherzo on Shakespeare's sparkling little poem *Queen Mab*. He, too, was surprised, and I was very sorry I had put the idea into his head. For years I lived in dread that he had used it, for he would have made it impossible--or, at any rate, very risky--for anyone to attempt it after him. Luckily he forgot.

My usual remedy for spleen was a trip to Subiaco, which seemed to put new life into me.

An old grey suit, a straw hat, a guitar, a gun and six piastres were all my stockin-trade. Thus I wandered, shooting or singing, careless where I might pass the night; sometimes hurrying, again stopping to investigate some ancient tomb, to listen silently to the distant bells of St Peter's, far away in the plain; interrupting my hunt for a flock of lapwing to jot down a note for a symphony, and, in short, enjoying to the full my absolute freedom.

Sometimes--a glorious landscape spread before me--I chanted, to the guitar accompaniment, long-remembered verses of the AEneid, the death of Pallas, the despair of Evander, the sad end of Amata, and the death of Lavinia's noble lover, and worked myself up to an incredible pitch of excitement that ended in floods of tears. Elicited originally by the woes of these mythical beings, my overwhelming grief ended by becoming personal, and my tears flowed in self-pity for my sorrows, my doubtful future, my broken career.

The odd thing was that, all the time, I was quite able to analyse my feelings, although I ended by collapsing under these chaotic miseries, murmuring a mixture of Virgil, Dante and Shakespeare--"Nessun maggior dolore--che ricordarsi--O poor Ophelia!--good-night, sweet ladies--vitaque cum gemitu--sub umbras--" and so fell fast asleep.

How crazy, you say? Yes, but how happy. Sensible people cannot understand this intensity of being, this actual joy in existing, in dragging from life the uttermost it has to give in height and depth. Here, in the

Parisian whirlpool, how well I recall the wild Abruzzi country where I spent so long.

Bitter-sweet memories of days now passed for ever. Days of utter irresponsible freedom to abolish time, to scorn ambition, to forget love and glory.

Oh strong, grand Italy! Wild Italy! Heedless of that sister Italy--the Italy of Art!

In time I became friendly with many of the villagers; one in particular, named Crispino, grew very fond of me; he not only got me perfumed pipe-stems (I had not then found out that I disliked the sort of excitement produced by tobacco) but balls, powder and even percussion caps. I first won his affection by helping to serenade his mistress and by singing a duet with him to that untameable young person; then fixed them by a present of two shirts and a pair of trousers. Crispino could not write, so when he had anything to tell me he came to Rome. What were thirty leagues to him?

At the Academy we usually left our doors open; one January morning--having left the mountains in October I had had three months' boredom--on turning over in bed, I found, standing over me, a great sun-burnt scamp with pointed hat and twisted leggings, waiting quite quietly till I woke.

"Hallo, Crispino! What brings you here?"

"Oh, I have just come to--see you."

"Yes; what next?"

"Well--just now----"

"Just now?"

"To tell the truth--I've got no money."

"Now come! That's something like the truth. You have no money; what business is that of mine, oh mightiest of scamps?"

"I'm no scamp. If you call me a scamp because I have no money, you are right, but if it is because I was two years at Civita Vecchia, you are wrong. I wasn't sent to the galleys for stealing, but just for good honest shots at strangers in the mountains."

It was all nonsense, of course, I don't believe he ever shot so much as a monk. However, he was hurt in his feelings and would only accept three piastres, a shirt and a neckerchief.

The poor fellow was killed two years ago in a brawl. Shall I meet him in a better world?

* * * * *

In the miserable oblivion and dishonour into which music has sunk in Rome I found but one small sign of honest life. It was among the pfifferari, players of a little popular instrument, a surviving relic of antiquity. They were strolling musicians who, at Christmastide, came down from the mountains in groups of four or five armed with bagpipes and *pfifferi*, a kind of oboe, to play before the images of the Virgin.

I used to spend hours in watching them, there was something so quaintly mysterious in their wild aspect as they stood--head slightly turned over one shoulder, their bright dark eyes fixed devoutly on the holy figure, almost as still as the image itself.

At a distance the effect is indescribable and few escape its spell. When I heard it in its native haunts, among the volcanic rocks and dark pine forests of the Abruzzi, I could almost believe myself transported back through the ages to the days of Evander, the Arcadian.

Of this time, musically, I have little to tell. I wrote a long and incoherent overture to *Rob Roy*, which I burnt immediately after its performance in Paris; the *Scene aux Champs* of the *Symphonie Fantastique*, which I rewrote entirely in the Borghese gardens; the *Chant de Bonheur* for *Lelio*, and lastly a little song called *La Captive*, inspired by Victor Hugo's lovely poem.

One day I was at Subiaco with Lefebvre, the architect. As he drew, he knocked over a book with his elbow; it was *Les Orientales*. I picked it up and it opened at that particular page. Turning to Lefebvre I said:

"If I had any paper I would write music to this exquisite poem; I can *hear it*."

"That is soon done," said he, and he ruled a sheet whereon I wrote my song. A fortnight later I remembered it and shewed it to Mademoiselle Vernet, saying:

"I wish you would try this, for I have quite forgotten what it is like."

I scribbled a piano accompaniment, and it took so well that, by the end of the month, M. Vernet, driven nearly mad by its reiteration, said:

"Look here, Berlioz. Next time you go up to the mountains don't evolve any more songs; your *Captive* is making life in the Villa impossible. I can't go a yard without hearing it sung or snored or growled. It is simply distracting! I am going to discharge one of the servants to-day, and I shall only engage another on condition that he does not sing the *Captive*."

The only other thing I did was the *Resurrexit* that I sent as my obligatory work to Paris. The Powers said that I had made *great progress*. As it was simply a piece of the mass performed at St Roch several years before I got the prize, it does not say much for the judgment of the Immortals!

To HUMBERT FERRAND.

"*January 1832*.--Why did you not tell me of your marriage? Of course, I believe, since you say so, that you did not get my letters, but--even so--how could you keep silence?

"Your *Noce des Fees* is exquisite; so fresh, so full of dainty grace, but I cannot make music to it yet. Orchestration is not sufficiently advanced; I must first educate and dematerialise it, then perhaps I may think of treading in Weber's footsteps. But here is my idea for an oratorio--the mere carcase, that you must vitalise:

"'The World's Last Day.'

"The height of civilisation, the depth of corruption, under a mighty tyrant, throughout the earth.

"A faithful handful of God's people, left alive by the tyrant's contempt, under a prophet, Balthasar, who confronts the ruler and announces the end of the world. The tyrant, in amused scorn, forces him to be present at a travesty of the Last Day, but during its performance, the earth quakes, angels sound gigantic trumpets, the True Christ appears, the Judgment has come.

* * * * *

"That is all. Tell me if the subject appeals to you. Do not attempt detail, it is lost in the Opera House. And, if possible, do not be tied down by the absurd bond of rhyme--use it or not, as seem best.

"I want to leave here in May; if possible, I will get the whole of my pension; if I cannot I must just go on a tour here. I have just finished an important article on the state of music in Italy for the *Revue Europeenne*.

* * * * *

"*March*.--Many thanks for your confession of colossal idleness. Will you never be cured?

"You have read me a fine homily, but you are entirely out in your conjecture.

"I shall never admire ugliness in art. What I said about rhyme was only to make things easier for you. I could not bear you to waste time and talent over unnecessary difficulties. You know as well as I do that, in hundreds of cases, in verses set to music the rhymes disappear entirely--then why bother about them?

"As for the literary side of the question, I am quite sure it is only custom and education that make you dislike blank verse.

"Just think! Three quarters of Shakespeare is so written, so is Klopstock's *Messiah*. Byron used it, and lately I read a translation of *Julius Caesar* that ran perfectly, although you had prepared me to be utterly shocked.

"So my subject appeals to you? It is new, grand and fertile, so imagine into it all that you like. As far as the music is concerned I am exploring a virgin Brazilian forest and great are the treasures I hope to find."

XX

NAPLES--HOME

AGAIN did that wretched malady--call it moral, nervous, imaginary, what you will, *I* call it spleen--which is really the fever of loneliness, seize upon me.

I had first felt it at La Cote Saint-Andre, when I was sixteen. One lovely May morning I was sitting in a meadow, under the shade of a spreading oak, reading Montjoie's *Manuscript found at Posilippo*. Engrossed in my story, I only gradually became aware of sweet and plaintive songs trembling in the breeze. It was the Rogation procession; in the old time-honoured way, that has always seemed to me most poetical and touching, the peasants were going round the fields, praying for the blessing of heaven on their crops. I watched them kneel before a green-wreathed wooden cross, while the priest blessed the land, then they passed on, and the sweet voices died in the distance.

Silence--the gentle rustling of the flowering wheat, the faint cry of the quail to his mate, a dead leaf floating from an oak, the deep throbbing of my own heart. Life seemed so very far away!

On the horizon the Alpine glaciers shone in the rising sun. Here was Meylan; far over those mountains lay Italy, Naples, Posilippo--the whole world of my story. Oh! for the wings of a dove, to leave this clogging earth-bound body! Oh! for life at its highest and best; for love, for rapture, for ecstasy; for the clinging clasp of hot embraces! Love! glory! where is my bright particular star, O my heart? my Stella Montis? Gone for ever?

Then came the crisis with crushing force. I suffered horribly, rolling on the earth, spreading wide my empty arms, tearing up handfuls of grass and daisies--that opened wide their innocent eyes--as I fought my awful sense of oppression and desolation and bereavement.

Yet what was all this compared to the agony I have suffered since, to the torment of my soul that increases daily?

I never thought of death; suicide had no place in my mind. I wanted life, life in its fullest capacity of love and joy and happiness--furious and all-devouring--life that would use to the uttermost my superabundant energies.

That is not spleen. Spleen follows upon it; it is the mental, moral and physical exhaustion that is the inevitable sequence to such a crisis.

* * * * *

One day as I slept, worn out by this reaction, in the laurel wood of the Villa, rolled up like a hedgehog in a heap of dry leaves, two of my comrades woke me.

"Now then, Silenus, get up and come to Naples. We're off."

"Off to the devil! You know I have no money."

"Idiot! Can't we lend you some? Come, Dantan, help me to heave him up or we shall get no sense out of him. There you are! Brush him down a bit. Now be off and get a month's leave from Monsieur Horace."

And I went.

What shall I say of Naples? Clear bright sky, fecund earth, dazzling sunlight!

So many have described this lovely land that I need not do it again. I wandered in the grounds of the Villa Reale, pondering on the woes of Tasso, and rowed to Nisita to watch the sun go down behind Capo Miseno to the accompaniment of the thousand minor chords of the rippling sea. As I stood, a soldier, who spoke very fair French, came up and offered to show me the curiosities of the island. I accepted gratefully, and after an hour's stroll together I took out my purse. Drawing back, he put my hand aside, saying:

"Monsieur, I want nothing. I ask nothing but--but--that you will pray God for me."

"Indeed I will," I said; "it's an odd notion, but I will do it."

And that night I seriously did say a Paternoster for him after I got to bed. I was beginning a second when I went into fits of laughter. So I am afraid that, as far as my intervention is concerned, the poor man is still a plain sergeant.

Next day the wind had freshened, and our passage back was stormy. However, we landed at last, and my sailors, overjoyed at the thirty francs I had promised them, insisted on my dining with them. They were such ruffianly-looking creatures that, when they led me through a lonely poplar wood, I began to doubt them, poor lazzaroni! However, we soon came to a cottage where my amphitryons gave orders for the feast--a mountain of macaroni, into which I plunged my hand with them; a great pot of Posilippo wine, from which we drank in turn--I after a toothless old man, the eldest of the family, for, with these good fellows, respect for age comes before even courtesy to guests.

Then the old man began discussing politics, and talking of King Joachim, who was very near his heart, until he got so deeply affected that, to turn his thoughts, his children made him tell me of a long and dangerous voyage he had once made when, after *three days and two nights* at sea, he had been thrown on a far-off island which the aborigines called Elba, and where it was rumoured Napoleon had once been kept prisoner. Of course I sympathised, and congratulated the old man on his wonderful escape.

The young men were greatly delighted at my interest and attention; they whispered together, there was a mysterious hurrying to and fro, and I gathered that some surprise was in store.

As I rose to leave, the tallest of the lazzaroni, with shy politeness, begged me to accept a present, the best they had to offer, calculated to make the most callous of men weep.

It was a gigantic--onion! which I received with modest dignity worthy of the occasion, and which I carried off in triumph, after a thousand vows of eternal friendship.

That night I went to San Carlo, and, for the first time, heard music in Italy. It was at least meritorious, though the noise made by the conductor tapping his desk bothered me greatly. I was assured, however, that without this support, the musicians *could not possibly keep in time*!

The musical attractions of Naples could not rival those of the surrounding country, so I passed most of my time in exploring until one day, breakfasting at Castellamare with Munier, the marine painter, whom we had christened Neptune, he said:

"What shall we do? I am sick of Naples. Don't let us go back."

"Shall we go to Sicily?"

"By all means. Give me time to finish a study I have begun, and I can catch the five o'clock boat."

"All right. Let's see how much money we have."

Upon investigation there turned out to be enough to take us to Palermo, but for coming back we should have had to trust to Providence, as the monks say. So we separated, he to paint the sea, I to walk back to Rome over the mountains, in company with two Swedish officers whom I knew.

Thus by way of Isola di Sora, Alatri, Subiaco, and Tivoli, and with but few adventures we got back to the Eternal City, and my life of stagnation began once more.

I dreamed of Paris, finished my monodrama, and revised the *Symphonie Fantastique*, then, considering that the time had come to have them performed, I obtained M. Vernet's permission to go back to France before my two years expired. I sat for my portrait, took a last trip to Tivoli, Albano, and Palestrina; sold my gun, broke my guitar, wrote in several albums, gave a punch-party to my fellow-students, spent a lot of time stroking M. Vernet's two dogs--faithful companions of my shooting excursions--had an attack of profound sorrow at the thought that I might see this poetic land no more; climbed into a wretched old chaise, and then--good-bye to Rome!

I went by Florence, Milan, and Turin, and at last, on the 12th May 1832, coming down the slopes of Mont Cenis, I beheld at my feet that smiling Gresivaudan valley, where my happiest hours and brightest dreams of childhood had passed. There was St Eynard, there the house where shone my Stella Montis; there, through the shimmering blue haze, my grandfather's place bade me welcome. Surely Italy had naught to show as lovely as this! Yet what is this strange oppression on my heart? Afar I hear the dull and ominous murmur of Paris commanding my presence.

To FERDINAND HILLER.

"FLORENCE, *May 1832*.--I arrived yesterday, and found your letter. Why do you not say whether the sale of my medal realised enough to pay the two hundred francs I owe you?

"I left Rome without regret. The Academy life had grown intolerable, and I spent all my evenings with the Director's family, who have been most kind. Mademoiselle Vernet is prettier, and her father younger than ever.

"I am glad to be here, yet my sensations are so curiously confused that I cannot explain them even to myself. I know no one, have no adventures, am utterly alone. Perhaps that is what affects me so oddly. I seem to be not myself but some stranger--some Russian or Englishman--sauntering along the Lung 'Arno. Berlioz is merely a distant acquaintance.

"This cursed throat of mine is still troublesome; it would be the death of me if I would allow it.

"I shall not be in Paris till November or December, as I go straight home from here. Many thanks for your invitation to Frankfort; sooner or later I mean to accept it."

To MADAME HORACE VERNET.

"LA COTE ST ANDRE, *July 1832*.--You have set me, Madame, a new and most agreeable task.

"An intellectual woman not only desires that I should write her my musings, but undertakes to read them without emphasizing too much their ridiculous side.

"It is hardly generous of me to take advantage of your kindness, but are we not all selfish?

"For my part, I must own that whenever such a temptation comes I shall fall into it with the utmost alacrity.

"I should have done so sooner had I not, on my descent from the Alps, been caught like a ball on the bound and tossed from villa to villa round Grenoble.

"My fear was that, on returning to France, I might have to parody Voltaire and say: 'The more I see of other lands, *the less* I love my country.' But all the glories of the glorious kingdom of Naples are powerless beside the ineffable charms of my beautiful vale of the Isere.

"Of society, however, I cannot say the same. The advantage is entirely with the absent, who are not 'always wrong' in spite of the proverb.

"Despite my herculean efforts to turn the conversation, the good folks here *will* insist on talking art, music and poetry to me, and you may imagine how provincials talk! They have most weird notions, theories and ideas that make an artist's blood curdle in his veins, and, withal, the calmest assumption of infallibility.

"One would think to hear them talk of Byron, Goethe, Beethoven, that they were respectable bootmakers or tailors, with a little more talent than their compeers.

"Nothing is good enough, there is no reverence, no respect, no enthusiasm!

"Thus living in a crowd, I am utterly, cruelly alone and am parched for want of music.

"No longer can I look forward to my evening's pleasure with Mademoiselle Louise and her piano; no more can I try her sweet patience by demanding and re-demanding those sublime adagios.

"You smile, Madame? No doubt you murmur that I know neither what I want nor where I would be--that I am, in fact, half demented.

"My father devised a charming cure for my malady; he said I ought to marry and forthwith unearthed a rich damsel, informing me that, since he could leave me but little, it was my duty to marry money.

"At first I laughed, but finding that he was in sober earnest, I was obliged to say firmly that, since I could not love the lady in question, I would not sell myself at any price.

"That ended the discussion, but it upset me terribly, for I thought my father knew me better.

"Madame, do you not think I am right?

"As I promised Monsieur Horace, I will go to Paris at the end of the year to fire my musical broadside, after which I intend to start at once for Berlin.

"But indeed, Madame, I am taking unmerciful advantage of your kindness and will conclude by asking your pardon for my garrulity.

To FERDINAND HILLER.

"LA COTE ST ANDRE, *August 1832*.--What a dainty, elusive, piquant, teasing, witty creature is this Hiller! Were we both women, I should detest her; were she, alone, a woman I should simply hate her, for I loathe coquettes. As it is--'Providence having ordered all for the best' as the good say--we are luckily both masculine.

"No, my dear fellow, you, being you, naturally 'could not do otherwise' than make me wait two months for your letter; naturally, also, I 'could not do otherwise' than be angry with you therefor. However, as I was not wounded to the quick by your neglect, I wrote you a second letter which I burnt, remembering Napoleon's wise saying, 'Certain things should never be said.' If so, still less should they be written.

"Come now! Since you are learning Latin I will turn schoolmaster.

"There are mistakes in your letter.

"No. 1. No accent on *negre*.

"No. 2. DE *grands amusements,* not *des*.

"No. 3. *Il est possible que Mendelssohn* L'AIT, not *l'aura*.

"Take thou good heed unto my lesson. Ouf!

"I am in the bosom of my family, by whom (particularly by my younger sister) I allow myself to be adored in an edifying manner. But oh! I long for liberty and love and money! They will come some day and perhaps also one little luxury--one of those superfluities that are necessities to certain temperaments--*revenge,* public and private. One only lives and dies once.

"I spend my time in copying my *Melologue;* I have been two months at it hard and have still sixty-two days' work. Am I not persevering? I am ill for want of music, positively paralysed; then I still suffer from that choleraic trouble that sometimes keeps me in bed. However, I am up to-day, getting ready for the next attack.

"I am going to see Ferrand; we have not met for five years. You see extremes meet. He is more religious than ever and has married a woman who adores him and whom he adores.

XXI

MARRIAGE

AFTER spending the summer in Dauphiny, copying my monodrama, I went on to Paris, hoping to give two concerts before starting on my German wanderings.

Apropos of the *Chorus of Shades* in this same composition, a rather comical thing happened in Rome. In order to have it printed it was necessary for it to pass the Papal censor. Now for this language of the dead, incomprehensible to the living, I had written pure gibberish (I have since substituted French, saving my unknown tongue for the *Damnation de Faust*) of which the censor demanded a translation.

They tried a German, who could make nothing of it; an Englishman, the same; Danes, Swedes, Russians, Spaniards--equally useless. Deadlock at the censorial office! At last, after much cogitation one of the officials evolved an argument that appealed forcibly and convincingly to his colleagues: "Since none of these people understand the language, perhaps the Romans will not understand it either. In that case I think we might authorise the printing, without danger to religion or morals."

So the *Shades* got printed. Oh reckless censors! Suppose it had been Sanscrit!

* * * * *

One of my first visits in Paris was to Cherubini, whom I found much aged and enfeebled. He received me with such affection that I was quite disarmed and said:

"I fear me the poor man is nigh unto death!"

It was not long before I found my forebodings quite uncalled for; as far as I was concerned he was as lively as ever.

As my old rooms in the Rue Richelieu were let, some influence compelled me to cross the road to the house in which Miss Smithson had lived, Rue Neuve St Marc, where I found a lodging. Next day, meeting the old servant, I said:

"Do you know what has become of Miss Smithson?"

"Why, monsieur, she is in Paris; she only left the rooms you are in a few days ago to go to the Rue de Rivoli. She is manageress of an English theatre that is to open in a few days."

Dumfoundered, I felt that this was indeed the hand of fate. For more than two years I had heard no word of "fair Ophelia" and here I arrive in Paris at the very moment she returns from her tour in Northern Europe.

A mystic might well find arguments in defence of his cult in this strange coincidence. What I said was this:

"I have come to Paris to perform my monodrama. If I go to the theatre before the concert, I shall certainly have another attack of that *delirium tremens;* all volition will be taken from me; I shall be incapable of the thought and care essential to the success of my work. So first my concert, then I will see her if I die for it and will fight no more against this strange destiny."

And, despite the Shakespearian names staring at me daily from all the walls in Paris, I kept sternly to my purpose.

The programme was to consist of the *Symphonie Fantastique* followed by *Lelio,* the monodrama which is the complement of the former and is the second part of my *Episode in an Artist's Life.*

Now trace the extraordinary sequence.

Two days before the concert--which I felt would be my farewell to life and art--I was in Schlesinger's music-shop, when an Englishman came in and went out almost at once.

"Who is that?" I asked, in idle curiosity.

"Schutter, of *Galignani's Messenger.* Ah!" cried Schlesinger, "give me a box for your concert. He knows Miss Smithson, I will get him to persuade her to go."

I trembled, but dared not refuse; so, running after M. Schutter, he explained matters and got his promise to do his best to induce Miss Smithson to go.

Now while I had been busy over my preparations the unfortunate actress had been also busy--in ruining herself.

She did not realise that Shakespeare was no longer new to the changeable, frivolous Parisian public and innocently counted on a reception such as she had had three years before.

The Romantic School was now on the rising tide and its apostles were not anxious that it should be stemmed by the colossus of dramatic poetry nor that their wholesale filchings from his works should be brought to light.

Hence, sparse audiences, mean receipts and considerable running expenses that swallowed up all the poor manageress's savings.

Schutter, long afterwards, told me that he found Miss Smithson too dejected to accept his invitation; her sister, however, persuaded her that the change would be good and she at length allowed him to take her down to the carriage. On the way to the Conservatoire her eyes fell on the programme; even then, as she read my name (which they had taken care not to mention) she little knew that she was, herself, the heroine of my work. But, in her box, she could not help seeing that she was the subject of conversation in the hall and when Habeneck came on to conduct with me--gasping with excitement--behind him, she said to herself:

"It is indeed he--poor young man! But he will have forgotten me--at least--I hope so."

The symphony made a tremendous sensation; that was the day of great enthusiasms and the hall of the Conservatoire (from which I am now shut out) echoed with the applause of that crowd of musicians. The success, the fiery *motifs* of my work, its cries of love and passion and the mere vibration of such a gigantic orchestra at close quarters, all worked upon Miss Smithson's sensitive organisation, and in her heart of hearts she cried:

"Ah! If he but loved me now!----"

During the interval Schutter and Schlesinger made thinly-veiled allusions to my sorrows and when, in the *Monodrama,* Lelio said:

"Shall I never meet this Juliet, this Ophelia, for whom my heart wearies?"

"Juliet! Ophelia!" she thought, "he must be thinking still of me! He loves me yet!"

From that moment she heard no more; in a dream she sat till the end; in a dream she returned home. That was the 9th December 1832. But while the web of one part of my life was being woven on one side of the hall, on the other side another was in the weaving--compounded of the hatred and wounded vanity of Fetis.

Before going to Italy I used to earn money by correcting musical proofs. Troupenas, having given me some Beethoven scores to do that had previously been revised by Fetis, I found them full of the most impertinent and unmeaning corrections. I was so furious that I went off to Troupenas and said:

"M. Fetis' corrections are criminal. They are entirely opposed to Beethoven's intention, and if this edition is published, I warn you that I shall denounce it to every musician I meet."

Which I accordingly did and there was such an outcry that Troupenas was obliged to suppress the corrections and Fetis thought it politic to tell a lie and announce in the *Revue Musicale* that there was no truth in the rumour that he had corrected Beethoven's symphonies. In *Lelio* I gibbeted him still farther by putting into my hero's mouth quotations of his own that the audience recognised and applauded, with much laughter. Fetis, sitting in the front row of the gallery, got the blow full in the face, and needless to say, was thereafter more my inveterate enemy than ever.

But I forgot all this next day when I went to call upon Miss Smithson and began that long course of torturing hopes and fears that lasted nearly a year.

Her mother and sister and my parents were all opposed to our marriage, and while various distressing scenes were in progress, the English theatre closed in debt.

To add to her misfortunes, getting out of her carriage, she missed her footing, and falling, broke her leg just above the ankle. The injury was most severe and it was feared that she would be lame for life.

Her accident elicited the greatest sympathy in Paris. Mademoiselle Mars, particularly, came forward, placing her purse, influence, everything she had at poor Ophelia's disposal. I managed to organise a benefit, in which Chopin and Liszt took part, which brought in enough to pay the most pressing debts.

At last, in the summer of 1833, Henriette being still weak and quite ruined, I married her in the face of the opposition of our two families. All our resources on the wedding day were three hundred francs lent me by Gounet. But what did it matter, since she was mine?

To H. FERRAND.

"PARIS, *12th June 1833*.--It is really too bad of me to cause you anxiety on my account. But you know how my life fluctuates. One day calm, dreamy, rhythmical; the next bored, nerve-torn, snappy and snarly as a mangey dog, vicious as a thousand devils, sick of life and ready to end it, were it not for the frenzied happiness that draws ever nearer, for the odd destiny that I feel is mine; for my staunch friends; for music, and lastly, for *curiosity*. My life is a story that interests me greatly.

"You ask how I pass my days? If I am well I read or sleep on the sofa (for I am in comfortable lodgings) or scribble a few well-paid pages for the *Europe Litteraire*. About six I go to see Henriette who, to my sorrow, is still ailing. I must tell you all about her some day. Your opinion of her is quite wrong; her life, also, is a strange book, of which her points of view, her thoughts, her feelings, are by no means the least interesting part.

"I am still meditating the opera I asked you to write in my letter from Rome eighteen months ago. As, in all this time, you have not sufficiently conquered your laziness to write it, don't be angry that I have given it to Deschamps and Saint-Felix. I really *have* been patient!"

"*August 1833.*--You true friend, not to despair of my future! These cowards cannot realise that, all the time, I am learning, observing, gathering ideas and knowledge. Bending before the storm, I still grow; the wind does but blow off a few leaves; the green fruit upon my branches holds too firmly to be shaken off. Your trust helps and encourages me.

"Have I told you of my parting with Henriette--of our scenes, despair, reproaches, which ended in my taking poison? Her protestations of love and sorrow brought back my desire to live; I took an emetic, was ill three days and am still alive! In her self-abasement she offered to do anything I chose, but now she begins to hesitate again. I will wait no more and have written that, unless she goes with me to the Town Hall on Saturday to be married, I leave for Berlin at once. She shall see that I, who for so long have languished at her feet, can rise, can leave her, can live for those who love and understand me.

"To help me to bear this horrible parting a strange chance has thrown in my way a charming girl of eighteen, who has fled from a brute who bought her--a mere child--and has kept her shut up like a slave for four years. Rather than go back to him, she says she will drown herself and my idea is to take her to Berlin, and by Spontini's influence, place her in some chorus. I will try and make her love me, and if I succeed, I will fan into life the smouldering embers in my own heart and persuade myself that I love her. My passport is ready; I must make an end of things here. Henriette will be miserable but I have nothing to reproach myself with.

"I would give my life this minute for a month of *perfect love* with her.

"She must abide the consequences of her unstable character; she will weep and despair at first, then will dry her tears and end by believing me in the wrong."

* * * * *

"*11th October 1833.*--I am married! All opposition has been in vain. Henriette has told me of the hundred and one lies they spread abroad. I was epileptic, I was mad--nothing was too bad. But we have listened to our own hearts and all is well.

"This winter we are going to Berlin, but before leaving I must give a horrid concert.

"How *awfully* I love my poor Ophelia! When once we can get rid of her troublesome sister, life will be hard but quite happy.

"We are at Vincennes, where my wife can spend her days in the Park, but I go to Paris every day. Our marriage has made the devil's own row there.

"My little fugitive is provided for. Jules Janin has arranged to send her away.

"Write soon. I love to answer, in order to tell you of the heaven I live in--it needs but you! Surely love and friendship like yours and mine is one of the supreme joys of this world!"

XXII

NEWSPAPER BONDAGE

AT the time of our marriage our sole income was my scholarship, which still had a year and a half to run; but the Minister of the Interior absolved me from the regulation German tour. I had a fair number of friends and adherents in Paris and firm faith in the future.

To pay my wife's debts, I had to start *benefit-mongering*. My friends rallied round me--amongst them Alexandre Dumas, who was all his life my most devoted helper--and after untold annoyances we arranged a theatrical performance, followed by a concert at the Theatre Italien.

The programme was Dumas' *Antony*, played by Firmin and Madame Dorval, followed by the fourth act of *Hamlet*, by my wife and some English amateurs; then a concert consisting of my *Symphonie Fantastique*, *Francs-Juges*, *Sardanapalus*, a chorus of Weber and his *Concert-Stuck*, played by Liszt.

If the concert had ever come off entirely it would have lasted till one in the morning. But it did not, and for the sake of young musicians I must tell what happened.

Not being versed in the manners and customs of theatrical musicians, I arranged with the manager to take his theatre and orchestra, adding to the latter some players from the Opera, an impossibly dangerous combination, since the theatre *employes* were bound by contract to take part gratuitously in concerts in their own house, and, therefore, naturally look upon them as a burden. By engaging paid artists, I simply added to their grievance, and they determined to be revenged.

Then, my wife and I being equally ignorant of the petty intrigues of the theatrical world we took no precautions to insure her success. We never even sent a ticket to the *claque*, and Madame Dorval, believing Henriette's triumph secured, of course took measures to arrange for her own. Besides, she played splendidly, so it was no wonder she was applauded and recalled.

The fourth act of *Hamlet*, separated from its context, was incomprehensible to French people and fell absolutely flat. They even noticed (although her talent and grace were as great as ever) how difficult my poor wife found it to raise herself from her kneeling position by her father's bier, by resting one hand on the stage. Gone was her magnetic power to thrill her audience, and, at the fall of the curtain, those who had idolised her did not even recall her once! It was heart-breaking. My poor Ophelia, the twilight had indeed crept on!

As to the concert, the *Francs-Juges* was poorly played but well received; the *Concert-Stuck*, played by Liszt with the passionate impetuosity he always put into it, created a furore, and I, carried away by enthusiasm, was idiotic enough to embrace him on the stage, a piece of stupidity fortunately condoned by the audience.

From then things went badly, and by the time we arrived at the symphony not only were my pulses beating like sledge-hammers, but it was very late indeed. I knew nothing of the rule of the Theatre Italien, that its musicians need not play after midnight, and when, after Weber's *Chorus*, I turned to review my orchestra before raising my baton, I found that it consisted of five violins, two violas, four 'cellos, and a trombone, all the others having slipped quietly away.

In my consternation I could not think what to do. The audience did not seem inclined to leave and loudly called for the symphony, one voice in the gallery shouting, "Give us the *Marche au Supplice*!"

"How can I," cried I, "perform such a thing with five violins? Is it my fault that the orchestra has disappeared?"

I was crimson with rage and shame.

With disappointed murmurs the people melted away. Of course my enemies announced that my music "drove musicians out of the place."

That miserable evening brought in seven thousand francs, which went into the gulf of my wife's debts without, alas! filling it up. That was only done after years of struggle and privation.

I longed to give Henriette a splendid revenge, but there were no English actors in Paris to help her with a complete play, and we both saw that mutilated Shakespeare was worse than useless. I was, therefore, obliged to content myself with taking vengeance for the malicious reports about my music, and, with Henriette's full approval, I arranged for a concert of my own works at the Conservatoire.

It was a terrible risk for a penniless man, but here, as ever, my wife shewed herself the courageous opponent of half-measures and steadfastly determined to face the chance of positive penury.

The concert, for which I engaged the very best artists, amongst whom were many of my friends, was a triumphant success. I was vindicated.

My musicians (none of whom came from the Italien) beamed with joy, and, to crown all, when the audience had dispersed I found waiting for me a man with long black hair, piercing eyes, and wasted form--genius-haunted, a colossus among giants--whom I had never seen before, yet who stirred within me a strange emotion.

Catching my hand, he poured forth a flood of burning praise and appreciation that fired my heart and head.

It was Paganini.

This was on the 22nd December 1833.

Thus began my friendship with that great artist to whom I owe so much and whose generosity towards me has given rise to such absurd and wicked reports. Some weeks later he said:

"I have a beautiful Strad. viola which I long to play in public. Will you write me a solo for it? I could not trust anyone but you."

"To do that one ought to play the viola," I objected. "You alone could do it satisfactorily."

But he insisted:

"I am too ill to compose; it would be useless to try. You will do it properly."

So to please him I tried to write a viola solo with orchestral accompaniment, feeling sure that his power would enable him to dominate the orchestra. It seemed to me an entirely new idea, and I burned to carry it through. However, he called soon after and asked to see a sketch of his part.

"This won't do," he said, looking at the pauses, "there is too much silence. I must be playing all the time."

"Did I not tell you so?" I answered. "What you want is a viola concerto, and you are the only one who can write it."

He seemed disappointed and dropped the subject; a few days later, suffering from the throat trouble of which he afterwards died, he left for Nice and did not come back for three years.

Still ruminating over my idea, I wove round the viola solo a series of scenes, drawn from my memories of wanderings in the Abruzzi, which I called *Childe Harold*, as there seemed to me about the whole symphony a poetic melancholy worthy of Byron's hero. It was first performed at my concert, 23rd November 1834, but Girard, the conductor, made a terrible hash of the *Pilgrim's March*. However, being doubtful of my own powers, I still allowed him to direct my concerts until, after the fourth performance of *Harold*, seeing that he would not take it at the proper *tempo*, I assumed command myself, and never but once after that broke my rule of conducting my own compositions.

We shall see how much cause I had to regret that one exception.

To HUMBERT FERRAND.

"MONTMARTRE, *30th August 1834*.--You are not forgotten--not the least little bit, but you cannot know what a slave I am to hard necessity. Had it not been for those confounded newspaper articles I should have written to you a dozen times.

"I will not write the usual empty phrases on your loss yet, if anything could soften the blow, it would be that your father's death was as peaceful as one could wish. You speak of my father. He wrote kindly and quickly in answer to my letter announcing the birth of my boy. Henriette thanks you for your messages; she, too, understands the depth of our friendship. I could write all night but, as I have to tug at my galley-oar all day, I must go to sleep."

* * * * *

"*30th November 1834*.--I quite expected a letter from you to-day, and although I am dropping with fatigue, I must snatch half an hour to answer it. The *Symphonie Fantastique* is out, and, as our poor Liszt has dropped a terrible lot of money over it, we arranged with Schlesinger that not one copy was to be given away. They are twenty francs. Shall I buy one for you?

"Would to heaven I could send it you without all this preface, but you know we are still very straitened. My wife and I are as happy as it is possible to be, in spite of our worldly troubles, and little Louis is the dearest and sweetest of children."

* * * * *

"*10th January 1835*.--If I had had time I should already have begun another work I am thinking of, but I am obliged to scribble these wretched, ill-paid articles. Ah! if only art counted for something with the Government perhaps I should not be reduced to this. Never mind, I must find time somehow."

* * * * *

"*April 1835*.--I wrote, about a month ago, an introduction to you for a young violinist named Allard, who is on his way to Geneva.

"So you have been in Milan! Not a town I like, but it is the threshold of Italy. I cannot tell you how much, when the weather is fine, I long for my ancient Campagna and the wild hills that I loved.

"You ask for news of us.

"Louis can nearly walk alone and Henriette is more devoted to him than ever. I work like a nigger for the four papers whence I get my daily bread. They are the *Renovateur*, which pays badly; the *Monde Dramatique* and *Gazette Musicale* which pay only fairly; the *Debats*, which pays well.

"Added to this is the nightmare of my musical life; I cannot find time to compose.

"I have begun a gigantic piece of work for seven hundred musicians, to the memory of the great men of France.

"It would soon be done if I had but one quiet month, but I dare not give up a single day to it, lest we should want for absolute necessaries.

"Which concert do you refer to? I have given seven this season and shall begin again in November.

"At present we sit dumb under the triumph of Musard,[12] who, puffed up by the success of his dancing-den concerts, looks upon himself as a superior Mozart. Mozart never composed anything like the 'Pistol-shot Quadrille,' consequently Mozart died of want.

"Musard is earning twenty thousand francs a year, and Ballanche, the immortal author of *Orpheus* and *Antigone* was nearly thrown into prison, because he owed two hundred francs.

"Think of it, Ferrand; does not madness lie that way? If I were a bachelor, so that my rash doings would recoil on myself alone, I know what I would do.

"Never mind that now, though. Love me always and, to please me, read de Vigny's *Chatterton*."

"*December 1835*.--Do not think me a sinner for leaving you so long in silence. You can have no idea of my work--but I need not emphasise that, for you know how much pleasure I have in writing to you and that I should not lightly forego it.

"I have seen Coste, who is publishing serially *Great Men of Italy*, and he is going to approach you about contributing some articles. Among those now out is a life of Benvenuto Cellini. Read it, if you are not already familiar with the autobiography of that bandit of genius.

"*Harold* is more successful even than last year, and I think it quite outdoes the *Fantastique*.

"They have accepted my *Cellini* for the Opera; Alfred de Vigny[13] and Auguste Barbier have written me a poem full of dainty vivacity and colour. I have not begun to work at the music yet, because I am in the same predicament as my hero, Cellini--short of money. Good reports from Germany, thanks to Liszt's piano arrangement of my Symphony.

* * * * *

"*April 1826*.--I still work frightfully hard at journalism. You know I write concert critiques for the *Debats*, which are signed 'H.'

"They seem to be making a stir. Parisian artists call them epoch-making.

"In spite of M. Bertin (the editor's) wish, I refused to review either *I Puritani* or that wretched *Juive*. I should have had to find too much fault, and people would have put it down to jealousy.

"Then there is the *Renovateur*, wherein I can hardly control my wrath over all these 'pretty little trifles'; and *Picturesque Italy* has dragged an article out of me.

"Next, the *Gazette Musicale* plagues me for a *resume* of the week's inanities every Sunday.

"Added to that I have tried every concert room in Paris, with the idea of giving a concert, and find none suitable except the Conservatoire, which is not available until after the last of the regular concerts on the 3rd May.

"We often talk of you to Barbier; he is a kindred soul whom you would love. No one understands better than he the grandeur and nobility of an artist's calling.

"Germany still talks of me; Vienna asks for a copy of the score of the *Fantastique*, but I tell them I cannot possibly let them have it, as I propose to give it on tour myself.

"All the poets in Paris, from Scribe to Victor Hugo, offer me subjects, but those idiotic directors stand in the way. Some day I will set my foot upon their necks.

"Now I must be off to the office of the *Debats* with my article on Beethoven's *C Minor*.

"Meyerbeer is coming soon to superintend his *Huguenots*, which I am most anxious to hear. He is the only recognised musician who has shown a keen interest in me.

"Onslow has been paying me his usual bombastic compliments on the *Pilgrim's March*. I am glad to think there was not a word of truth in them, I prefer open hatred to honeyed venom."

XXIII

THE REQUIEM

IN 1836 M. de Gasparin, Minister of the Interior, feeling that religious music should be better supported, allocated, yearly, a sum of 3000 francs to be given to a French composer, chosen by the Minister, for either a mass or an oratorio; his idea being also to have it executed at the expense of the Government.

"I shall begin with Berlioz," he said, "I am sure he could write a good Requiem."

A friend of M. de Gasparin's son told me this. My surprise was only equalled by my delight, but, to make sure, I asked an audience of M. de Gasparin.

"It is quite true," he said, "I am going out of office, and this is my last bequest. You have, of course, received the official notification."

"No, monsieur; it was by a mere chance that I heard of your kind intentions towards me."

"What! you ought to have had it a week ago. It must be an official oversight; I will look into it."

But nothing happened, and I finally spoke to the Minister's son, who told me that there was an intrigue on foot to put off my commission until his father's retirement, after which the Director of Fine Arts--who had no love for me, but whom I need not name since he is dead--hoped that it would be shelved.

This Monsieur X. was a Rossinist. One day I heard him giving his opinion of composers, ancient and modern, and rejecting them all, except Beethoven, whom he forgot. Suddenly he bethought him and said:

"Let's see. I believe there is another--a German--what is his name? They play his symphonies at the Conservatoire. You may know him, Monsieur Berlioz?"

"Beethoven."

"Ah yes, Beethoven. I believe he has a certain amount of talent."

I heard that myself. *Beethoven not devoid of talent!*

M. de Gasparin had no intention of being ignored; therefore, finding that nothing had been done, he sent for M. X. and ordered him sternly to make out my appointment at once.

Naturally this snub did not increase M. X.'s friendly feeling towards me but, armed with my decree, I set to work with the greatest ardour.

I had so long ached to try my hand at a Requiem that I flung myself into it body and soul. My head seemed bursting with the ferment of ideas, and I actually had to invent a sort of musical short-hand to get on fast enough.

All composers know the bitter despair of losing beautiful ideas through want of time to jot them down.

In spite of the rapidity with which I wrote, I afterwards made but few corrections.

Is it not strange that, during that volcanic time, I should twice over have dreamed that I was sitting in the Meylan garden, under a beautiful weeping acacia, alone. Estelle was not there, and I kept asking:

"Where is she? Where is she?"

Who can explain it? Only those who recognise the affinity of the mysteries of the human heart with those of the magnet.

Here, briefly, is a list of the miseries I endured over that Requiem.

It was arranged that it should be performed at the memorial service held every July for the victims of the Revolution of 1830. I, consequently, had the parts copied, and was beginning rehearsals, when I was told to stop, as the service was to be held without music.

Of course the new Minister owed a certain amount to my copyists and chorus (without mentioning myself), yet will it be believed that for five months I had to besiege that department for those few hundred francs? At last, losing all patience, I had a pretty lively quarrel with M. X., and as I left his room the guns of the Invalides proclaimed the fall of Constantine.

Two hours later he sent for me in hot haste. A funeral service was to be held for General Damremont and the soldiers who had fallen in the siege.

Now mark! This being a military affair, General Bernard had charge of it, and in this way M. X. hoped to get rid of me and also of the necessity of paying his just debts.

Here the drama becomes complicated.

Cherubini, hearing that my Requiem was to be performed, worked himself into a fever, for he considered that *his* Requiem should have a monopoly of such ceremonies. His rights, his dignity, his genius, all set aside in favour of a hot-headed young heretic!! His friends, headed by Halevy, started a cabal to oust me.

Being one morning in the *Debats* office, I saw Halevy come in. Now M. Bertin, the editor, has always been one of my best and kindest friends, and the frigid reception he and his son Armand gave the visitor somewhat disconcerted him--my presence still more so--and he found a change of tactics advisable.

He followed M. Bertin into the next room, and I, through the open door, heard him say that "Cherubini took it so to heart that he was ill in bed, and he (Halevy) had come to beg M. Bertin to use his influence in getting him the consolation of the Legion of Honour."

M. Berlin's cold voice broke in:

"Certainly, my dear Halevy, we will do our best to get Cherubini such a well-merited distinction. But as far as the Requiem is concerned, if Berlioz gives way one jot, *I will never speak to him again*."

So much for that failure. Next came a blacker plot.

General Bernard agreed that I should have a free hand, and rehearsals had already begun when M. X. sent for me again. This time it was:

"Habeneck has always conducted our great official performances, and I know he would be terribly hurt at being left out of this. Are you on good terms with him?"

"Why, no. We have quarrelled, goodness only knows why--I don't! He has not spoken to me for three years. I never troubled to find out the reason, but he began by refusing to conduct one of my concerts. Still, if he wishes to conduct this one, he may, but I reserve the right of conducting one rehearsal."

On the great day princes, ministers, peers, deputies, the press--home and foreign--and a mighty crowd gathered in the Invalides. It was most important that I should have a real success, failure would have crushed me irretrievably.

My performers were rather curiously arranged. To get the right effect in the *Tuba mirum*, the four brass bands were placed one at each corner of the enormous body of instrumentalists and choristers. As they join in, the *tempo* doubles, and it is, of course, of the utmost importance that the time should be absolutely clearly indicated. Otherwise, my Titanic cataclysm--prepared with so much thought and care by means of original and hitherto unknown combinations of instruments to represent the Last Judgment--becomes merely a hideous pandemonium.

Suspicious as usual, I took care to be close to Habeneck--in fact, back to back with him--keeping an eye on the group of kettledrums (which he could not see) as the critical moment drew near.

There are about a thousand bars in my Requiem; will it be believed that at this--the most important of all--Habeneck *calmly laid down his baton and, with the utmost deliberation, took a pinch of snuff*.

But my eye was upon him; turning on my heel, in a flash I stretched out my arm and marked the four mighty beats. The executants followed me, all went right, and my long-dreamed-of effect was a magnificent triumph.

"Dear me," bleated Habeneck, "I was quite in a perspiration; without you we should have been done for."

"Yes, we should," I answered, eyeing him steadily.

Could it be that this man, in conjunction with M. X. and Cherubini, planned this dastardly stroke?

I do not like to think so, yet I have not the slightest doubt. God forgive me if I wrong them.

The Requiem had succeeded, but then began the usual sordid trouble about payment.

General Bernard, a thoroughly honourable man, had promised me ten thousand francs for the performance as soon as I brought from the Minister of the Interior a promise to pay the sum ordered by the late Minister--M. de Gasparin--and also that due to the copyists and choristers.

But do you think I could get this letter? It was written out ready for his signature, and from ten to four I waited in his ante-room. At last he emerged and, being button-holed by his secretary, scrawled his name to the precious document, and without a moment's loss of time I hurried off to General Bernard, who promptly handed me the ten thousand francs, which I spent entirely in paying the performers.

Of course I thought the Minister's three thousand would soon follow.

Sancta simplicitas! Will it be credited that only by making most unpleasant, almost scandalous, scenes could I, at the end of *eight months*, get that money?

Later on, when my good friend, M. de Gasparin, again came into office, he tried to make up for my mortification by giving me the Legion of Honour. But by that time I was past caring for such a commonplace distinction.

Duponchel, manager of the Opera and Bordogni, the singing-master, got it at the same time.

When the Requiem was printed, I dedicated it to M. de Gasparin, all the more willingly that he was not then in power.

What added greatly to the humour of the situation was that the opposition newspapers dubbed me a "Government parasite," and said I had been paid thirty thousand francs. They only added a nought.

Thus is history written.

Ere long Cherubini played me another charming trick.

A professorship of Harmony was vacant at the Conservatoire, for which I applied. Cherubini sent for me, and, in his most honeyed voice, said:

"Is it zat you present yourself for ze 'armonee?"

"Yes, monsieur."

"Zen you vill get it. You 'ave a reputation, influence----"

"Since I asked for it because I want it, I am glad, monsieur."

"Yes, but zat is vhere I am bothair; I vill zat anozzer get it."

"Then, monsieur, I withdraw."

"No, no! I vill not 'ave zat, because you see zey will say I am ze cause zat you vizdraw."

"Then I won't withdraw."

"But--but--zen you vill get ze place--and I did not vish it for you."

"Then what am I to do?"

"You know zat you must be pianist, for teach ze 'armonee at Conservatoire, my tear fallow."

"Ah, I never thought of that. That is a capital excuse. You want me to say that, not being a pianist, I withdraw?"

"Just so! just so, my tear fallow! But *I* am not ze excuse zat you vizdraw----"

"Certainly not, monsieur; it was stupid of me to forget that only pianists could teach Harmony."

"Yes, my tear boy; embrace me, for I lof you much."

A week after he gave the place to Bienaime, who played the piano as well as I do!

Now I call that a thoroughly well-planned trick, and I was among the first to laugh at it.

Soon after, I seriously hurt the feelings of the friend who "lofed me much."

It was at the first performance of his *Ali Baba*, about the emptiest, feeblest thing he ever wrote. Near the end of the first act, tired of hearing nothing striking, I called out:

"Twenty francs for an idea!"

In the middle of the second I raised my bid.

"Forty francs for an idea!"

The finale commenced.

"Eighty francs for an idea!"

The finale ended and I took myself off, remarking:

"By Jove! I give it up. I'm not rich enough!"

Of course indignant friends of Cherubini told him of my insolence and, considering how he "lofed" me, he must have thought me an ungrateful wretch.

I had better explain here how I got on to the staff of the *Debats*. One day, being utterly wretched and not knowing where to turn for money, I wrote an extravagantly amusing tale called "Rubini at Calais." These contrasts happen sometimes.

A few days after it came out in the *Gazette Musicale*, the *Journal des Debats* reproduced it, with a few words of cordial appreciation from the editor.

I went to thank M. Bertin, who offered me the proud post of musical editor. This enabled me to throw up my least well-paid work; yet, all the same, I abominate criticism, and feel quite ill from the moment I see the advertisement of a new performance until I have written my article on it. The ever-recurring task poisons my life. I hate circumlocution, diplomacy, trimming, and all half-measures and concessions. They are so much gall and wormwood to me.

People call me passionate, rude, spiteful, prejudiced. O scrubby louts! If you but knew all I *want* to write of you, you would find your present bed of nettles a couch of roses compared to the gridiron on which I long to toast you!

At least I can truly say that never have I grudged the fullest, most heartfelt praise to all that aims at the good and true and beautiful --even when it emanates from my bitterest foes.

One day Armand Bertin, who was grieved at my narrow circumstances, told me he had heard that I was to be appointed professor of composition at the Conservatoire, in spite of Cherubini. M. X., whom I met at the Opera, confirmed it, and I begged him to tender my thanks to the Minister for a position that would be to me assured comfort.

That was the last I heard of it.

Still I got something--the post of librarian, which I still hold and which brings me in 118 francs a month.

While I was in England,[14] several worthy patriots tried to eject me, and it was only the kind intervention of Victor Hugo--who had some authority in the Chamber--that saved it for me. Another good friend of mine was M. Charles Blanc, who became Director of Fine Arts, and frequently helped me with a ready warmth I shall never forget.

XXIV

FRIENDS IN NEED

AND now for my opera and its deadly failure.

The strange career of Benvenuto Cellini had made such an impression on me that I stupidly concluded that it would be both dramatic and interesting to other people. I therefore asked Leon de Wailly and Auguste Barbier to write me a libretto on it. I must own that even our friends thought it had not the elements essential to success, but it pleased me, and even now I cannot see that it is inferior to many others that are played daily.

In order to please the management of the *Debats*, Duponchel, manager of the Opera--who looked upon me as a species of lunatic--read the libretto and agreed to take my opera. After which he went about saying that he was going to put it on, not on account of the music, which was ridiculous, but of the book, which was charming.

Never shall I forget the misery of those three months' rehearsals. The indifference of the actors, riding for a fall, Habeneck's bad temper, the vague rumours I heard on all sides, all betrayed a general hostility against which I was powerless. It was worse when we came to the orchestra. The executants, seeing Habeneck's surly manner, were cold and reserved with me. Still they did their duty, which he did not. He never could manage the quick *tempo* of the saltarello; the dancers, unable to dance to his dragging measure, complained to me. I cried:

"Faster! Faster! Wake up!"

Habeneck, in a rage, hit his desk and broke his bow.

After several exhibitions of temper of this sort I said, calmly:

"My good sir, breaking fifty bows will not prevent your time being twice as slow as it ought to be. This is a saltarello."

He turned to the orchestra.

"Since it is impossible to please M. Berlioz," said he, "we will stop for to-day. You may go."

If only I could have conducted myself! But in France authors are not allowed to direct their own works in theatres.

Years later I conducted my *Carnaval Romain*, where that very saltarello comes in, without the wind instruments having any rehearsal at all; and

Habeneck, certain that I should come to grief, was present. I rushed the allegro at the proper time and everything went perfectly.

The audience cried "encore," and the second time was even better than the first. I met Habeneck as we went out, and threw four words at him over my shoulder.

"That's how it goes." He did not reply.

I never felt so happy conducting as I did that day; the thought of the torments Habeneck had made me suffer increased my pleasure.

* * * * *

But to return to *Benvenuto*.

Gradually the larger part of the orchestra came over to my side, and several declared that this was the most original score they had ever played. Duponchel heard them and said:

"Was ever such a right-about face? Now they think Berlioz' music charming, and the idiots are praising it up to the skies."

Still some malcontents remained, and two were found one night playing *J'ai du bon tabac* instead of their parts.

It was just the same on the stage. The dancers pinched their partners, who, by their shrieks, upset the chorus. When, in despair, I sent for Duponchel he was never to be found; attending rehearsal was beneath his dignity.

The opera came on at last. The overture made a furore, the rest was unmercifully hissed. However it was played three times.

It is fourteen years (I write in 1850) since I was thus pilloried at the opera, and I have just read over my poor score, carefully and impartially. I cannot help thinking that it shows an originality, a raciness and a brilliancy that I shall, probably, never have again and which deserve a better fate.[15]

Benvenuto took me a long time to write and would never have been ready--tied as I was by my bread-earning journalistic work--had it not been for the help of a friend.

It was heart-breaking, and I had almost given up the opera in despair when Ernest Legouve came to me, asking:

"Is your opera done?"

"First act not even ready yet. I have no time to compose."

"But supposing you had time----"

"I would write from dawn till dark."

"How much would make you independent?"

"Two thousand francs."

"And suppose someone--If someone--Come, do help me out!"

"With what? What do you mean?"

"Why, suppose a friend lent it to you?"

"What friend could I ask for such a sum?"

"You needn't ask when I offer it----"

Think of my relief! In real truth, next day Legouve lent me two thousand francs, and I finished *Benvenuto*. His noble heart--writer and artist as he was--guessed my trouble and feared to wound me by his offer! I have been fortunate in having many staunch friends.

Paganini was back in Paris when *Benvenuto* was slaughtered; he felt for me deeply and said:

"If I were a manager I would commission that young man to write me three operas. He should be paid in advance, and I should make a splendid thing by it."

Mortification and the suppressed rage in which I had lived during those everlasting rehearsals, brought on a bad attack of bronchitis that kept me in bed, unable to work.

But we had to live, and I determined to give two concerts at the Conservatoire. The first barely paid its expenses so, as an attraction, I advertised the *Fantastique* and *Harold* together for the 16th December 1838.

Now Paganini, although it was written at his desire, had never heard *Harold*, and, after the concert, as I waited--trembling, exhausted, bathed in perspiration--he, with his little son, Achille, appeared at the orchestra door, gesticulating violently. Consumption of the throat, of which he afterwards died, prevented his speaking audibly and Achille alone could interpret his wishes.

He signed to the child, who climbed on a chair and put his ear close to his father's mouth, then turning to me he said:

"Monsieur, my father orders me to tell you that never has he been so struck by music. He wishes to kneel and thank you."

Confused and embarrassed, I could not speak, but Paganini seized my arm, hoarsely ejaculating, "Yes! Yes!" dragged me into the theatre where several of my players still lingered--and there knelt and kissed my hand.

Coming away in a fever from this strange scene, I met Armand Bertin; stopping to speak to him in that intense cold sent me home to bed worse than ever. Next day, as I lay, ill and alone, little Achille came in.

"My father will be very sorry you are ill," he said, "if he had not been ill himself he would have come to see you. He told me to give you this letter."

As I began to open it, the child stopped me:

"He said you must read it alone. There is no answer." And he hurried out.

I supposed it just a letter of congratulation; but here it is:

"DEAR FRIEND,--Only Berlioz can recall Beethoven, and I, who have heard that divine work--so worthy of your genius--beg you to accept the enclosed 20,000 francs, as a tribute of respect.--Believe me ever, your affectionate friend,

NICCOLO PAGANINI.

"PARIS, *18th Dec. 1838*."

I knew enough Italian to make out the letter, but it surprised me so greatly that my head swam, and, without thinking of what I was doing, I opened the little note which was enclosed and addressed to M. de Rothschild. It was in French and ran:

"MONSIEUR LE BARON,--Would you be so good as to hand over the 20,000 francs that I deposited yesterday to M. Berlioz.

PAGANINI."

Then I understood.

My wife, coming in, thought that some new trouble had fallen upon us.

"What is it now?" she cried. "Be brave! we have borne so much already."

"No, no--not that----"

"What then?"

"Paganini--has sent me--20,000 francs!"

"Louis! Louis!" cried Henriette, rushing for her boy, "come here to your mother and thank God."

And together they knelt by my bed--grateful mother and wondering child. Oh Paganini! why could you not be there to see?

Naturally, my first thought was to thank him. My letter seemed so poor, so inadequate, that I am ashamed to give it here. There are feelings beyond words.

His munificent kindness was soon noised abroad and my room besieged by friends anxious to know the facts. All rejoiced and some were jealous--not of me, but of Paganini, who was rich enough to do such deeds. Then began the comments, fury and lies of my opponents, followed by the congratulatory letter of Janin and his eloquent article in the *Debats*.

For a week I lay in bed, burning with impatience to see and thank my benefactor. Then I hurried to his house and found him in the billiard-room. We embraced in silence then, as I poured forth broken thanks, he spoke and--thanks to the silence of the room--I was able to make out his words.

"Not a word! It is so little and has given me the greatest pleasure of my life. You cannot tell how much your music moves me. Ah!" he cried, with a blow of his fist on the table, "now your enemies will be silenced for they know I understand and am not easily satisfied."

But great as was his name it was not great enough to silence the dogs of Paris; in a few weeks they were again baying at my heels.

My earnest wish, now that all debts were paid and a handsome sum remained in hand, was to write a masterpiece, grand, impassioned, original, worthy of dedication to the master to whom I owed so much.

But Paganini, growing worse, had left for Nice, whence alas! he returned no more. I consulted him as to a suitable theme, but he replied:

"I cannot advise you. You best know what suits you best."

After much wavering I fixed on a choral symphony on Shakespeare's *Romeo and Juliet*, and wrote the prose words for the choral portion, which Emile Deschamps, with his usual kindness and extraordinary versatility, put into poetry for me.

Ah! the joy of no more newspaper articles!--or at least hardly any. Paganini had given me money to make music, and I made it. For seven months, with only a few days' intermission, did I work at my symphony.

And, during those months, what a burning, exhilarating life I led! Ah! the joy of floating on the halcyon sea of poetry; wafted onward by the sweet soft breeze of imagination; warmed by the rays of that golden sun of love unveiled by Shakespeare! I felt within me the god-like strength to win my way to that blessed hidden isle, where the temple of pure art raises its soaring columns to the sky.

To others must I leave it to say whether I ever truly looked upon its glories.

Such as it was, my symphony was performed three times running, and each time appeared to be a great success. To my sorrow, Paganini never heard it nor read it. I hoped to see him again in Paris; then to send him the printed score; but he died at Nice leaving to me the poignant sorrow that he would never judge whether the work, undertaken to please him and to justify his faith in its author, was worthy of his great trust.

He, too, seemed sorry not to have known it, and in his letter of the 7th January 1840, he wrote:

"Now it is well done; jealousy can but be silent."

Dear, noble friend! He never saw the ribald nonsense written about my work; how one called my *Queen Mab* music a badly-oiled squirt, how another--speaking of the *Love-Scene,* which musicians place in the forefront of my work--said I *did not understand Shakespeare*!

Empty-headed toad, bursting with stupid self-importance! If you could prove that....

Never was I more deeply hurt by criticism, and yet none of these high priests of art deigned to point out the faults, which I thankfully corrected, when told of them.

For instance, Ernst's secretary, M. Frankoski, wrote from Vienna saying that the end of *Queen Mab* was too abrupt; I therefore wrote the present coda and destroyed the original one.

The criticisms of M. d'Ortigue I also appreciated. The rest of the alterations were my own.

But the symphony is enormously difficult for the executants, both in form and style, and needs most careful, conscientious practice and perfect conducting--which means that none but first-rate artists in each department could possibly do it.

For this reason it will never be given in London. They do not give enough time to rehearsals. The musicians there have no time for music.[16]

XXV

BRUSSELS--PARIS OPERA CONCERT

To FRANZ LISZT.

"PARIS, *6th August 1839*.--I long, dear friend, to tell you all the musical news--at least all that I know. Not that you will find anything new in it. You must be quite *blase* with studying Italian modes of thought; they are dreadfully like Parisian ones.

"I know you have not the heart to laugh at them, for you are not of those who find subject for mirth in the insults offered to our Muse--you would rather, at any cost, hide the blemishes upon her snowy robes and the woful rents in her shimmering veil of light.

"So I will content myself with calmly stating facts and retailing news, whereby I can preserve a dignified quiet, and can simply deal out remarks without theorising.

"The day before yesterday, as I was smoking a cigar in the Boulevard des Italiens, Batta caught me by the arm.

"'What are they up to in London?' I asked.

"'Nothing whatever. They despise music and poetry and drama--everything. They go to the Italian Opera because the Queen goes, and that's all. I feel quite thankful not to be out of pocket and to have been clapped at two or three concerts. That is all the British hospitality I can boast of. Even Artot, in spite of his Philharmonic success, was horribly bored.'

"'And Doehler?'

"'Bored also.'

"'Thalberg?'

"'Is cultivating the provinces.'

"'Benedict----'

"'Encouraged by the success of his first attempt, is writing an English opera.'

"'Well, I'm off. Come to Halle's to-night, we are going to drink and have some music.'

"M. Halle is a young German pianist--tall, thin, and long-haired--who plays magnificently, and seems to get at music by instinct rather than by notes--that is to say, he is rather like you. Real talent, immense knowledge, perfect execution, are among the gifts we all recognise in him.

"Halle and Batta played Mendelssohn's B flat sonata, then we had a chorus over our beer, then Beethoven's A major sonata, of which the first movement excited us wildly, and the minuet and finale drove us to the verge of lunacy.

"Oh you untiring vagabond! when will you return, once more to preside over our nights of music?

"Between ourselves, you always had too many people at your gatherings--too much talk, too little listening. You, alone, wasted an amount of inspiration that was enough to turn one giddy, without all the rest of the folks in addition.

"Do you remember that evening at Legouve's when--the lights put out--you played the C sharp minor sonata, we five lying in the dark on the floor? My tears and Legouve's, Schoelcher's wondering respect, Goubeaux's astonishment! Ah me! you were indeed sublime that night!

"But to get back to news.

"There is a glorious row toward between our Opera troupe and the Italian; they want to unite them in the Rue Le Pelletier. It will be rather a shock. Lablache against Levasseur, Rubini against Duprez, Tamburini against Derivis, Grisi against Mdlle. Naudin and the whole lot against the big drum.

"We mean to be there to pick up the dead and the dying. Lots of people find fault with the Opera orchestra, they say they do not keep in tune, that the right-hand side tends to get a quarter-tone higher than the left--which these gentlemen consider most unreasonable----

"'You seem to suffer in silence,' one of them said to me the other day.

"'I? I did not say I suffered at all,' I replied. 'First, because I never said a word, and secondly, because....'

"Sometimes when they are at their wit's end they play *Don Giovanni*. If Mozart could come back to this world, he would tell them (like Moliere's president) that he would not have it *played*.

"The other day, Ambroise Thomas, Morel, and I were saying we would give five hundred francs for a good performance of Spontini's *Vestale*; that set us off--we know it by heart--and we went on singing it till midnight.

"But we missed you for our accompaniments.

"I am just pouring out news as it comes into my head. Hiller has sent me part of his *Romilda* from Milan. One of our enemies wished to throw himself off the Vendome Column the other day. He gave the keeper forty francs to let him go up--then changed his mind and walked down again.

"Chopin is still away; they said he was very ill, but there is no truth in it. Dumas has just written an exquisite thing--*Mademoiselle de Belle Isle*--but that is out of my province. There! no more news.

"My indifferentism does not extend to you and your long absence. Come back soon. It is high time you did, both for us and, I hope, for yourself too. Adieu."

In 1840 the Government proposed celebrating the tenth anniversary of the Revolution by exceptional ceremonies, and the Minister of the Interior, M. de Remusat, who, like M. de Gasparin, had a soul for music, commissioned me to write a symphony, leaving form and all details entirely to me.

I planned a great symphony, on broad, simple lines, and as it was to be played in the open air where delicate orchestral effects would be lost, I engaged a military band of two hundred men.

Habeneck was anxious to conduct but, remembering the snuff trick, I preferred to do my own conducting.

Most fortunately, I invited a large audience to the final rehearsal, feeling sure that my work could not be properly judged on the day of performance.

And so it proved. On the great Place de la Bastille, ten yards away, you could make out nothing, and to make things worse, the legions of the National Guard marched off right in the middle, to the rattle of fifty kettledrums. That is the way music is always honoured in France at public *fetes,* apparently they think it is meant to please--the eye.

Towards the end of this year I made my first musical venture out of France, as M. Snel, of Brussels, asked me to direct some of my works for the *Societe de la Grande Harmonie* in the Belgian capital.

Nothing but a regular *coup d'etat* at home made the execution of this plan possible. On one pretext or another, my wife had always set her face against my leaving Paris, her real reason being a most foolish and unfounded jealousy, for which there was absolutely no cause.

But constant accusations forced me, in time, to justify them and to take advantage of the position with which she credited me.

Smuggling my music out of the house by degrees, I finally departed secretly, leaving a letter of explanation and, accompanied by the lady who has since been my constant travelling companion,[17] I went off to Brussels.

To cut short these sad and sordid details--after many painful scenes, an amicable separation was arranged. I often saw my wife, my affection for her remained unchanged--indeed, the miserable state of her health but made her dearer to me.

This is sufficient to explain my conduct to those who have only known me since that time; I shall not recur to the subject as I am distinctly not writing confessions.

I gave two concerts in Brussels, where opinions were, as usual, divided about me as in Paris. Fetis chose to find fault with my (perfectly correct) harmony, and I was rather tempted to reply to him in one of the papers, but finally decided to stick to my invariable rule to reply to no criticism whatsoever.

This being merely a trial trip, I arranged to spend five or six months on tour in Germany, and therefore returned straight to Paris to give a colossal farewell concert.

I explained my wish to M. Pillet, director of the Opera, who was quite willing to allow me the use of the theatre.

But it was necessary to keep it secret so that Habeneck might not have time to counterplot, as he would hardly look with a favourable eye on anyone who supplanted him at the conductor's desk.

I, therefore, prepared all my music and engaged my performers without telling them where the concert would be held, and when all was ready I asked M. Pillet to tell Habeneck that the concert was entirely in my hands. But he dared not face his terrible chief, and it fell to my lot to write and inform him of our arrangements.

He received my letter during a rehearsal, read it several times, looked very black, then went down to the office and said that the plan suited him exactly, as he wished to go into the country the day of the concert. Still his disgust was quite evident, and it was shared by a part of his orchestra, who thought to pay court to him by shewing it.

The concert was for the benefit of the Opera, but I was to have five hundred francs for my share and the Opera staff were to get no extra remuneration whatever. Mindful of my experience with the Theatre Italien, I determined to devote my five hundred francs to the payment of these men, all the more readily that I felt thunder in the air in the form of Habeneck's savage looks, the numbers of the *Charivari* (which cut me up tremendously) on the desks, and the constant little confabulations that went on in odd corners.

I engaged six hundred performers from different theatres and from the Conservatoire, and in a week managed to drill them into something like order, how I cannot imagine.

I was on foot, baton in hand, the whole day, going from the Opera to the Theatre Italien, whence I engaged the chorus; thence to the Opera Comique and to the Conservatoire to superintend different parts, for I dared not relegate a single department to anyone else.

Then, in the foyer of the Opera, I took the stringed instruments from eight till twelve, and the wind from twelve to four. My throat was on fire, my voice gone, my right arm almost paralysed. One day I should have been ill with thirst and fatigue had not a kind chorus-singer had the humanity to bring me a large glass of hot wine.

The players of the Opera made me as much trouble as possible; they learnt that the outside performers were to have twenty francs a piece, so they demanded a like sum.

"Not for the money," said they, "but for the honour of the Opera."

"You shall have your twenty francs," I cried; "but for heaven's sake go on and let me have a little peace."

On the day of the grand rehearsal all went fairly well, except the *Queen Mab* scherzo, which is too dainty to be treated by so large a body of players. Unfortunately I did not think, at the time, of entrusting it to a small band of picked musicians, so was reluctantly obliged to cut it altogether out of the programme.

On the day of the performance I had hoped to keep quiet until the evening, but my friend, Leon Gatayes, came in to tell me that a plot was being hatched by Habeneck's partizans (who were indignant at his being passed over) to ruin the whole affair. The drum parchments were to be slit, the bows of the double-basses greased, and in the middle of the concert a section of the audience was to shout for the *Marseillaise*.

After this, needless to say, I did not take much rest. Prowling restlessly round the Opera, I had the good luck to meet Habeneck; I caught him by the arm.

"I hear your musicians are going to play me some tricks. I have my eye on them."

"Oh, it's all right," he answered. "I have talked to them; you need not be afraid."

"I am not afraid: on the contrary, I am comforting *you*. You see, if anything happened, it would fall pretty heavily on you. But make your mind easy; they won't do anything."

And they did not. My copyist had been all day in the theatre guarding the drum and double-basses, and I myself went round to all the desks to ensure each man having his own part.

Indeed I was made quite ashamed of myself when I got to the Dauverne brothers; one of them looked up and said reproachfully:

"Berlioz, surely you don't doubt us? Aren't we decent fellows and your friends?"

I grew quite hot and stopped my investigations, for which, it must be owned, there really was some excuse.

Nothing went wrong and my *Requiem* produced its due effect, but during the interval, according to rumour, Habeneck's cabal howled for the *Marseillaise*. I went to the front of the stage and shouted at the top of my lungs:

"We will *not* play the *Marseillaise*; that is not what we are here for," and peace reigned once more.

Although the receipts were eight thousand five hundred francs, the sum put aside to pay the musicians was not sufficient to fulfil my promises to them, and I had to supplement it by three hundred and fifty out of my own pocket, as the red ink entry in the cashier's book at the Opera testifies to this day.

Thus I organised the most tremendous concert Paris had ever known, and was three hundred and fifty francs put of pocket for my pains. I was likely to grow rich!

M. Pillet is a gentleman and I never could understand how he allowed it; perhaps the cashier never told him.

I left for Germany a few days later on my pilgrimage. It was hard work truly, but it was at least *musical* hard work, and I had the untold happiness of being safe away from the intrigues and platitudes of Paris and among sympathetic musical people.

XXVI

HECHINGEN--WEIMAR

MY tour began with trouble; I had intended giving a concert in Brussels, as Madame Nathan-Treillet, the idol of the Bruxellois, had kindly promised to come from Paris purposely to sing for me. But she fell seriously ill, and we knew that not all the symphonies in the world would make up for her absence.

When the catastrophe was announced the Grande Harmonie promptly fainted *en bloc*, pipes went out as if from want of air, and people dispersed groaning. In vain did I say, "Be calm! There will be no concert; you will be spared the misery of listening to my music. Surely that compensation is not to be despised!" It availed naught. *Their eyes wept tears of beer et nolebant consolari* because she came not. So my concert went to the devil.

Time passed; I was obliged to go on leaving the poor Belgians to their fate. My anxiety for them, however, soon melted as I embarked on my Rhine journey and went up to Mainz, hoping to be able to arrange a concert there.

I first went to Schott, patriarch of music publishers, who seemed rather as if he belonged to the household of the Sleeping Beauty, his somnolent sentences being interspersed with long silences.

"I don't think--you hardly will be able--give a concert--there is--no orchestra--no public--no money."

Not being overburdened with patience, I went straight to the station and off to Frankfort. To add fuel to my fire, the train was asleep too; it "made haste slowly"; it did not *go*; it dawdled and, particularly that day, made interminable organ pedal-points at each station. But every adagio has an end, and finally I got to Frankfort--a well-built, bright town, very much alive and up to date.

Next day, crossing the square on my way to the theatre, I came up with some young men carrying wind-instruments and asked them--since they evidently belonged to the orchestra--to take my card to Guhr, the chief.

"Ah," said one, who spoke French, "we are glad to see you. M. Guhr told us you were coming. We have done *King Lear* twice, and though we cannot offer you your Conservatoire orchestra, perhaps you will not be very displeased with us."

Guhr appeared, sharp, incisive, with snapping dark eyes and quick gestures; it was easy to see that he would not err on the side of indulgence with his orchestra. He spoke French but not fluently enough for his wishes, so he tumbled over his sentences, which were interlarded with oaths in a thick German accent, with most ludicrous results.

The upshot of his flow of eloquence was that the two Milanollo girls were creating such a furore that no other music would have the slightest chance of success.

He was voluble in excuses and ended:

"What can I do, my dear fellow? These infant prodigies make money; French Vaudevilles make money--I can't refuse money, can I? But do stay till to-morrow and you shall hear *Fidelio* with Pischek and Mdlle. Capitaine and you can give me your opinion of them."

So it was arranged that I should go on to Stuttgart and try my fortunes with Lindpaintner, leaving the Frankfurters to cool down after the fever caused by the charming little sisters, whom I had praised and applauded in Paris but who got sadly in my way in Frankfort.

Fidelio was beautifully sung by Mdlle. Capitaine; she is not a brilliant singer, but of all the women I heard in Germany I like her best in her own style. In a box I espied my old friend, Ferdinand Hiller, and a moment we were back on our student-comrade footing of years before. He is at work on an oratorio *The Fall of Jerusalem*; I am sorry that I have never been in Frankfort for one of his concerts to hear and judge of his compositions, which I am told are of a very high order.

My first care was to get as much information as I could on the musical resources of Stuttgart, for I found the expenses of carrying so much concerted music about with me something enormous and only wished to take what I might fairly expect to be performed. I finally decided on two symphonies, an overture and some choral pieces, leaving all the rest with that unlucky Guhr, who seemed fated to be bothered with me and my music in some way or other.

I had a letter of introduction to a Dr Schilling, whose title made me shudder. I pictured an aged pedant in spectacles and red wig, armed with a snuff-box and astride his hobbies, fugue and counterpoint, caring for nothing but Bach and Marpurg and hating modern music in general and mine in particular.

So much for preconceived ideas.

Dr Schilling was young, wore no spectacles, had a handsome crop of black hair, smoked, took no snuff, never mentioned fugues or canons and showed no dislike for modern music--not even mine.

He spoke French about as badly as I did German and our intercourse was not precisely on the lines of Herder and Kant. I made out that I could either apply for the loan of the theatre, which would mean freedom from expense and ensure the presence of the King and Court or else could engage the *Salle de la Redoute*, where I should have everything to manage and which the King never entered.

I sought an interview with Baron von Topenheim, superintendent of the theatre, who most kindly assured me that he would speak to the King that evening:

"But," he added, "I think I ought to tell you that the acoustic of the theatre is vile and that of the *Salle de la Redoute* is good."

I was nonplussed and could only go and see if Lindpaintner would advise me what to do. I do not know how to express my feelings towards him, but at the end of ten minutes we might have been friends of ten years' standing.

"First," said he, "do not be deceived as to the musical importance of our town--we have neither money nor public. (I thought of Mainz and father Schott)! But since you are here we certainly cannot let you go without hearing some of your works, about which we are very curious. So you must take the *Redoute* and as far as players are concerned, if you will only give about eighty francs to their pension fund, they will think it an honour to rehearse and to perform under your baton. Come to-night and hear *Freyschutz* and I will introduce you and you will see that I am right."

He was as good as his word and all my fears melted away. Here was a young, fiery, enthusiastic orchestra. I saw that from the way they played Weber.

They were intrepid readers, too, nothing upset, nothing disconcerted them, they never missed a single sign of expression either. I had chosen the *Symphonie Fantastique* and *Francs-Juges* and trembled for my syncopations, my four notes against three, my unusual rhythms; but they plunged straight in without a single mistake.

I was astounded, for with two rehearsals the whole thing was done.

It would have been grand had not illness on the day of the concert taken away half my violins and left me with four firsts and four seconds to fight that mass of wind and percussion. It was the more harrowing, in that the King and Court were there in full force; still it was intelligent and sympathetic, and the audience applauded everything warmly except the *Pilgrim's March* from *Harold*, which fell flat. I found it do so again when I separated it from the rest of the symphony, which shows what a mistake it is to divide up some compositions.

After the concert I was congratulated by the King, by Prince Jerome Bonaparte and by Count Niepperg, but I am afraid Lindpaintner, whose approval was more to me than all, hated everything but the overture. I am sure Dr Schilling found it hideous and was quite ashamed of having introduced such a musical freelance to his quiet town.

However, being Councillor of State to the Prince of Hohenzollern-Hechingen, he wrote and told His Highness of the savage he had in tow, thinking that the said savage would find a more appropriate setting in the wilds of the Black Forest than in civilised Stuttgart.

The savage therefore--receiving a cordial invitation from the Prince's Privy Councillor, Baron de Billing--and being avid of new sensations, took his way through the snow and the great pine woods to the little town of Hechingen, without in the least troubling about what he should do when he got there.

I never recall this Black Forest journey without a medley of pleasant, sad, sweet and troubled remembrances that strangely stir my heart. The double mourning--white of the snow and black of the trees--spread over the mountains; the cold wind's dreary moan among the shivering, restless pines; the ceaseless gnawing of sorrow at my heart, grown stronger in this solitude, the bitter cold, then the arrival at Hechingen, bright faces, gracious prince, *fetes*, concerts, laughter, promises to meet in Paris, then--good-bye--and once more the darkness and the cold!

Ah! what do I suffer even yet! What demon started me thinking of it? But that is my way--without apparent cause, I am tormented, possessed, just as in certain electric states of the air the leaves rustle without wind.

But back to Hechingen. The ruler of this minute principality was an intellectual young man who seemed to have but two objects in life--to make his people happy and to worship music.

Can one imagine a more perfect existence?

His subjects adored him and music loved him, for he understood her both as poet and musician, and had composed some touching songs.

He had a tiny orchestra, conducted by Taglichsbeck, whom I had met five years earlier in Paris, and who received me with open-hearted kindness.

It was most amusing to see me adapting my big orchestral works to this little band, but, by dint of patience and goodwill all round, we did wonders and gave *King Lear*, the *Pilgrims' March*, the *Ball Scene*, and other excerpts in really good style.

Still, of course, I could not help longing for wider scope, and when the Prince came to compliment me, I said:

"Ah! I would give two years of my life if Your Highness could hear that with my Conservatoire orchestra."

"Yes! yes!" he said. "I know that you have an imperial orchestra that calls you 'Sire,' while I am but a Highness. I mean to go to Paris and hear it one day--one day."

After the concert we supped at his villa, and his charming brightness infected us all. Wishing me to hear a trio he had composed for piano, tenor, and 'cello, Taglichsbeck took the piano, the Prince the air, and I, amid laughter and applause, tried to sing the 'cello part. My high A simply brought down the house.

Two days later I returned to Stuttgart.

The snow was melting on the mourning pines, stained was the fair white mantle of the mountains--all was dreary and woe-worn--again at my heart gnawed the worm that dieth not----

The rest is silence.

To FRANZ LISZT.

"You, my dear Liszt, know nothing of the uncertainties of the wandering musician. You never have a moment's anxiety as to whether, when you get to a town, there will be a decent orchestra or a theatre ready for you. To parody Louis XIV. you can say:

"'Orchestra, chorus, conductor are myself.'

"A grand piano and a large hall are the extent of your needs. But a poor travelling composer like myself depends upon a combination most difficult to arrange and at any moment liable to be upset. How much thought, precaution, fatigue it all requires. Yet look at the reward!

"Think of the compensation of *playing on an orchestra*, of having under one's hand this vast living instrument!

"You *virtuosi* are princes and kings by the grace of God, you are born on the steps of the throne; we composers must fight and conquer before we reign. Yet the difficulties and dangers surmounted add brilliance to our victories, and we should perhaps be happier than you--if we always had soldiers.

"But this is a digression.

"At Stuttgart I waited, hardly knowing what plans to make, until a favourable answer came to my letter of enquiry addressed to Weimar.

Meanwhile I had another experience of the coldness of Germans towards Beethoven.

"Lindpaintner conducted a magnificent performance of the Leonore overture at the Redoute Society's concert, which elicited but the faintest applause, and I heard a gentleman say afterwards that he wished they would give Haydn's symphonies instead of that noisy music without any tune in it!!!

"Really now, we do not own such Philistines as that in Paris!

"I went to Weimar *via* Carlsruhe (where there was nothing to be done) and Mannheim--a cold, calm, respectable town, where love of music will never keep the inhabitants awake.

"The younger Lachner, a real artist, both modest and talented, is director there; he hurriedly arranged a concert for me, and was deeply grieved because the ineptitude of his trombones forbade our giving the *Orgie* in *Harold*.

"Mannheim bored me horribly, and it was an intense relief to get away and breathe freely once more.

"Behold me then again afloat on the Rhine--I meet Guhr, still swearing--I leave him--meet our friend Hiller, who tells me his *Fall of Jerusalem* is ready--I leave, in company with a magnificent sore throat--sleep on the way--dream frightful things that I will not repeat--reach Weimar, thoroughly ill--Lobe and Chelard try in vain to prop me up--preparations for concert--first rehearsal--I rejoice and am cured.

"There is something broad, cultivated, liberal about the very air of Weimar. Calm, luminous, peaceful, dreamy--how my heart beat as I paced the streets!

"Here is the summer-house of Goethe where the late Grand Duke used to come to take part in the discussions of Schiller, Herder, and Wieland. There, a Latin inscription traced by the author of *Faust*. Those two attic windows, are they indeed those of Schiller? Was it this humble roof that sheltered the mighty enthusiasm of the author of *Don Carlos*? Was it right of Goethe, the rich and powerful minister, thus to leave his friend in poverty? I fear me that it was true friendship on the side of Schiller only--Goethe loved himself too well, he lived too long and death was to him a terror.

"Schiller! Schiller! you deserved a less human friend!

"It is one in the morning, with bitter cold and a brilliant moon. I stand entranced before that small dark house; all is silent in this city of the dead.

"Within me surges up that passion of respect, regret, and love for the genius that stretches out a hand from beyond the cold dark grave, and lays a mighty finger on us poor obscure earth wanderers, and upon that humble threshold I kneel, murmuring brokenly, 'Schiller! Schiller!'

"But I am no nearer the subject of my letter, dear friend; to soothe myself I must think of another dweller in Weimar, the talented but cold Hummel.

"That calms me; I feel better!

"Chelard, as Frenchman, artist, and friend, has done everything possible to help me, and the Baron von Spiegel, the superintendent, has most kindly offered me the theatre and orchestra. He did not add the chorus, which was just as well, for I heard them trying to do Marschner's *Vampire*, and a more ghastly collection of squallers I never heard.

"Of the women soloists, too, the less said the better.

"But are there words to describe the bass--Genast? Is he not a true artist, a born tragedian? I wish I could have stayed long enough to hear him in Shakespeare's *King Lear*, which they were mounting.

"The orchestra is good, but, to do me special honour, Chelard and Lobe hunted up every available extra instrument in the place; there was no harp to be found, but a good pianist and perfect musician, named Montag, kindly arranged my harp parts and played them on the piano.

"Everyone was eagerly ready to help, and you may imagine the rare and extreme joy of being promptly understood and followed. I will spare you a description of the applause and recalls, the compliments of their Highnesses, and the many new friends who, waiting at the stage door, bore me off and kept me till three o'clock next morning.

"Where, oh where is my modesty that I retail all this? Adieu!"

XXVII

MENDELSSOHN--WAGNER

To STEPHEN HELLER.

"On leaving Weimar, my dear Heller, my easiest plan seemed to be to go to Leipzig, but I hesitated because Felix Mendelssohn was musical dictator there, and, in spite of our Roman days together, we had since followed such divergent lines that I could not be sure of a sympathetic reception. Chelard, however, made me ashamed of my misgivings. I wrote, and Mendelssohn replied so warmly and promptly, bidding me welcome to Leipzig, that I could not resist such an invitation, but set off at once, regretfully leaving Weimar and my new friends.

"My relations with Mendelssohn in Rome had been rather curious. At our first meeting I had expressed a great dislike to the first allegro in my *Sardanapalus*.

"'Do you really dislike it?' he said, eagerly. 'I am so glad. I was afraid you were pleased with it, and I think it simply horrid.'

"Then we nearly quarrelled next day because I spoke enthusiastically of Gluck. He said disdainfully:

"'Do you like Gluck?' as much as to say, 'How can a music-maker like you appreciate the majesty of Gluck?'

"I took my revenge a few days after by putting on Montfort's piano a manuscript copy of an air from *Telemaco* without the author's name to it. Mendelssohn came, picked it up thinking it was a bit of Italian opera, and began parodying it. I stopped him in assumed astonishment, saying:

"'Hallo, don't you like Gluck?'"

"'Gluck?'"

"'Why yes, my dear fellow. That is Gluck, not Bellini as you seem to think. You see I know him better than you do, and am more of your own opinion than you are yourself.'"

"One day, speaking of the uses of the metronome, he broke in--

"'What's the good of one? A musician who can't guess the time of a piece of music at sight is a duffer.'"

"I might have replied, but did not, that there were lots of duffers. Soon after he asked to see my *King Lear*. He read it through slowly, then, just as he was going to play it (his talent for score-reading was incomparable), said:

"'Give me the time.'

"'What for? You said yesterday that only duffers needed to be told the time of a piece.'

"He did not show it, but these home thrusts annoyed him intensely. He never mentioned Bach without adding ironically, '*your little pupil*.' In fact, over music he was a regular porcupine; you could never tell where to have him. In every other way he was perfectly charming and sweet-tempered.

"In Rome I learnt to appreciate the beauties of his marvellous *Fingal's Cave*. Often, worn out by the scirocco and thoroughly out of sorts, I would hunt him out and tear him away from his composition. With perfect good humour--seeing my pitiable state--he would lay aside his pen, and, with his extraordinary facility in remembering intricate scores, would play whatever I chose to name--he properly and soberly seated at the piano, I curled up in a snappy bunch on his sofa.

"He liked me, with my wearied voice, to murmur out my setting of Moore's melodies. He always had a certain amount of commendation for my--little songs!

"After a month of this intercourse--so full of interest for me--he disappeared without saying good-bye, and I saw him no more.

"His Leipzig letter, therefore, the more agreeably surprised me, for it showed an unexpected and genial kindness of heart that I found to be one of his most notable characteristics.

"The Concert Society has a magnificent hall--the Gewandhaus--of which the acoustic is perfect. I went straight to see it, and stumbled into the middle of the final rehearsal of Mendelssohn's *Walpurgis Nacht*.

"I am inclined to think[18] that this is the finest thing he has yet done, and I hardly know which to praise most--orchestra, chorus, or the whole combined effect.

"As Mendelssohn came down from his desk, radiant with success, I went to meet him. It was the right moment for our greetings, yet, after the first words, the same thought struck us both--'Twelve years since we wandered day-dreaming in the Campagna!'

"'Are you still a jester?' he asked.

"'Ah no! my joking days are past. To show you how sober and in earnest I am, I hereby solemnly beg a priceless gift of you.'

"'That is ---'

"'The baton with which you conduct your new work.'

"'By all means, if I may have yours instead?'

"'It will be copper for gold, still you shall have it.

"Next day came Mendelssohn's musical sceptre, for which I returned my heavy oak cudgel with the following note, which I hope would not have disgraced the Last of the Mohicans:--

"'Great Chief! To exchange our tomahawks is our word given. Common is mine, plain is yours. Squaws and Pale-faces alone love ornament. May we be brethren, so that, when the Great Spirit calls us to the happy hunting grounds, our warriors may hang our tomahawks side by side in the door-way of the Long House.'"

To JOSEPH D'ORTIGUE.

"*28th February 1843.*--My trade of galley-slave is my excuse for not having written sooner. I have been, and am still, ill with fatigue, the work involved in conducting rehearsals in both Leipzig and Dresden is incredible.

"Mendelssohn is most kind, friendly, and attentive--a master of the highest rank. I can honestly say this in spite of his admiration for my *songs*--of my symphonies, overtures, and *Requiem* he says never a word!

"His *Walpurgis Nacht* is one of the finest orchestral poems imaginable.

"Can you believe that Schumann, the taciturn, was so electrified by my *Offertorium* that he actually opened his mouth, and, shaking my hand, said:

"This *Offertorium* surpasses all.'"

To HELLER.

"It really pains me to see a great master like Mendelssohn worried with the paltry task of chorus-master. I never cease marvelling at his patience and politeness. His every remark is calm and pleasant, and his attitude is the more appreciated by those who, like myself, know how rare such patience is.

"I have often been accused of rudeness to the ladies of the Opera chorus--a reputation which I own I richly deserve--but the very minute there is question of a choral rehearsal a sort of dull anger takes possession of me, my throat closes up, and I glare at the singers very much like that Gascon who kicked an inoffensive small boy, and, when reproached because the child had done nothing, replied:

"'But just think if he *had*!'

"A charming little incident concluded my Leipzig visit. I had again been ill, and, on leaving, asked my doctor for his account. 'Write me the theme of your *Offertorium*,' he said, 'and sign it, and I shall be your debtor.'

"I hesitated, but finally did as he wished, and then, will you believe that I missed the chance of a charming compliment? I wrote: 'To Dr Clarus.'

"'Oh,' said he, 'you have added an *l* to my name.'

"I thought:

"'Patientibus *Carus*, sed inter doctes *Clarus*,' and had not the sense to say it!

"There are times when I am really quite idiotic.

"Now for your questions. You ask me to tell you--

"Is there a rival to Madame Schumann as a pianist? I believe not.

"Is the musical tendency of Leipzig sound? I will not.

"Is it true that the confession of faith here is 'there is no God but Bach, and Mendelssohn is his prophet?' I ought not.

"If the public is at fault in being contented with Lortzing's little operas? I cannot.

"If I have heard any of those old five-part Masses they think so much of here? I know not.

"Good-bye. Write more of your lovely capriccios, and the Lord preserve you from Choral Fugues!"

To ERNST.

"And now about Dresden. I was engaged to give two concerts there, and found chorus, orchestra, and a noble tenor all complete! Nowhere else in Germany have I happened on such wealth. Above all, I found a friend--devoted, energetic, and enthusiastic--Charles Lipinski, whom I knew in Paris. He so worked upon the musicians, by firing them with ambition to do better than Leipzig, that they were rabid for rehearsals. We had four, and they would gladly have had a fifth had there been time.

"The Dresden *Kapelle* is directed by Reissiger, of whom we know little in Paris, and by young Richard Wagner, who spent a long time with us, without, however, making himself known except by a few articles in the *Gazette Musicale*. He has only just received his appointment, and, proud and pleased, is doing his very best to help me.

"He bore endless privations in France, with the added bitterness of obscurity, yet he returned to Saxony and boldly wrote and composed a five-act opera, *Rienzi*, of which the success was so great that he followed it up with the *Flying Dutchman*.

"A man who could, twice over, write words and music for an opera must be exceptionally gifted, and the King of Saxony did well to give him the appointment.

"I only heard the second part of *Rienzi*, which is too long to be played in one evening, and I cannot, in one hearing, pretend to know it thoroughly, but I particularly noted a fine prayer and a triumphal march.

"The score of the *Flying Dutchman* struck me by its sombre colouring, and the clever effect of some tempestuous motifs. But there, as in *Rienzi*, I thought he abused the use of the *tremolo*--sign of a certain lazy attitude of mind against which he must guard.

"In spite of that, all honour to the royal remembrance that has saved from despair such a highly endowed young artist.

"My concerts were successful, the second even more so than the first. What the public liked best were the *Requiem*--although we could not give the most difficult numbers of it--and the *5th May Cantata*, no doubt because the memory of Napoleon is as dear to the Germans now as to us French.[19]

"I made the acquaintance of that wonderful English harpist, Parish-Alvars. He is indeed the Liszt of the harp! He produces the most extraordinary effects, and has written a fantasia on *Moses* that Thalberg has most happily arranged for the piano.

"Why on earth does he not come to Paris?

"When I left Dresden to go back to Leipzig, Lipinski heard that Mendelssohn had put the finale of *Romeo and Juliet* in rehearsal, and told me that if he could get a holiday he should go over and hear it.

"I thought it was a mere compliment, but judge of my consternation when, on the day of the concert, he turned up. He had travelled thirty-five leagues to hear a piece that was not given after all, because the singer who was entrusted with Friar Lawrence's part refused to learn his notes!

To H. HEINE.

"So great has been my happiness in your good town of Brunswick that I should like to tell it all to my dearest foes instead of to you, my friend, to whom it can hardly give pleasure!

"But a truce to irony; it is mere vanity that makes me begin like this, taking a leaf out of your book--inimitable satirist!

"How often in our talks have I regretted that nothing would make you serious, that nothing would stop the restless working of those feline claws, even when you were under the delusion that they were safely sheathed in your velvet paws--you tiger-cat!

"Yet look at the sensitive, delicate imagery of your writings--for you *can* sing major when you choose; at your enthusiasm when you let yourself go; at your tender hidden love for your old grandmother, Germany!

"She, too, speaks of you with wistful tenderness; her elder sons are dead and gone; there remains but you, whom she calls, with a smile, her naughty boy.

"It would be easy for you to make splendid travesties of my Brunswick visit, yet such is my fearless confidence in you, that to you I mean to tell everything.

"That ideal family of musicians, the Mullers, received me and arranged my concert. I counted altogether seven of them, brothers, sons, and nephews, and never in all my travels did I see so devoted and impassioned a set of men.

"As soon as they grasped the chief difficulties of my symphonies (which they did at the first rehearsal), their progress between each meeting was simply incredible. On my expressing surprise, I found that they were deceiving me about the time, and that the whole orchestra actually arrived each morning an hour before I did to practise the intricate passages.

"At Zinkeisen's request we actually dared to try *Queen Mab*, which I had never hitherto dared do in Germany. 'We will practise so hard,' said he, 'that we *must* do it.'

"He did not misjudge his colleagues; my dainty little lady in her microscopic car, drawn by humming gnats at full gallop, disported herself with all her tricksey caprices--to the delight of the good Brunswickers.

"You--own brother to fairies and will-o'-the-wisps and their chosen poet laureate--will realise my misgivings; but never did my tiny invisible queen glide more happily and gaily through her world of silent harmonies.

"Then, in contrast, with what magnificent fury did they not seize on the *Orgie* in *Harold*.

"There was something absolutely terrifying and supernatural in their diabolic rhythm as they bounded, roared, and clashed. Ah, you poets! No joy is yours equal to the joy of conducting!

"I longed to fold the whole orchestra in one comprehensive embrace, but all I could do was cry in French--

"'Gentlemen, you are sublime! You are stupendous brigands!'

"The concert was crowded and the audience quite carried away; hardly was the last chord struck when a frantic noise shook the hall; it was compounded of the shouts of the listeners, the discordant blare of the wind instruments, the tapping of bows on the violins, and the clang of percussion instruments.

"At first I felt perfectly savage at this ruin to my finale, but I calmed down when George Muller, laden with flowers, stepped forward and said in French:

"'Monsieur, allow me to offer these in the name of the Ducal Kapelle.'

"The shouts and noise redoubled, my baton fell from my hand, and my head whirled.

"Hardly had I left the theatre when I was invited to a supper given in my honour by artists and amateurs. There were a hundred and fifty guests.

"Toasts, speeches in French and German, to which I responded as well as I could, then a most musical and effective hurrah was chanted by all in chorus. The basses began on D, tenors on A, and the ladies following on F, made up the chord of D major, to which succeeded the sub-dominant, tonic, dominant, tonic. It was most beautiful, most worthy of a really musical nation. Will you laugh and call me a great simpleton for repeating all this, dear Heine? I must candidly own that I enjoyed it.

"From Brunswick I journeyed on to your native city of Hamburg, where I again had the pleasure of a crowded house and appreciative audience, and made many friends among the orchestra. Krebs alone was reserved in his praise. 'My dear fellow,' said he, 'in a few years your music will be all over Germany, and will be popular, and that will be an awful misfortune! Think of the imitations, the eccentricities, the style it will let us in for! For Art's sake it were better you had never been born!!'

"Let us hope my poor symphonies are not as contagious as he thinks. And so, O maker of poems, adieu!"

From Hamburg I went to Berlin and Hanover, finishing at Darmstadt where the Grand Duke insisted not only on my taking the full receipts from my concert (so far Weimar--city of artists--was the only one that had extended to me this courtesy) but, in addition, refused to let me pay any of the expenses.

Everywhere I met with success and made friends.

Thus ended the longest and perhaps the most arduous pilgrimage ever taken by a musician; its memory will, to me, be ever green.

How can I thank thee, Germany, noble foster-mother to the sons of music? How express my gratitude, admiration, and regret? I know not. I can but bow before thee humbly and murmur brokenly--

"Vale Germania, alma parens!"

XXVIII

A COLOSSAL CONCERT

WHEN I got back to Paris, I found M. Pillet planning a revival of *Der Freyschutz*. Now, by the rules of the Opera every word must be sung and as there are spoken dialogues in Weber's opera he engaged me to set them in the form of recitations.

"It is all wrong," I said, "but as that is the only condition on which it will be played and as, if I don't do it, you will give it to someone who does not know Weber as I do, I accept but with one stipulation--that you change neither music nor libretto."

"Certainly," he replied, "do you suppose I would revive *Robin des Bois*?"

"Very well, then I will get to work at once. How are you arranging the parts?"

"Madame Stolz, Agatha; Mdlle. Dobre, Annette; Duprez, Max."

"I bet he won't take it," I said.

"Why not?"

"You will see soon enough."

"Bouche will do well for Gaspard."

"And the Hermit?"

"Oh--well--" said he, awkwardly, "you know the Hermit isn't much use, I was going--to cut him out."

"H'm! Really? Yet you are going to act *Freyschutz* and not *Robin des Bois*. Evidently, since we sha'n't agree, it is better for me to retire at once for I can't stand that sort of correction."

"Dear me! how wholesale you are in your notions. Very well, we will keep the Hermit, we will keep everything, lock, stock, and barrel."

Then my troubles began. The actors would make their recitations as slow and stately as a tragedy; Duprez,--as I foretold--although ten years before he had been a light tenor and had managed Max perfectly--found it impossible to adapt his fine tenor voice to the music and demanded all sorts of unheard-of transpositions and alterations. I cut them short by refusing to disintegrate the role and it was handed over to Marie.

Then nothing would do but they must have a ballet, and as I could not stop it I tried to arrange a sort of scene from Weber's *Invitation to the*

Waltz; but that was not enough, so the dancers themselves took it into their heads that some bits out of my symphonies would come in nicely.

Pillet agreed. I did not; and, to stop discussion, I said:

"Now look here! I entirely object to introducing into *Der Freyschutz* music that is not Weber's. To prove that I am not unreasonable, go and ask Dessauer, who is over there; I will abide by his decision."

At Pillet's first words Dessauer turned sharply to me:

"Oh, Berlioz! don't do that!"

That ended the matter for the time and the opera was a success. But when I went to Russia they cut and chopped and gnawed it until it was simply a deformity.

And *how* they play what is left now! What a conductor! What a chorus! What utterly sleepy, disgraceful ineptitude and misinterpretation of everything by everybody!

When will a new Christ come to purge our temple and drive out the money changers with a scourge!

* * * * *

I returned to my treadmill--journalism--once more, and oh! the horror of it!

The misery of writing to order an article on nothing in particular--or on things that, as far as I was concerned, simply did not exist since they excited in me no feeling of any description whatsoever. Long ago I remember spending three days over a critique without being able to write one word. I cannot remember the subject but I well remember my torments.

I strode up and down, my brain on fire; I gazed at the setting sun, the neighbouring gardens, the heights of Montmartre--my thoughts a thousand miles away.

Then, as I turned and saw that confounded white paper without a line on it, I flew into the wildest rage.

My unoffending guitar leant against the wall. I kicked it to bits; my pistols stared at me from the wall with big round eyes. I gazed back, then, tearing my hair, burst into burning tears.

That soothed me somewhat, I turned those staring pistols face to the wall and picked up my poor guitar which gave forth a plaintive wail. Then my six-year-old boy, with whom I had unjustly found fault, tapped at the door. As I did not answer he cried:

"Father, is you friends?"

"Yes, yes, my boy, I is friends!" and I flew to let him in. I took him on my knee and laid his fair head on my shoulder; we dropped asleep together and my article was forgotten. Next morning I managed to write something. That is fifteen years ago and my martyrdom still lasts! It is not that I mind work. I can grind at rehearsals for hours at a time; can spend my nights in correcting proofs; can and will do anything and everything that pertains to my work as a musician.

But to eternally pamphleteer for a living! It is cruel!

To HUMBERT FERRAND.

"*3rd October 1844.*--I read in the *Debats* of your splendid agricultural success and can imagine how much work and perseverance it involves. You are a kind of Robinson Crusoe in your island,[20] and when the sun shines I long to be with you, to breathe the spicy air, to follow you from field to field, to listen with you to the sweet silence of your lonely groves--our affection is so sure, so whole-hearted, so perfect!

"Yet when dull days come and mists rise, the fever of Paris seizes me once more and I feel that here only is life possible. But can you believe that a strange sort of torpid resignation with regard to things musical has taken possession of me? It is as well, for this indifference saves my strength for the time when a passionate struggle may become necessary.

"You have doubtless heard of the marvellous success of my *Requiem* in St Petersburg. Romberg most bravely tackled the enormous expense and, thanks to the generosity of the Russian aristocracy, made a profit of five thousand francs. Give me a despotic government as nursing mother of Art!

"If you could but be here this winter! I long to see you. I seem to be going down hill so rapidly, life is so short! The end is often before my eyes now and I clutch with frenzied eagerness at the flowers beside my path as I slip quickly past.

"There was a rumour that I was to succeed Habeneck at the Opera, it is a dictatorship that I should enjoy in the interests of Art. But, for that, Habeneck would have to be translated to the Conservatoire, where Cherubini still goes to sleep. Perhaps when I am old and incapable I shall go to the Conservatoire. At present I am too young to dream of it!"

I was railing more than usual at my hard fate when Strauss proposed that we should give a concert at the close of the 1844 Exhibition, in the empty building.

It was a tremendous undertaking, for his original intention was to have also a ball and a banquet to the exhibitors. But, owing to the fixed idea of M. Delessert, chief of the police, that plots and risings were in the air, we were forced to reduce it to a classical concert for me and a popular promenade concert next day for Strauss.

Rushing all over Paris I engaged nearly every musician of any consequence and gathered a body of 1022 performers--all paid except the singers from the lyric theatres, who helped me for love of music.

The rehearsals and general arrangements were most arduous and my anxiety lest we should fail nearly killed me. The great day, the 1st August, came and at noon (the concert began at one o'clock) I went to the Exhibition, noticing with pleasure the stream of carriages all converging on the Champs Elysees. Everything inside the building was in perfect order, everyone in his or her appointed place, and my good friend and indefatigable librarian, M. Rocquemont, assured me that all would go perfectly.

Musical delirium seized me, I thought no more of public, receipts or deficit, but was just raising my baton to begin when a violent smashing of wood announced that the people had burst the barriers and filled the hall. This meant success and I joyfully tapped my desk, crying:

"Saved!"

To direct my mass of performers I had Tilmant to conduct the wind, Morel[21] the percussion instruments, and five chorus-masters, one in the centre and four at the corners to guide those singers who were out of my range. Thus there were seven deputy-conductors, whose arms rose and fell with mine with incredible precision.

The Blessing of the Daggers from the *Huguenots* was given with an imposing effect that surpassed my expectations. I wished Meyerbeer could have heard it. It worked upon me so that my teeth chattered and I shook with nervous ague. The concert had to be stopped while they brought me some punch and a change of clothes, and by making a little screen of the harps in their linen covers, I was enabled to dress right before the audience without being seen.

The concert finished triumphantly with the utmost satisfaction to artists and audience but, as I went out, I had the gruesome pleasure of seeing the hospital authorities counting our receipts and walking off with the *eighth gross*--that is, four thousand francs--which left me, when all was paid, with eight hundred francs for all my trouble and anxiety.

This mad experiment was hardly over when M. Amussat, my anatomy master and friend, called.

"Why, Berlioz!" he said, "what on earth is the matter? You are as yellow as a guinea and look thoroughly overdone."

He felt my pulse.

"You are on the verge of typhoid and must be bled."

"Very well, do it now."

He did, and then said:

"You will please leave Paris at once and go to the Riviera or somewhere south by the sea and forget all these exciting topics. Be off at once."

With my eight hundred francs I went to Nice. It moved me strangely to see those haunts of thirteen years earlier--the days of my youth.

I bathed, explored the well-known cliffs, paid my respects to the old cannon, still asleep in the sun; the room in which I wrote *King Lear* was let to an English family so I found shelter in an old tower adjoining the Ponchettes Rocks. After a month's lotus-eating I turned my face once more to Paris and took up again my Sisyphus burden.

After giving some concerts in the circus of the Champs Elysees, which fatigued me greatly I again took a rest on the Mediterranean shores then gave some more concerts in Marseilles, Lyons and Lille of which I have given a full account in my *Grotesques de la Musique*. Shortly afterwards I started on my tour through Austria, Bohemia and Hungary.

XXIX

THE RAKOCZY MARCH

OF my journey from Paris to Vienna I only have two distinct impressions--one of a violent pain in my side that I thought would be the death of me and the other of a species of god I saw at Augsbourg. This worthy man had founded a sort of neo-christianity which was rather popular: he looked a decent sort of fellow.

At Ratisbon the steamer had gone, so I was obliged to wait two days and then go on in a diligence, which made me feel as if I had gone back into the Dark Ages. At Linz, however, I set foot on a fine steam-boat, and found myself once more in A.D. 1845.

But I had time for reflection and could not help wondering why on earth we cannot all spell the names of places alike. There was I, hunting through a German map. Linz was graciously pleased to be the same in both languages, but where was Ratisbon? Who could possibly find it masquerading as Regensburg?

What should we say to the Germans if they persisted in calling Lyons, Mittenberg, and Paris, Triffenstein?

On landing at Vienna I at once got an idea of the passion for music of the Austrians.

The custom-house officer examining my trunks caught sight of the name on them and asked:

"Where is he? Where is he?"

"I am he, monsieur."

"*Mein Gott*, M. Berlioz, where in the world have you been? We have been waiting for you a week and couldn't think what had become of you."

I thanked my worthy friend as well as my limited vocabulary would allow, and could not help thinking that my non-appearance would never give rise to similar anxiety at the Paris Douane.

The first concert I went to was one in the Riding School, given by nearly a thousand performers--most of them amateurs--for the benefit of the Conservatoire, which has no, or very little, Government support. The verve and precision with which that musical crowd rendered Mozart's delicate *Flauto Magico* overture quite astonished me, I had not believed it possible.

I was delighted to make the acquaintance of Nicolai, conductor of the Karnthnerthor Theatre; he has the three gifts necessary--to my mind--for a perfect director. He is an experienced, enthusiastic composer, has perfect intuition for rhythms and clear-cut and precise mechanism. Finally, he is a clever organiser, sparing neither time nor trouble; hence the wonderful unity and perfection of the Karnthnerthor orchestra.

He arranged sacred concerts in the *Salle des Redoutes* similar to ours in Paris. There I heard a scena from *Oberon*, a fine symphony of Nicolai's own and the incomparable B flat of Beethoven.

It is in this fine hall that, thirty years since, Beethoven gave his masterpieces--now worshipped by Europe, but then despised by the Viennese, who crowded to hear Salieri's operas! How my knees trembled as I stood at the desk where once *he* had stood! Nothing is changed; the desk I used is the very one that he had used, by that staircase he had come up to receive the applause of his few admirers, looked upon by the rest of the audience as fanatics in search of eccentricity.

For recognition Beethoven had to wait, but how he suffered!

To my great delight Pischek, the splendid baritone I had met and admired in Frankfort, suggested that he should make his Viennese debut at my concert.

He had improved immensely; somehow his voice always gave rise in me to a sort of exaltation or intoxication which, now, was intensified by its splendid compass, passion and exquisite sweetness.

No wonder that his success in a great ballad by Uhland (which bore no resemblance to the inanities we call ballads in Paris) was instantaneous and, as an encore, he gave a song that drove the audience almost frantic. If only he would learn French what a furore he would make in Paris!

My reception by all in Vienna--even by my fellow-ploughmen, the critics--was most cordial; they treated me as a man and a brother, for which I am heartily grateful.

After my third concert at a grand supper my friends presented me with a silver-gilt baton, and the Emperor sent me eleven hundred francs with the rather odd compliment, "Tell Berlioz I was really amused."

The rest of my doings, are they not written in the newspapers of the day?

The first thing I did on leaving Vienna for Pesth was to get into trouble with the Danube, which, instead of remaining decently within its banks, chose to overflow and inundate that muddy Slough of Despond by courtesy called the Emperor's highway. Only with an extra team of horses had we been able to make way even so far, but at midnight I was aroused from my resigned drowsiness by the stoppage of the carriage and the boiling of waters all round.

The driver had gone straight into the river, and dared not stir a step. The water rose steadily.

There was a Hungarian captain in the coupe who had spoken to me once or twice through the little window between us; it was my turn to speak now:

"Captain!"

"Sir?"

"Don't you think we are going to be drowned?"

"Yes, I do. Have a cigar."

His calm insolent coolness made me long to smash his head in; in a fury I took his cigar and puffed violently. Still the water rose and the desperate driver turned, and at the risk of spilling us all in the river, climbed up the bank and took us straight-way--into a lake. This time I thought must be the end of all and I called out to the soldier:

"Captain, have you another cigar?"

"Yes, sir."

"Let me have it quick, for it's all up with us now!"

But it was not, for an honest country man passing by (where the devil could he have been going in such weather at such a time of night?) extricated us and gave our unhappy Phaeton directions whereby we made our way to Pesth. At least it was a big town of which I asked my captain the name.

"Buda," said he.

"What? In my map the town opposite Pesth is called Ofen. Look."

"Oh yes, that's Buda. Ofen is the German name for it."

"H'm, I see. German maps are as cleverly arranged as French ones; but I think they might give us both names anyway."

On reaching Pesth I had a little pleasure party all to myself, in accordance with a promise made to myself while soaking in the Danube mud. I took a bath, drank two glasses of Tokay and slept twenty hours--not, however, without visions of boiling waters and lakes of mud. After which I set out on the war-path of concert-promoting, greatly helped by the kindness of Count Raday, superintendent of the National Theatre.

Now the Hungarians are nothing if not patriotic. In every shop window things are ticketed *hony* (national) and, by the advice of an amateur in Vienna, who had brought me a volume of Hungarian national airs, I chose the Rakoczy March and arranged it as it now stands as finale to the first part of my *Faust*.

No sooner did the rumour spread that I had written *hony* music than Pesth began to ferment.

How had I treated it? They feared profanation of that idolised melody, which for so many years had made their hearts beat with lust of glory and battle and liberty; all kinds of stories were rife, and at last there came to me M. Horwath, editor of a Hungarian paper--who, unable to curb his curiosity, had gone to inspect my march at the copyist's.

"I have seen your Rakoczy score," he said, uneasily.

"Well?"

"Well; I feel horribly nervous about it."

"Bah! why?"

"Your motif is introduced *piano*, and we are used to hearing it started *fortissimo*."

"Yes, by the gipsies. Is that all? Don't be alarmed. You shall have such a forte as you never heard in your life. You can't have read the score carefully; remember the end is everything."

All the same, when the day came my throat tightened, as it did in times of great excitement, when this devil of a thing came on. First the trumpets gave out the rhythm, then the flutes and clarinets, with a *pizzicato* accompaniment of strings--softly outlining the air--the audience remaining calm and judicial. Then, as there came a long *crescendo*, broken by the dull beats of the big drum (as of distant cannon) a strange restless movement was perceptible among them--and, as the orchestra let itself go in a cataclysm of sweeping fury and thunder, they could contain themselves no longer.

Their overcharged souls burst with a tremendous explosion of feeling that raised my hair with terror.

I lost all hope of making the end audible,[22] and in the encore it was no better; hardly could they contain themselves long enough to hear a portion of the coda.

Horwath, in his box, was like one possessed, and I could not resist a smiling glance at him to ask--

"Are you still afraid or are you content with your *forte*?"

It was lucky that this was the end of the programme, for certainly these excitable people would have listened to nothing more.

As I mopped my face in the little room set apart for me, a poorly dressed man slipped quietly in. He threw himself upon me, his eyes full of tears, and stammered out:

"Ah, monsieur--the Hungarian--poor man--not speak French--Forgive, excited--understood your cannon--Yes, big battle--Dogs of Germans!"

Striking his chest vehemently--"In heart of me you stay--ah, French--Republican--know to make music of Revolution!"

I cannot describe his frenzy; it was almost sublime.

After that, of course, the Rakoczy ended every concert, and on leaving I had to present the town with my MS.

Later on I sent them a revised version, as some young Hungarians did me the honour to present me with a silver crown of most exquisite workmanship.

When I got back to Vienna, the amateur who had given me the idea of writing the march came to me in comical terror.

"For mercy's sake," he begged, "never tell that I gave you the idea. The excitement of it has reached Vienna, and I should get into dreadful trouble if it were known."

Of course I promised silence, but, as this terrible affair is long since done with, I may now add that he was called---- No, I only wished to frighten him. I won't tell!

* * * * *

I had not intended to include Prague in my round, but someone sent me the Prague *Musical Gazette* with three appreciative articles on my *King Lear* by Dr Ambros. I wrote to thank him and mentioned my doubts of my reception by his fellow-citizens who, I had been told, would hear no one but Mozart. His kind reply swept away my misgivings and made me as eager to go as I had hitherto been the reverse. Of Prague my recollections are golden. I gave six concerts, and at the last, had the great joy of having Liszt to hear my *Romeo and Juliet*.

At the close of the performance as I begged him to be my interpreter in thanking the artists for their devotion and patience in spending three weeks over my works, two or three of them came up to us and spoke to him.

"My office is changed," he said, turning to me; "these gentlemen request me to convey to you their thanks for the pleasure you have given them and their joy in your pleasure."

This was indeed a red-letter day for me! There are not many such in my life.

As the music lovers of Vienna had given me a banquet and a silver-gilt baton, those of Prague gave me a supper and a silver cup.

But this same cup poured out such floods of champagne that Liszt, who had made a charming and touching speech in my honour, was shipwrecked therein. At two o'clock in the morning Belloni, his secretary, and I were hard at work in the streets of Prague trying to persuade him to wait till daylight to fight a Bohemian who had drunk more than he had. We were rather anxious about him, as he had to give a concert at noon next day, and at half-past eleven was still asleep. At length he was awakened, jumped into a carriage, walked on to the platform, and played as I verily believe he had never played before. There certainly is a Providence over--pianists.

I cannot express my tender regrets for those good Bohemians.

"O Prague! when shall I see thee again?"

XXX

PARIS--RUSSIA--LONDON

WHILE trailing round Germany in my old post-chaise I composed my *Damnation de Faust*. Each movement is punctuated by memories of the place where it was written. For instance, the Peasant's Dance was written by the light of a shop gas-jet one night when I had lost myself in Pesth, and I got up in the middle of the night in Prague to write the song of the angelic choir.

Thinking that my foreign tour might have enhanced my home reputation, on my return to Paris I ventured to put it in rehearsal, going to enormous expense for copying and for the hire of the Opera Comique. Fatal reasoning! The indifference of the Parisians to art had increased by leaps and bounds, the weather in November 1846 was vile, and they preferred their warm homes to the unfashionable Opera Comique.

It was twice performed to half empty houses and elicited no more attention than if I had been the least of Conservatoire students. Nothing in all my career has wounded me as this did. The lesson was cruel but useful; I vowed that never again would I trust to the tender mercies of Paris.

I did not keep my vow, for later on I could not resist letting it hear my *Childhood of Christ*, which proved a great success.

[Berlioz does not mention the domestic troubles that added greatly to his dejection. His wife was paralysed and his son Louis, brought up in a divided household, naturally gave him anxiety, as the following letter shows]:

To LOUIS BERLIOZ.

"*October 1846*.--Your mother is a little better, but she is still in bed and unable to speak. As the least agitation would be fatal to her, do not write to her as you have done to me.

"You talk of being a sailor. Do you wish to leave me? for, once at sea, God knows when I shall see you again. Were I but free I would go with you, and we would seek our fortunes in India or some far-off land, but to travel one must have money, and only in France can I get my living--such as it is.

"I am speaking to you as if you were grown up. You must think over what I say and you will understand. But remember that, whatever happens, I am and always shall be your best and most devoted friend. It would indeed be sad if, when you came to be twenty years of age, you found yourself useless both to society and yourself. Good-bye, dear child. My heartfelt love."

Faust was my ruin. After two days of unutterable misery I decided to retrieve my fortunes by a tour in Russia, if I could but collect enough money first to pay my debts. Then did my kind friends rally round me and apply healing balm to my wounded spirit.

M. Berlin advanced me a thousand francs from the *Debats* funds; one friend lent me five hundred, others six or seven; M. Friedland, a young German I had met in Prague, twelve hundred, and Hetzel a thousand.

So, helped on all sides, I was able, with a clear conscience, to leave for Russia on the 14th February 1847, feeling that few men have been so blessed as I in the devoted generosity and kind-heartedness of my single-minded friends.

The time for concert-giving in Russia is Lent--March--as then the theatres are all closed. The cold was intense, and during my whole fortnight's journey I never lost sight of the snow, and made only one short stop in Berlin to beg a letter of introduction to the Empress of Russia from her brother, the King of Prussia, which, with his invariable kindness, he sent me at once.

Before leaving Paris, Balzac said to me:

"Be sure at Tilsit to hunt up the post-master, M. Nernst. He is a clever, well-read man and may be useful to you."

So at Tilsit I walked into his office and there found a big man perched on a high stool.

"M. Nernst?" I said, taking off my hat.

"Yes, monsieur; to whom have I the honour of speaking?"

"To Hector Berlioz."

"No! not really?" He bounced off his stool and landed before me, cap in hand.

How well I remember my poor father's happy pride in this story! "Not really?" he would repeat, and his laughter would ring out again and again.

We had a cordial meeting-ground in our mutual friendship with Balzac, and after some hours' rest I set out, warmed and comforted, in a horrible iron sledge wherein I endured a martyrdom till, four days later, I reached St Petersburg.

Hardly had I shaken off the traces of my journey when M. Lenz, an old acquaintance, came to take me to Count Michael Wielhorski, from whom

I received a most flattering welcome. He and his brother, by their love of art, their great connections and immense fortune, have made their palace a sort of little Ministry of Fine Arts.

By them I was introduced to Romberg, General Guedeonoff, superintendent of the Imperial theatres, and General Lwoff, aide-de-camp to the Emperor, a composer of rare talent.

Not to go into too many details, my visits both to St Petersburg and Moscow were the greatest success financially as well as artistically. My first concert (at which I was summoned, hot and dishevelled with my exertions, to the box of the Emperor, who was most gracious) made eighteen thousand francs; the expenses were six thousand, the balance was mine.

I could not resist murmuring, as I turned to the south-west, "Ah, dear Parisians!"

I must just recall one of my red-letter days--the performance of *Romeo and Juliet* in St Petersburg.

No wretched bargaining, no limitation of rehearsals here!

I asked General Guedeonoff:

"How many rehearsals can your Excellency allow me?"

"How many? Why! as many as you want. They will rehearse until you are satisfied."

And they did; consequently it was royally, imperially, organised and performed.

The vast theatre was full; diamonds, uniforms, helmets shone and glittered everywhere. I, too, was in good form, and conducted without a single mistake--a thing that, in those days, did not happen often.

I was recalled more times than I could count, but I must own that I paid small heed to the public, the divine Shakespearean poem that I myself had made affected me so deeply that, the moment I was free, I fled to a quiet room in the theatre, where my dear, good Ernst found me in floods of tears.

"Ah! nerves!" said he, "I know too well what it is."

And, holding my head, he let me sob like a hysterical girl for a quarter of an hour.

Despite its warm reception, I doubt that my symphony was rather over the heads of the audience, therefore, when it was to be repeated, on the advice of the cashier of the theatre, I added two scenes from *Faust*.

I heard of a funny incident at this second performance. One lady present sat and was bored with most exemplary patience; she would not have it thought that she could not understand this feast of music. Proud of having stayed to the end, she said, as she left her box:

"Yes, it is a tremendous thing, but quite intelligible. In that grand introduction I could absolutely *see Romeo driving up in his gig*!!!"

I spoke of Ernst just now--great artist and noble friend. He has been compared to Chopin--a comparison both true and false.

Chopin could never bear the restraints of time, and, I think, carried his independence too far; he simply *could not* play in time. Ernst, while employing *rubato*, kept it within artistic limits, retaining always a dignified sway over his own caprices.

In Chopin's compositions all the interest centres in the piano, his orchestral concerto accompaniments are cold and practically useless. Ernst is distinguished by quite the opposite--his concerted music is not only brilliant for the solo instrument, but the symphonic interest is thoroughly grateful and sustained.

Even Beethoven allowed the orchestra to overpower the soloist, and, to my mind, the perfect system is that adopted by Ernst, Vieuxtemps and Liszt.

Chopin was the delicate refined virtuoso of small gatherings, of groups of intimate friends. Ernst was master of crowds; he loved them, and, like Liszt, was at his very best with two thousand hearers to conquer.

* * * * *

The Great Feast being over, there was nothing to keep me in St Petersburg, which, however, I left with great regret.

Passing through Riga, I thought I would give a concert. The receipts hardly covered the expenses (I think I was twelve francs to the good), but it procured me the friendship of some pleasant artists and amateurs, amongst them the post-master, who turned out to be a constant reader of my newspaper articles. He looked me dubiously up and down, and said:

"You don't *look* a firebrand, but from your articles I should have expected quite a different sort of man, for, devil take me! you write with a dagger, not a pen!"

The King of Prussia wishing to hear my *Faust*, I arranged to stay ten days in Berlin. The Opera House was placed at my disposal, and I was promised half the gross receipts. The orchestra and choruses were capital, but I cannot say as much for the soloists, who were feeble in the extreme. The King of Thule ballad was hissed, but whether this was due to me or to the singer I cannot say--probably both--for the stalls were filled with a malicious crowd who objected to a Frenchman having the audacity to set to music a German classic.

However, by the time we got to the *Danse des Sylphes* I was in a bad temper and refused the encore they gave it.

The royalties were apparently satisfied; the Princess of Prussia said many nice things and the King sent me the Red Eagle by Meyerbeer and invited me to dinner at Sans Souci. I met with a cordial reception, gave him news of his sister in Russia and finally ventured to say after dinner was over: "Ah, sire, you are the true king of artists. Without you could Spontini and Meyerbeer have gained a hearing? Was it not at your suggestion that Mendelssohn composed his *Antigone* music? Did not you commission him to write the *Midsummer Night's Dream*? Does not your known love of art incite us all to do our best?"

"Well, perhaps so," he answered, "but there's no need to say so much about it."

But it is true. Now there are two other sovereigns who share his interest--the Grand Duke of Saxe-Weimar and the blind young King of Hanover.

* * * * *

On returning to France I took my boy to see his relations at La Cote Saint-Andre. Poor Louis! how happy he was; petted by relations and old servants and wandering about the fields, his little hand thrust in mine.

In a letter I had yesterday he says that that fortnight was the happiest of his life. And now he is at the blockade of the Baltic, on the eve of a naval battle--that hell upon the sea! The mere thought of it maddens me, yet he chose it himself--this noble profession. But we did not expect war then.

Dear noble boy! at this minute they may be bombarding Bomarsund--it will not bear thinking of, I must turn to other things--I can write no more.

* * * * *

From Paris and its usual weary round of jealousy and intrigue, it was a comfort to turn to London, whence I received the offer of an engagement to conduct the grand English Opera for Jullien. In his usual role of madman he got together orchestra, chorus, principals and theatre, merely forgetting a repertoire. To cover expenses he would have had to take ten thousand francs a night and this he expected to net out of an English version of *Lucia di Lammermoor*!

To TAJAN ROGE of St Petersburg.

"LONDON, *November 1847*.--Dear Roge,--Your letter should have been answered sooner had it not been for the thousand and one worries that overwhelmed me the minute I set foot in Paris.

"You can have no idea of my existence in that infernal city that thinks itself the home of Art.

"Thank heaven I have escaped to England and am, financially, more independent than I dared to hope.

"Jullien, the manager here, is a most intrepid spirit and seems to understand English people; he has made his fortune and is going to make mine, he says. I let him have his own way since he does nothing unworthy of art and good taste--but I have my doubts.

"I have come *alone* to London; you may guess my reasons. I badly needed a little freedom which, so far, I have never been able to get. Not one *coup d'etat* but a whole series was necessary before I succeeded in shaking off my bonds. Yet now, although I am so busy with rehearsals, my loneliness seems very odd.

"Since I am in a confidential mood, will you believe that I had a queer little love affair in St Petersburg with a girl--now don't laugh like a full orchestra in C major! It was poetic, heart-rending, and perfectly innocent.

"Oh, our walks! oh, the tears I shed when, like Faust's Marguerite, she said: 'What can you see in me--a poor girl so far beneath you?' I thought I should die of despair when I left St Petersburg, and was really ill when I found no letter from her in Berlin. She *did* promise to write, probably by now she is married.

"I can picture it all again--the Neva banks, the setting sun. In a maze of passion I pressed her hand to my heart, and sang her the Love Song from *Romeo*.

"Ah me! not two lines since I left her.

"Good-bye; you at least will write to me."

To AUGUSTE MOREL.

"76 HARLEY STREET, LONDON, *31st November 1847*.--Jullien asks me confidentially to get your report on the success of Verdi's new opera.[23] We begin next week with the *Bride of Lammermoor*, which can hardly help going well with Madame Gras and Reeves. He has a beautiful voice, and sings as well as this awful English language will allow.

"I had a warm reception at one of Jullien's concerts, but shall not begin my own until January.

"Your friend, M. Grimblot, has given me the *entree* to his club, but heaven only knows what amusement is to be found in an English club.

Macready gave a magnificent dinner in my honour last week; he is charming and most unassuming at home, though they say he is terrible at rehearsal. I have seen him in a new tragedy, *Philip van Artevelde*; he is grand, and has mounted the piece splendidly.

"No one here understands the management and grouping of a crowd as he does. It is masterly."

* * * * *

"*8th December.*--The opening of our season was a success. Madame Gras and Reeves were recalled frantically four or five times, and they both deserved it.

"Reeves is a priceless discovery for Jullien; his voice is exquisite in quality, he is a good musician, has an expressive face, and plays with judgment."

* * * * *

"*14th January.*--Jullien has landed us all in a dreadful bog, but don't mention it in Paris, as we must not spoil his credit. It is not the Drury Lane venture that has ruined him; that was done before; now he has gone off to the provinces and is making a lot of money with his promenade concerts, while we take a fair amount each night at the theatre, none of which goes into our pockets, for *we are not paid at all.* Only the orchestra, chorus, and work-people are paid every week in order to keep the thing going somehow.

"If Jullien does not pay me on his return, I shall arrange with Lumley to give some concerts in Her Majesty's Theatre, for there is a good opening here since poor Mendelssohn's death."

* * * * *

"*12th February 1848.*--My music has taken with the English as fire to gunpowder. The *Rakoczy* and *Danse des Sylphes* were encored. Everyone of importance, musically, was at Drury Lane for my concert, and most of the artists came to congratulate me. They had expected something diabolic, involved, incomprehensible. Now we shall see how they agree with our Paris critics. Davison himself wrote the *Times* critique; they cut half of it out from want of space; still the remainder has had its effect. Old Hogarth of the *Daily News* was truly comical: 'My blood is on fire,' said he; 'never have I been excited like this by music.'"

Jullien, coming finally to the end of his resources, was obliged to call a council of war. It consisted of Sir Henry Bishop, Sir George Smart, Planche, Gye, Marezeck, and myself.

He talked wildly of the different operas he proposed to mount, and finally came to *Iphigenia in Tauris*, which, like many others, is promised yearly by the London managers. Impatient at my silence he turned upon me:

"Confound it all! surely you know that?"

"Certainly I know it. What do you want me to tell you?"

"How many acts there are, how many characters, what voices and, above all, the style of setting and costume."

"Take a pen and paper and I will tell you. Four acts, three men: Orestes, baritone; Pylades, tenor; Thoas, high bass; a grand woman's part, Iphigenia, soprano; a small one, Diana, mezzo-soprano. The costumes you will not like, unfortunately; the Scythians are ragged savages on the shores of the Black Sea; Orestes and Pylades are shipwrecked Greeks. Pylades alone has two dresses--in the fourth act he comes in in a helmet----"

"A helmet!" cried Jullien, excitedly; "we are saved! I'll write to Paris for a golden helmet with a pearl coronet, and an ostrich plume as long as my arm. We'll have forty performances."

"Prodigious!" as good Dominie Sampson says.

Needless to say, nothing happened. Reeves, the divine tenor, laughed at the bare idea of singing Pylades, and Jullien quitted London shortly after, leaving his theatre to go to pieces.

XXXI

MY FATHER'S DEATH--MEYLAN

ALREADY saddened on my return to Paris by the havoc and ruin caused by the Revolution, it was but my usual fate to suffer in addition, the terrible sorrow of losing my father.

My mother had died ten years before, and, bitter as was that blow, it was but light in comparison with the wrench of parting with this dearly loved and sympathetic friend.

We had so much in common, our tastes were similar in so many ways, and, since he had gladly acknowledged himself in the wrong over my choice of a profession, we had been so entirely at one.

Ah! that I could have gratified his ardent wish to hear my *Requiem*, but it was not to be.

I pass over the sorrow of my home-coming, the meeting with my grief-worn sisters, the sight of his empty chair, of his watch--still living, though he was dead!

A strange wish to indulge the luxury of grief crept over me; I must drink this wormwood cup to the dregs; I must revisit Meylan--the early home of my Mountain Star--and live over again my early love and sorrow.

Even now my heart beats faster as I recall my journey. Thirty-three years ago and I, a ghost, come back to my early haunts! As I climb through the vineyards the thoughts, the aspirations, the desires of my childish days crowd in upon me.

Here did I sit with my father, playing *Nina* to him on my flute; there did Estelle stand.

I turn and take in the whole picture; that blessed house, the garden, the valley, the river, and the far-off Alpine glaciers.

Once more I am young; life and love--a glorious poem--lie before me; on my knees I cry to the hills, the valleys, the heavens: "Estelle! Estelle!"

Bleed, my heart, bleed! but leave me still the power to suffer!

I rise and wander on, noting each familiar point. Here is her cherry tree; there still flowers the plant of everlasting pea from which she plucked blossoms. Sweet plant! bloom on in thy solitude! Good-bye! good-bye!

Good-bye to my childhood, to my lost love--Time sweeps me on; Stella! Stella!

The cold hand of Death lies heavy on my heart, yet around me are soft sunlight, solitude, and silence.

* * * * *

Next day I asked my cousin Victor:

"Do you know Madame F----?"

"The lovely Estelle D----, do you mean?"

"Yes, I loved her so when I was twelve--I love her yet."

"You idiot," said Victor, laughing, "she is fifty-one, and has a son of twenty-two."

He laughed again, and I laughed too, but mine was the cry of despair, an April gleam through the rain.

"Nevertheless I want to see her."

"Hector, I beg you will do no such thing. You will make a fool of yourself and upset her."

"I want to see her," I repeated doggedly, with clenched teeth.

"Fifty-one!" he cried again, "you had much better keep your bright, fresh, youthful memory of her."

"Well, then, I will write."

He gave me a pen, and subsided into an armchair in fits of laughter, while my incoherent, despairing letter was composed. I sent it, but no reply came. When next I go to Grenoble I mean to see her.

* * * * *

In May 1851 I was commissioned by Government to judge instruments at the London Exhibition, and wrote to Joseph d'Ortigue in June 1851--

"I want to tell you of the extraordinary impression made on me by the singing of six thousand Charity School children in St Paul's Cathedral. It is an annual affair, and is, beyond compare, the most imposing, the most *Babylonian* ceremony I ever witnessed.

"It was a realisation of part of my dreams, and proof positive of the unknown power of vast musical masses.

"This fact is no more understood on the Continent than is Chinese music.

"By-the-bye, France is easily first in the manufacture of musical instruments. Erard, Sax and Vuillaume lead; all the others are of the reed-pipe and tin-kettle tribe."

To LWOFF.

"*January 1852.*--It is impossible to do anything in Paris, so next month I shall go back to England, where, at least, the *wish to love music* is real and persistent. If I can be of the least use to you in my newspaper articles, commend me, dear master. It will be a pleasure to tell our few earnest French readers of the great and good things that are done in Russia. It is a debt I shall gladly pay, since I never shall forget the warmth of my reception and the kindness of your Empress and your great Emperor's family.

"What a pity he himself does not like music!"

To J. D'ORTIGUE.

"LONDON, *March 1852*.--Just a line to tell you of my colossal success. Recalled I know not how often, and applauded both as composer and conductor. This morning, in the *Times*, the *Morning Post*, the *Advertiser*, and others, such effusions as never were written before about me! Beale is wild with joy, for it really is an event in the musical world. The orchestra at times surpassed all that I have heard in *verve*, delicacy and power.

"All the papers except the *Daily News* puff me, and now I am preparing Beethoven's *Choral Symphony*, which, so far, has been sadly mutilated here.

"But can you believe that all the critics are against the *Vestal*, of which we performed the first part yesterday?

"I am utterly cast down at this *lapsus judicii*--am I not weak?--and am ashamed of having succeeded at such a cost. Why can I not remember that the good, the beautiful, the true, the false, the ugly, are not the same to everyone?"

* * * * *

"*May 1852*.--You speak of the expenses of our concerts; they are enormous. Every impresario in London expected to lose this year. In fact Beale, in the programme of the last concert, actually told the public that the *Choral Symphony* rehearsals had swallowed more than a third of the subscription.

"However, it has had a miraculous effect, and my success as conductor was great also; indeed, it was such an event in the musical world that people greatly doubted whether we should carry it through."

* * * * *

"*June 1852*.--I leave to-morrow. How I shall regret my glorious chorus and orchestra! Those beautiful women's voices!

"If only you had been here to hear our second performance of the *Choral Symphony*. The effect in that enormous Exeter Hall was most imposing.

"Paris once more! where I must forget these melodious joys in my daily task of critic--the only one left me in my precious native land!

"A naif Birmingham amateur was heard the other day regretting that I had not been engaged for the Birmingham Festival. 'For I hear,' said he, 'that Berlioz really is better than Costa!!!'"

To LOUIS BERLIOZ.

"1852.--You say you are going mad! You must actually *be* mad to write me such letters in the midst of the strenuous fatigue of my present life.

"In your last letter from Havana you say you will arrive home with a hundred francs. Now you say you owe forty. Now remember! I shall take no notice in future of the nonsense you talk.

"You chose your own profession--a hard one, I grant you, but the hardest part is over. Only five more months, and you will be in port for six months studying, after which you will be able to earn your own living.

"I am putting aside money for your expenses during those six months. I can do no more.

"What is this about torn shirts? Six weeks in Havana, and all your clothes ruined! At that rate you will want dozens of shirts every five months. You must be laughing at me.

"Please weigh your language in writing to me. I do not like your present style. Life is not strewn with roses, and I can give you no career but *that which you yourself chose*. It is too late to alter now."

To J. D'ORTIGUE.

"*January 1854*.--Yes, dear d'Ortigue, you are right. It is my ungovernable passion for Art that is the cause of all my trouble, all my real suffering. Forgive me for letting you read between the lines. I knew it would hurt you, and yet I could not hold back the words that burnt me, although I might have known that your opinions on Art would be in accord with your religious feelings.

"You know that I love the beautiful and the true, but I have another love quite as ardent--the love of love.

"And when for some idea, some misunderstanding, I feel that my love may be lessened, something within me bursts asunder, and I cry like a child with a broken toy.

"I know it is puerile, but it is true, although I do my best to cure myself. Like a true Christian, you have punished me by returning good for evil.

"Your notes are capital, and I think I shall be able to use them, though never did I feel less in the mood for writing.

"I cannot make a beginning. And I am sad--so sad! Life is slipping away. I long to *work*, and am obliged to *drudge* in order to live. Adieu, adieu."

XXXII

POOR OPHELIA

I WOULD I were done with these wearisome reminiscences! When I have written a few pages more I shall have said enough to give a fair sketch of the mill-round of thought, work and sorrow wherein I am fated to turn, until I cease to turn for ever. However long may still be the days of my pilgrimage, they can but resemble those that are past. The same stony roads, the same Slough of Despond, with here and there a blessed oasis of

Montmartre Cemetery

rest or a mighty rock that I may painfully climb, thereon to forget, in the evening sunshine, the cold rains of the plain beneath. So slow are changes in men and things that one would need to live two hundred years to mark any difference.

Nanci, my sister, died of cancer, after six months' frightful suffering. Adele, worn out with the fatigue and anxiety of nursing, nearly followed her.

Why had no doctor the humanity to put an end to that awful martyrdom with a little chloroform? They administer it to avoid the pain of an operation that lasts, perhaps, an hour, and they refuse it when they know cure to be impossible, to spare months of torture, when death would be the supreme good. Even savages are more humane.

But no doubt my sister would have refused the boon had it been offered. She would have said, "God's will be done!" Would not God's will have been as well interpreted by a calm, swift death as by these months of useless agony?

* * * * *

My wife, too, died--mercifully without much suffering.

After four years' death-in-life, unable to speak or move, she passed quietly away at Montmartre on the 3rd March 1854. Her last hours were sweetened by Louis' presence. He was home on leave from Cherbourg four days before she died.

I had been out for two hours when one of her nurses came to tell me all was over, and I returned but to draw aside the shroud and kiss her pale forehead.

Her portrait, painted in the days of her radiant beauty, and which I had given her the year before, hung above her bed, looking calmly down on the poor shell that had once enshrined her brilliant genius.

My sufferings were indescribable. They were intensified by one feeling that has always been the hardest for me to bear--that of pity.

Again and again I went over Henriette's troubles and their crushing weight bore me to the earth. Her losses before our marriage, her accident, the fiasco of her second appearance, her lost beauty and renown, our home quarrels, her jealousy--not, in the end, without cause--our separation, her son's absence, her helplessness and dreary years of retrospection, of contemplating approaching death and oblivion.

Oh, the pity of it! It turns my brain.

Shakespeare! Shakespeare! Thou alone couldst have understood us both, thou alone couldst have pitied us--poor children of Art--loving, yet wounding each other through our love! Thou art our God, if that other God sits aloof in sublime indifference to our torments. Thou art our father. Help us! Save us!

De profundis ad te clamo!

Alone I went about my sorrowful task.

The Protestant pastor lived at the other side of Paris and I went to him that evening. As my cab passed the Odeon I thought of how, in that theatre twenty-six years before, my poor dead wife had burst like a meteor upon Paris and had come forward, trembling and awed at her own success, to receive the plaudits of all that was best and brightest in France. Ophelia! Ophelia!

Through that door I saw her pass to a rehearsal of *Othello*. I was nothing to her then. She would have thought the prophet mad who pointed out a worn, distraught, unknown youth and said:

"Behold your husband!"

Yet he it is, my poor Ophelia, he who loved and suffered with you, who tends you on this last long journey.

"... Forty thousand brothers

Could not, with all their quantity of love,

Make up my sum."

Shakespeare! Shakespeare! The waters have gone over me. Father! Father! where art thou?

* * * * *

Next day, out of love for me, came d'Ortigue, Brizeux, Leon de Wailly, some artists brought by good Baron Taylor and other kind friends to accompany Henriette to her last rest. Twenty-five years earlier all intellectual Paris would have been there--now, he, who loved her and had not the courage to go with her to the little Montmartre God's-acre, sits and weeps alone in her deserted garden, and her young son wanders afar on the dreary ocean.

They turned her face towards the north, to that England she never saw again, and her humble grave bears only--

Henriette Constance Berlioz-Smithson, born at Ennis, Ireland, died at Montmartre, 3rd March 1854.

The papers barely noticed her death, but Jules Janin remembered and wrote in the *Debats*:

"These stage divinities how soon they pass!

"How short a time it seems since we sat with Juliet on that balcony above the Verona road. Juliet, so fair, so ethereal, listening dreamily as Romeo speaks, her golden voice vibrating with the undying poetry of Shakespeare, the whole world bound by her magic spells!

"She was barely twenty, this Miss Smithson, and, without knowing it, she was a poem, a passion, a revolution--By her absolute truth she conquered.

"She it was who gave the lead to Dorval, Malibran, Victor Hugo and Berlioz. To her Delacroix owed his conception of sweet Ophelia.

"Now she is dead and her dream of glory--that glory which passes so rapidly--is over and done.

"In my young days they used to sing a funeral dirge to Juliet, wherein recurred, like an old Greek chorus, the heart-breaking refrain, 'Throw flowers! Throw flowers!'

"'Juliet is dead. Throw flowers!

Death lies upon her, softly as frost on April grass. Throw flowers!

Her love song is a funeral knell. Throw flowers!

Her marriage feast the feast of Death. Throw flowers!

Her marriage blossoms deck her tomb. Throw flowers!'"

Liszt wrote from Weimar as only he can write:

"She inspired you, you loved and sang of her. Her work is done!"

To LOUIS BERLIOZ.

"*6th March 1854.*--My poor dear Louis,--You know all. I am alone and writing to you in the large sitting-room next to her deserted bedroom. I have just been to the cemetery where I laid two wreaths upon her grave--one for you and one for myself. The servants are still here and are arranging things for the sale; I want to realise as much as possible for you.

"I have kept her hair.

"You will never know how much we made each other suffer; our very suffering bound us one to the other. I could neither live with her nor without her.

"Alexis and I talked much of you yesterday. How I wish you were more rational! It would make me so happy to feel that you were sure of yourself.

"I shall be able to do more for you now than has hitherto been possible, but I shall take every precaution to prevent your squandering money. Alexis agrees that I am right.

"At present I am penniless and shall be for at least six months; I must pay the doctor and the sale will bring in but little. The King of Saxony's director wishes me to be in Dresden next month and I shall have to borrow money for my journey."

* * * * *

"*23rd March.*--Your letter is an unexpected pleasure, dear boy. With seventy francs a month you can easily save, if you give up your habit of squandering money. Tell me whether you can get back the watch you pawned at Havre. My father gave it to you. If you cannot, I will buy you another. I have had a watch chain made for you of your mother's hair; keep it carefully. I also had a bracelet made for my sister, the rest of the hair I shall keep.

"Did you see Jules Janin's touching words on your poor mother and his exquisite reference to my *Romeo* 'Throw flowers?' I hope for another letter from you before Saturday.

"God grant that my German trip may bring in something! The Montmartre house is not let and I may have to pay rent there a year longer."

* * * * *

What more can I say of the two great passions that influenced my life? One was a childhood's memory--yet not to be despised since, with my love for Estelle, awoke my love of nature. The other--coming in my manhood with my worship of Shakespeare--took possession of me and overwhelmed me completely. Love of Art and the artist intermingled, each acting upon and intensifying the other.

Those who cannot understand this will still less understand my vague poetic longings at the scent of a lovely rose, the sight of a beautiful harp. Estelle was the rose that bloomed alone, Henriette the harp that shared my music, my joys, my sorrows and of which alas! I snapped so many, many strings!

To LOUIS BERLIOZ.

"*October 1854.*--I am sad this morning, dear Louis. I dreamt that we were walking--you and I--in the garden at La Cote, and not knowing exactly where you are, my dream troubles me.

"I have some news that will not, I think, surprise you. Two months ago I married again.

"I could not live alone, neither could I desert the woman who, for fourteen years, has been my companion.

"My uncle and all my friends agree with me.

"I need not tell you that your interests are safe. If I die first my wife will have but a quarter of my small fortune and even that I know she intends to leave to you.

"If you still have any painful thoughts of Mademoiselle Recio I know you will hide them for my sake.

"We were married very quietly without fuss or mystery. If you mention this in your letters, write nothing that I cannot show to my wife; I must have no cloud in my home. But your own heart will tell you what to do.

"Admiral Cecile tells me he has received your letter. You cannot enter the Marines until the end of your three years' cruise.

"I am overwhelmed with rehearsals and arrangements for producing my new work, the *Childhood of Christ*. It bristles with difficulties.

"Good-bye, dear Louis."

XXXIII

DEAD SEA FRUIT

THE end of my career is in sight, or if not the end, yet are my feet set on the steep slope leading to the goal; worn and tired, I am consumed by a burning fire that sometimes rages with such violence as to frighten me.

I begin to know French, to write fairly a page of verse, prose or score; I love an orchestra, and can direct it; I worship Art in every form. But I belong to a nation that cares for none of these things. Parisians are barbarians; not one rich man in ten has a library, no one buys books--they hire feeble novels at a penny a volume from circulating libraries--this is sufficient mental food for all classes. For a few francs a month they hire from the music shops the flat and dreary compositions with which they overflow.

What have I to do with Paris? That Paris--the apotheosis of industrialism in Art--that casts a scornful eye upon me, holding me only too honoured in fulfilling my calling of pamphleteer, for which alone, it holds, I came into the world. I *know* what I could do with dramatic music, but to try it would be both useless and dangerous.

There is no suitable theatre; I must be absolute dictator of a grand orchestra; I must have the eager good-will of all, from prima-donna to sceneshifter; my theatre must be a gigantic musical instrument.

I could play it.

But this will never be; it would give too much scope to the cabals of my foes, and not only should I have to face the hatred of my critics but also the vindictive fury caused by my original style.

People would naturally ask, "If he becomes popular, where will our compositions be?"

I proved this at Covent Garden, where a crew of Italians nearly wrecked *Benvenuto Cellini* by hissing from beginning to end. Costa was credited with this cabal, since I had fallen foul of him in newspaper articles for the liberties he took with the scores of the great masters. However, guilty or not, he knew how to quiet my doubts by doing his best to help me during my rehearsals.

Indignant at my treatment, the artists of London tried, unsuccessfully, to arrange a testimonial concert for me, and through my good friend Beale offered me a present of two hundred guineas, the subscription list being headed by Messrs Broadwood. Although greatly moved at the kindly generosity of the present, I was unable to accept it. French ideas would not permit.

For three years I have been worried by the vision of a grand opera to which I want to write both words and music, as I have done in the *Childhood of Christ*.

So far I have resisted temptation. May I hold out until the end![24]

To me the subject is magnificent, soul-stirring, which means that the Parisians would find it flat and wearisome.

Even if I could believe they might like it, where should I find a woman with beauty, voice, dramatic talent and fiery soul to fill the chief part? The very thought of hurling myself once more against the obstacles raised by the crass stupidity of my opponents makes my blood boil. The shock of our collision would be too dangerous, for I feel I could kill them all like dogs.

Even from concert-giving in Paris I am excluded, for, thanks to the machinations of my enemies in the Conservatoire, the Minister of the Interior at the prize-giving took occasion to state that in future the hall of the Conservatoire (the only possible one for my purpose) would be lent to *no one*. The no one could only be me, for, with two or three exceptions in twenty years, I was the only one who so used it.

Although most of the executants in this celebrated society are my friends, they are overborne by a hostile chief and a small clique; my compositions, therefore, are never given. Once, six or seven years ago, they did ask me for some excerpts from *Faust*, then tried to damn them by sandwiching them between Beethoven's *C minor Symphony* and Spontini's finale to the *Vestal*. Fortunately they were disappointed, the Sylph scene was enthusiastically encored; but Girard, who had conducted the whole thing clumsily and colourlessly, pretended he could not find the place, so it was not repeated.

After that they avoided my works like the plague.

Of all the millionaires in Paris none thinks of doing anything for music. Paganini's example was not followed, and the great artist's gift to me stands alone.

No; a composer of classical music must be absolutely independent or must resign himself to all the miseries from which I suffered--to incomplete rehearsals, to inconvenient concert halls, to checks of every foreseen and unforeseen kind, and to the rapacity of the hospital tax-gatherers, who seize one-eighth of the *gross* receipts. Usually I am willing and anxious to make every possible sacrifice, but sometimes occasions arise when such sacrifices cease to be generous and become criminal.

Two years ago, when there was still some hope of my wife's recovery, and therefore expenses were greatly increased, I dreamt one night of a symphony.

On waking I could still recall nearly all the first movement, an allegro in A minor. As I moved towards my writing-table to put it down, I suddenly thought:

"If I do this I shall be drawn on to compose the rest, and, since my ideas always expand, it will end by being enormously long; it will take me three or four months; I shall write no articles, and my income will fail. When the symphony is written I shall, weakly, have it copied and so incur a debt of a thousand or twelve hundred francs.

"Then I shall be impelled to give a concert that it may be heard; the receipts will hardly equal half the expenditure, and I shall lose money. I have not got it. My poor invalid will be without necessary comforts, and my son's expenses on board ship will not be met."

With a shudder of horror I threw aside my pen, saying:

"To-morrow I shall have forgotten the symphony."

But no! Next night that obstinate motif returned more clearly than before--I could even see it written out. I started up in feverish agitation, humming it over and--again my decision held me back, and I put the temptation aside. I fell asleep and next morning my symphony was gone for ever.

"Coward!" cries the young enthusiast, "brave all and write! Ruin yourself! Dare everything! What right have you to push back into oblivion a work of art that stretches out to you its piteous hands crying for the light of day?"

Ah, youth, youth! never hast thou suffered as I suffer, else wouldst thou understand and be silent.

Never was I backward, when I stood alone, to bear the brunt of my own actions, never did I fail when my wife stood beside me, alert and hopeful, to help me on, to face with me privation and suffering in the cause of Art. But when she lay half dead, a doctor and three nurses in attendance, when I knew that my musical venture *must* end in disaster, was I cowardly to hold back? Did I not do more honour to my divine goddess, Music, in crediting her with sweet reasonableness than in treating her as an all-devouring Moloch, greedy for human victims?

If I have lately been carried away in writing my trilogy *The Childhood of Christ*, it is that I no longer have these heavy calls upon me, and also that, owing to my warm and generous reception in Germany, I can count upon the performance of my works.

Since writing this, M. Benazet of Baden has invited me several times to conduct the annual festival there, and, with unequalled generosity, has given me *carte blanche* in the engagement and payment of my performers.

Each year Germany receives me more cordially; I have been there four times during the last eighteen months.

So interested were the blind King of Hanover and his Antigone, the Queen, in my rehearsals that they would appear at eight o'clock in the morning and sometimes stay till noon, as the King said:

"In order the better to get at the heart of my meaning and to grasp more thoroughly my new ideas."

How warmly, too, he spoke of my *King Lear*--of the storm, the prison scene, the fateful sorrows of sweet Cordelia.

"I did not believe there was anything so beautiful in music," he said, "but you have enlightened me. And how you conduct? I cannot see you but I feel it. I owe much to Providence," he added, simply; "this love of music is a compensation for all I have lost."

I never saw Henriette in that part, which was her best, but from her recital of some scenes I can imagine what it must have been.

On my last visit to Hanover the Queen asked me to include two pieces from *Romeo* in my programme, and the King desired me to return next winter to superintend a theatrical performance of the same work, allowing me to requisition artists from Brunswick, Hamburg, and even Dresden.

It was the same with the Grand Duke of Saxe-Weimar, who said, as I took my leave:

"M. Berlioz, shake hands with me and remember my theatre is always open to you."

M. de Luttichau, superintendent to the King of Saxony, has offered me the post of director when it shall be vacant.

Liszt strongly advises me to accept, but I cannot say. Time enough to decide when the place is at my disposal.

At present in Dresden they talk of reviving *Benvenuto Cellini,* which Liszt has already given in Weimar, and of course I should have to go and superintend the first performances.

Blessed Germany, nursing mother of Art; generous England; Russia, my saviour; good friends in France, and you--noble hearts of all nations whom I have known--I thank and bless you all; your memory will be my comfort to my latest hour.

As for you, idiots and blind! You, my Guildenstern, Rosencrantz, Iago and Osric! You, crawling worms of all kinds! Farewell, my friends--I scorn you; may you be forgotten ere I die!

Note.--This was originally the ending of Berlioz' *Memoires*, but his correspondence was voluminous after this date and he also added some chapters to his Life.

To AUGUSTE MOREL.

"*June 1855.*--You ask me to describe my *Te Deum*, which is rather embarrassing. I can only say that its effect both on the performers and myself was stupendous. Its immeasurable grandeur and breadth struck everyone, and you can understand that the *Tibi omnes* and *Judex* would have even more effect in a less sonorous hall than the church of St Eustache.

"I start for England on Friday. Wagner, who is directing the old London Philharmonic (a post I was obliged to refuse, being engaged by the other society) is buried beneath the vituperations of the whole British press. He remains calm, for he says that *in fifty years he will be master of the musical world*."

"*July.*--"My trip to London, where, each time, I become more comfortably established, was a brilliant success.

"I mean to go back next winter after a prospective short tour through Austria and Bohemia--at least if we are not at war with Austria."

"I do nothing but correct proofs from morning to night, and see, hear, know nothing."

"Meyerbeer ought to be pleased with the reception of the *Etoile du Nord* at Covent Garden. They threw him bouquets, as though he were a prima-donna."

To RICHARD WAGNER.

"*September 1855.*--Your letter has given me real pleasure. You do well to deplore my ignorance of German, and I have often told myself that, as you say, this ignorance makes it impossible for me to appreciate your writings. Expression melts away in translation, no matter how daintily it is handled."

"In *true music* there are accents that belong to special words, separated they are spoilt."

"But what can I do? I find it so devilishly hard to learn languages; a few words of English and Italian are all I can manage."

"So you are busy melting glaciers with your Nibelungen! It must be glorious to write in the presence of great Mother Nature--a joy withheld from me, for, instead of stimulating, the sea, the mountain peaks, the glories of this beautiful earth absorb me so completely that I have no room, no outlet for expression. I only feel. I can but describe the moon from her reflection at the bottom of a well."

"I am sorry I have no scores to send you, but you shall have the *Te Deum*, *Childhood of Christ* and *Lelio* as soon as they come out. I already have your *Lohengrin* and should be delighted if you would let me have *Tannhauser*.

"To meet as you suggest would be indeed a pleasure, but I dare not think of it. Since Paris offers me but Dead Sea fruit I must of necessity earn my bread by travelling for bread--not pleasure.

"No matter. If we could but live another hundred years or so we might perhaps understand the true inwardness of men and things. Old Demiurge must laugh in his beard at the continual triumph of his well-worn, oft-repeated farce.

"But I will not speak ill of him, since he is a friend of yours and you have become his champion. I am an impious wretch, full of respect for the *Pies*. Forgive the atrocious pun!

"*P.S.*--Winged flights of many tinted thoughts crowd in upon me and I long to send them, were there but time.

"Write me down an ass until further orders."

XXXIV

1863--GATHERING TWILIGHT

NEARLY ten years since I finished my memoir and during that time my life has been as full of incident as ever.

But since, for nothing on earth would I go through the labour of writing again, I must just indicate the chief points.

My work is over; Othello's occupation's gone. I no longer compose, conduct, write either prose or verse. I have resigned my post of musical critic and wish to do nothing more. I only read, think, fight my deadly weariness of soul and suffer from the incurable neuralgia that tortures me night and day.

To my great surprise I have been elected a member of the Academy and my relations with my colleagues are, throughout, pleasant and friendly.

In 1855 Prince Napoleon desired me to arrange a great concert in the Exhibition building for the day upon which the Emperor was to distribute the prizes.

I accepted on condition that I had no pecuniary responsibility, and M. Ber, a generous and brave impresario, came forward and treated me most liberally.

These concerts (for there were several besides the official one) brought me in eight thousand francs.

In a raised gallery behind the throne I had placed twelve hundred musicians, who were barely heard. Not that that mattered much on the day of the ceremony, for I was stopped at the most interesting point of the very first piece (the *Imperial Cantata* which I had written for the occasion) because the Prince had to make his speech and the music was lasting too long!!

However the next day the paying public was admitted and we took seventy-five thousand francs. This time I brought the orchestra down into the body of the hall, with fine effect.

I sent to Brussels for an electrician I knew, who made me a five-wired metronome so that by the single movement of my left hand, I could mark time for the five deputy conductors placed at different points of the enormous space.

The *ensemble* was marvellous.

Since then most of the theatres have adopted electric metronomes for the guidance of chorus-masters behind the scenes. The Opera alone refused; but, when I undertook the supervision of *Alcestis,* I introduced it.

In these Palais de l'Industrie concerts the finest effects were obtained from broad, grand, simple and somewhat slow movements, such as the chorus from *Armida*, the *Tibi omnes* of my *Te Deum* and the *Apotheosis* of my *Funeral Symphony*.

Letters to FERRAND and LOUIS BERLIOZ from
1858 to 1863.

To HUMBERT FERRAND.

"*November 1858*.--I have nothing to tell you, I simply want to write. I am ill, miserable (how many *I's* to each line!) Always *I* and *me*! One's friends are for *oneself*, it ought to be oneself for one's friends.

"My dejection melts away as I write; for pity's sake let us write oftener! These years of silence are insupportable.

"Think how horribly quickly we are dying and how much good your letters do me!

"Last night I dreamt of music, this morning I recalled it all and fell into one of those supernal ecstasies.... All the tears of my soul poured forth as I listened to those divinely sonorous smiles that radiate from the angels alone. Believe me, dear friend, the being who could write such miracles of transcendent melody would be more than mortal.

"So sings great Michael as, erect upon the threshold of the empyrean, he dreamily gazes down upon the worlds beneath.

"Why, oh, why! have I not such an orchestra that I, too, could sing this archangelic song!

"Back to this lower earth! I am interrupted. Vulgar, commonplace, stupid life! Oh! that I had a hundred cannon to fire all at once!

"Good-bye. I feel better. Forgive me!"

* * * * *

"*6th July 1861.--The Trojans* has been accepted for the Opera, but I cannot tell when they will produce it as Gounod and Gervaert have to come first. But I am determined to worry myself no more; I will not court Fortune, I will lie in bed and await her.

"All the same, I could not resist a little uncourtly frankness when the Empress asked me when she should hear *The Trojans*.

"'I do not know, madame, I begin to think one must live a hundred and fifty years in order to get a hearing at the Opera.'

"The annoying part is that, thanks to these delays, my work is getting a sort of advance reputation that may injure it in the end.

"I am getting on with a one-act opera for Baden, written round Shakespeare's *Much Ado About Nothing*. It is called *Beatrice and Benedict*; I promise there shall not be much *Ado* in the shape of noise in it. Benazet, the king of Baden, wants it next year.

"An American director has offered me an engagement in the *Dis*united States; but his proposals are unavailing in view of my unconquerable antipathy to his great nation, and my love of money is not sufficiently great to prick me on. I do not know whether your love for American *utilitarian* manners and customs is any more intense than my own.

"In any case, it would be a great mistake to go far from Paris now; at any moment they might want *The Trojans*."

* * * * *

"*30th June 1862*.--In my bereavement I can write but little.

"My wife is dead--struck down in a moment by heart disease. The frightful loneliness, after the wrench of this sudden parting, is indescribable. Forgive me for not saying more."

To LOUIS BERLIOZ.

"*January 1858*.--Perhaps you have heard that a band of ruffians surrounded the Emperor's carriage as he went to the opera. They threw a bomb that killed and wounded both men and horses, but, by great good luck, did not touch the Emperor; and the charming Empress did not lose her head for a moment. The courage and presence of mind of both were perfect.

"I have just had a long letter from M. von Bulow, Liszt's son-in-law, who married *Mlle.* Cosima. He tells me that he performed my *Cellini* overture with the greatest success at a Berlin concert. He is one of the most fervent disciples of that crazy school of the 'Music of the Future,' as they call it in Germany."

"They stick to it, and want me to be their leader and standard-bearer, but I write nothing, say nothing, but just let them go their way. Good sense will teach reasonable people the truth."

* * * * *

"*May 1858*.--The foreign mail leaves to-morrow, and I must have a chat with you, dear Louis. I long for news. Are you well? happy?

"Here we are rather miserable. I am somewhat better, but my wife is nearly always in bed and in pain."

* * * * *

"*November 1860.*--Dear Boy,--Here is a hundred-franc note. Be sure to acknowledge it. I am thankful you are better. I, too, think my disease is wearing itself out. I am certainly better since I gave up remedies. Ideas for my little opera throng in so fast that I cannot find time to write; sometimes I begin a new one before I finish the old."

"You ask how I manage to crowd Shakespeare's five acts into one. I have taken only one subject from the play--the part in which Beatrice and Benedict, who detest each other, are mutually persuaded of each other's love, whereby they are inspired with true passion. The idea is really comic."

* * * * *

"*14th February 1861.*--It worries me to hear of your state of mind.

"I cannot imagine what dreams have made your present life so impossible. All I can say is that I was, at your age, far from being as well off as you are.

"Nay, more; I never dared to hope that, so soon after getting your captain's certificate, you would find a berth.

"It is natural that you should wish to get on, but sometimes the chances of one year bring more change into a man's life than ten years of strenuous endeavour.

"How can I teach you patience? Your mania for marriage would make me laugh were I not saddened by seeing you striving after the heaviest of all fetters and after the sordid vexations of domestic life--the most hopeless and exasperating of all lives. You are twenty-six, and have eighteen hundred francs, with a prospect of rapid promotion. When I married your mother I was thirty, and had but three hundred francs in the world--lent me by my friend Gounet--and the balance of my Prix de Rome scholarship.

"Then there were your mother's debts--nearly fourteen thousand francs--which I paid off gradually, and the necessity of sending money to her mother in England, besides which I had quarrelled with my family, who cast me off, and was trying hard to make my first small mark in the musical world.

"Compare my hardships with your present discontent! Even now, do you think it is very lively for me to be bound to this infernal galley-oar of journalism?

"I am so ill I can hardly hold my pen, yet I am forced to write for my miserable hundred francs, the while my brain teems with work and plans and designs that fall dead--thanks to my slavery.

"You are well and strong, while I writhe in ceaseless, incurable pain. Marie[25] thanks you for your kind messages. She, too, is ill. Dear boy! you have at least a father, friend, devoted brother, who loves you more than you seem to think, but who wishes that your character were firmer, your mind more decided.

* * * * *

"*21st February 1861.*--Wagner is turning our singers into goats. It seems impossible to disentangle this *Tannhauser*. I hear that the last general rehearsal was awful, and only finished at one in the morning. I suppose they will get through somehow.

"Liszt is coming to prop up the charivari.

"I have refused to write the critique, and have asked d'Ortigue to do it. It is best for every reason, and besides, it will disappoint them! Never did I have so many windmills to run a-tilt of as I have this year. I am deluged with fools of every species, and am choking with anger.

* * * * *

"*5th March 1861.*--The *Tannhauser* scandal grows apace. Everyone is raging. Even the Minister left the rehearsal in a towering passion. The Emperor is far from pleased; yet there are still a few honest enthusiasts left--even among French people.

"Wagner is decidedly mad. He will die of apoplexy, just as Jullien did last year.

"Liszt never came after all. I think he expected a fiasco. They have spent a hundred and sixty thousand francs over mounting the opera. Well, we shall see what Friday brings forth."

* * * * *

"*21st March 1861.*--The second performance of *Tannhauser* was worse than the first. No more laughter, the audience was too furious, and, regardless of the presence of the Emperor and Empress, hissed unmercifully. Coming out, Wagner was vituperated as a scoundrel, an idiot, an impertinent wretch. If this goes on, one day the performance will stop abruptly in the middle, and there will be an end of the whole thing.

"The press is unanimous in damning it."

* * * * *

"*18th April 1861.*--Write, dear Louis, if you can, without the cruel knife-thrusts you gave me in your last letter.

"I am worse than usual to-day, and have not strength to begin my article. I had an ovation at the Conservatoire after the performance of

Faust. I dined with the Emperor a week ago, and exchanged a few words with him. I was magnificently bored."

* * * * *

"*2nd June 1861*.--You are worried, and I can do nothing for you. Alexis is trying to find you a position in Paris, but is unsuccessful. I am as inefficient as he is. You alone can command your fate. They wish me to bring out *Alcestis* at the Opera as I did *Orpheus* at the Theatre Lyrique, and offer me full author's rights, but I have refused for various reasons.

"They believe that, for money, artists will stultify their consciences; I mean to prove that their belief is false.[26]

"My obstinacy has offended many. Instead of amusing themselves by spoiling Gluck's *chef d'oeuvre*, I wish they would spend their money over mounting *The Trojans*. But of course they won't, since it is the obvious thing to do! Liszt has conquered the Emperor; he played at Court last week, and has been given the Legion of Honour.

"Ah, if one only plays the piano!"

* * * * *

"*28th October 1861*.--Dear Louis,--Did I not know what a terrible effect disappointment has on even the best characters, I should really feel inclined to let you have some home truths. You have wounded me mortally with a deliberate calmness that shows you were master of your language. But I can forgive, for you are not a bad son after all.

"You go too far. Is it my fault that I am not rich, that I could not let you live idly in Paris with a wife and children? Is there a shadow of justice in reproaching me as you do? For nearly three months you keep silence, then comes this ironical letter! My poor dear boy, it is not right.

"Don't worry about your debt to the tailor; send me the bill and I will pay him.

"You ask me to beg a post for you. From whom? You know there never was a more awkward man than I at asking favours.

"Good-bye, dear son, dear friend, dear unlucky boy--unlucky by your own fault, not by mine."

* * * * *

"*17th June 1862*.--You have received my letter and telegram,[27] but I write to ask whether you can come to me in Baden on the 6th or 7th August, as I know you would enjoy hearing the last rehearsals and first performance of my opera. In my leisure moments you would be my companion, you would see my friends, we should be together.

"Could you leave your ship so near its date for sailing?

"I am not sure how much money I can send you. The expenses of that sad ceremony--the transference from St Germain--will be great.

"I am rather afraid, too, of trusting you in a gambling town, but if you will give me your word of honour not to stake a single florin I will trust you.

"My mother-in-law came back yesterday just after I had left home to find only her daughter's body. She is nearly frantic and is constantly watched by a friend who came to our help. Think of the anguish! Write soon, my dear, dear boy."

* * * * *

"BADEN, *10th August 1862*.--*Beatrice* was applauded from end to end, and I was recalled more times than I could count. My friends were delighted, but I was quite unmoved, for it was one of my days of excruciating pain and nothing seemed to matter.

"To-day I am better and can enjoy their congratulations.

"You will be pleased too, but why have you left me so long without a letter? Why do they keep transferring you from boat to boat? Do not write here again as I soon go back to Paris. Now I am called and must go and thank my radiant singers."

To H. FERRAND.

"PARIS, *21st August 1862*.--I am just home from Baden, where *Beatrice* obtained a real triumph.

"I always fly to you, be my news good or evil, I am so sure of your loving interest. Would you had been there! it would have recalled the night of the *Childhood of Christ*.

"Foes and conspirators stayed in Paris, artists and authors journeyed to Baden to be present; Madame Charton-Demeur was perfect, both as singer and actress.

"But can you believe that my neuralgia was too bad that day for me to take interest in anything? I took my place at the conductor's desk, before that cosmopolitan audience, to direct an opera of which I had written both words and music, absolutely, deadly impassible. Whereby I conducted better than usual. I was much more nervous at the second performance.

"Benazet, who always does things royally, spent outrageously in every department. He has splendidly inaugurated the new theatre and has created a furore. They want to give *Beatrice* at the Opera Comique, but there is no one to do the heroine since Madame Charton-Demeur is going to America.

"You would laugh at the critiques. People are finding out that I have melody; that I can be gay--in fact, really comic; that I am not *noisy*, which is rather obvious, since the heavy instruments are conspicuous by their absence.

"How much patience I should need were I not so completely indifferent. Dear friend, I suffer a perfect martyrdom daily from four in the morning till four in the afternoon. What is to become of me? I do not tell you this to make you patient under your own afflictions--my woes are no compensation to you.

"I simply cry unto you as one does to those who love and are loved. Adieu! Adieu!"

* * * * *

"*26th August 1862.*--How I should love to come to you, as Madame Ferrand wishes! But I have much to do here owing to my wife's death, and Louis has resigned his commission and is stranded. Besides, I am busy enlarging my *Beatrice.*

"I am trying to cut or untie all the bonds that hold me to Art, that I may be able to say to Death, 'When thou wilt.'

"I dare not complain when I think of what you bear.

"Are sufferings like ours the inevitable result of our organisation? Must we be punished for having worshipped the Beautiful throughout our lives? Probably.

"We have drunk too deeply of the enchanted cup; we have pursued our ideals too far.

"Still, dear friend, you have a devoted wife to help you to bear your cross. You know nothing of the dread duet beating, night and day, into your brain--the joint voices of world-weariness and isolation!

"God grant you never may! It is saddening music.

"Good-bye! My gathering tears would make me write words that would grieve you yet more. Again, good-bye!"

* * * * *

"*3rd March 1863.*--Your suppositions with regard to my depression are fortunately wrong; Louis has certainly worried me terribly, but I have forgiven him; he has found a ship and is now in Mexico.

"No; my trouble was Love. A love unsought that met me smiling, that I did not seek, that I even fought against for awhile.

"But my loneliness, my unceasing yearning for affection, conquered me; first I let myself be loved, then I more than loved in return, and at last a separation became inevitable--a separation absolute as death. That is all. I am slowly recovering, but health such as this is sad. I will say no more....

"I am glad my *Beatrice* pleases you. I am going to Weimar, where it is now in rehearsal, to conduct a few performances in April, then I shall come back to this wilderness--Paris.

"Pray, dear friend, that my apathy may become complete, for otherwise I shall have a hard time while *The Trojans* is in rehearsal.

"Good-bye; when I see your dear writing on my desk it calms me for the day. Never forget that."

XXXV

THE TROJANS

BY this time (1863) I had finished the dramatic work on which I had been engaged. Four years earlier, being in Weimar with Liszt's devoted friend, the Princess of Sayn-Wittgenstein--a woman whose noble heart and mind had often been my comfort in my darkest hours--I was drawn on to speak of my love of Virgil and of my wish to compose a grand opera in Shakespearian style on the second and fourth books of the *AEneid*. I added that I knew too well the misery and worry that would be my fate to dare to embark on such a project.

Said the Princess:

"Your passion for Shakespeare and love for the classics would indeed produce a work both grand and original. You must do it."

As I demurred, she continued:

"Listen! If you draw back from fear of petty troubles, if you are so weak as not to suffer in the cause of Cassandra and Dido, come here no more. I will never see you again!"

Once back in Paris I began the poem of *The Trojans*. Then I started on the score, and at the end of three years and a half it was finished. As I polished and repolished it I read it to many of my friends, profiting by their criticism; then I wrote to the Emperor begging him to read it and, should he judge it suitable, to use his influence to secure it a hearing at the Opera.

However, M. de Morny dissuaded me from sending my letter, and when finally *The Trojans* saw the footlights the Emperor was not even present.

After many cruel disappointments with regard to the opera,[28] I at last succumbed to the persuasion of M. Carvalho and allowed him to set *The Trojans at Carthage* (the second section of the opera) at the Theatre Lyrique.

Although he received a Government subsidy of a hundred thousand francs a year, neither his theatre, singers, chorus, nor orchestra was equal to the task. Both he and I made great sacrifices, and I, out of my small income, paid some extra musicians and cut up my orchestration to bring it within his limits.

Madame Charton-Demeur, the only possible woman for Dido, most generously accepted fees far below those offered her in Madrid, but despite everything the production was incomplete; indeed, the sceneshifters made such a muddle of the storm scene that we were obliged to suppress it entirely.

As I said before, if I am to superintend a really fine representation I must have an absolutely free hand, and the good-will of every one around, otherwise I get worn out with storming at opposition, and end by resigning and letting everything go to the devil as it will.

I cannot describe what Carvalho[29] made me suffer in demanding cuts that he deemed necessary. When he dared ask no more he worked upon me through friends, whose niggling, peddling criticism drove me nearly mad. Said one:

"How about your rhapsodist with the four-stringed lyre? I daresay you are right as to archaeology, but----"

"Well?"

"It is rather dangerous; people are certain to laugh."

"H'm! laughable is it that an antique lyre should have only four notes?"

Another:

"There is a risky word in your prologue that I fairly tremble over."

"What's that?"

"*Triomphaux.*"

"Well, why not? Is not it the plural of *triomphal* just as *chevaux* is of *cheval*?"

"Yes, but it is not much used."

"Oh, confound it all! If, in an epic poem, I were to use words suited to vaudevilles and variety shows, I should not have much choice of language."

"Well, people will certainly laugh."

"Ha! ha! triomphaux! It is really almost as funny as Moliere's *tarte a la creme*. Ha! ha!"

A third:

"I say! You really must *not* let AEneas come on in a helmet."

"And why not?"

"Why, Mangin, the gutter pencil-seller, wears one. Certainly his is a mediaeval one, but that doesn't matter. The gallery cads will certainly howl 'Hallo! there's Mangin!'

"I see--a Trojan hero may not wear a helmet, lest he should be like Mangin!"

Number four:

"Old fellow, do something to please me!"

"What is it now?"

"Suppress Mercury. Those wings on his head and his heels are really too comical. No one ever saw anybody with wings anywhere but on their shoulders."

"Ah, you have seen people with wings on their shoulders? I have not, but I can quite understand that wings in unexpected places are awkward. One does not often meet Mercury strolling about the streets of Paris."

Can any one conceive what these crass idiots made me endure? In addition, I had to fight the musical ideas of Carvalho, who could not believe that, after studying opera for forty years, I knew just a little about it.

The actors alone loyally abstained from worrying me, for which forbearance I give them all most hearty thanks.

The first performance took place on the 4th November 1863. There was no hostile demonstration except the hissing of one man, and he kept on regularly up to the tenth night. Five papers said everything insulting that they could think of, but, on the other hand, fifty articles of admiring criticism--among them those of my friends, Gasperini, d'Ortigue, L. Kreutzer, and Damcke--filled me with a joyous pride to which I had too long been a stranger.

I also received many appreciative letters, and was frequently stopped in the street by strangers who begged to shake hands with the author of *The Trojans.*

Were these not compensations for the diatribes of my foes? In spite of the cutting and polishing (I called it mutilation) that my *Trojans* suffered at the hands of Carvalho, it only ran twenty-one nights. The receipts did not reach his expectations; he cancelled the engagement of Madame Charton-Demeur, who left for Madrid, and to my great comfort my work disappeared from the play-bills.

Nevertheless, being both author and composer, my royalties for those twenty-one performances and the sale of the piano score in Paris and London amounted--to my unspeakable joy--to about the annual income I derived from the *Journal des Debats*, and I was, therefore, able to resign my post as critic.

Freedom, after thirty years of slavery! No more articles to concoct, no more platitudes to excuse, no more commonplaces to extol, no more righteous wrath to bottle up, no more lies, no more farces, no more cowardly compromises! Free! I need never more set foot in theatre! Gloria in excelsis! Thanks to *The Trojans* the wretched quill-driver is free!!

* * * * *

My *Beatrice*, having been a success at Baden in August 1862, was translated into German, and, at the request of the Grand Duchess of Saxe-Weimar, was given at Weimar in April 1863. Their Serene Highnesses desired me to direct the two first performances, and, as usual, overwhelmed me with kindness.

So did the Prince of Hohenzollern-Hechingen, who sent his Kapellmeister to invite me to conduct a concert at Lowenberg, his present residence.

He told me that his orchestra knew all my symphonies, and wished for a programme drawn exclusively from my own works.

"Your Highness," I said, "since your orchestra knows all, be pleased to choose for yourself. I will conduct whatever you wish."

He therefore chose *King Lear*, the festival and love-scene from *Romeo*, the *Carnaval Romain* overture, and *Harold in Italy*. As he had no harpist, Madame Pohl of Weimar, with her husband, was invited.

The Prince had greatly changed since my visit in 1842; he was a martyr to gout, and was, after all, unable to be present at the concert he had planned. He was keenly disappointed, for, said he, "You are not a mere conductor; you are the orchestra itself; it is hard that I cannot reap the benefit of your stay here."

He has built a splendid music-room in the castle, with a musical library; the orchestra is composed of about fifty *musical* musicians, and their conductor, M. Seifriz, is both patient and talented. They are not worried with lesson-giving, church or theatre work, but belong exclusively to the Prince.

My rooms were close to the concert hall, and the first afternoon, at four, a servant came to say:

"Monsieur, the orchestra awaits you."

There I found the forty-five silent artists, instruments in hand and all in tune!!

They rose courteously to receive me, *King Lear* was on the desk, I raised my baton and everything went with spirit, smoothness, and precision, so that--not having heard the piece for ten or twelve years--I said to myself in amazement: "It is tremendous! Can I really have written it?"

The rest was just as good, and I said to the players:

"Gentlemen, to rehearse with you is simply a farce; I have not a single objection to make."

The Kapellmeister played the viola solo of *Harold* perfectly (in the other pieces he returned to his violin), and I can truly say that never have I heard it more perfectly done.

And ah! how they sang the *adagio* of *Romeo*! We were transported to Verona, Lowenberg was gone. At the end Seifriz rose and, after waiting a moment to conquer his emotion, cried in French: "There is nothing finer in music!"

Then the orchestra burst into storms of applause, and I bit my lip.... Messengers passed constantly back and forth to the poor Prince in his bed to report progress, but nothing consoled him for his absence. Every few minutes during dinner he would either send for me or a big, powdered lacquey would bring me a pencilled note on a silver salver. Sometimes I would spend half an hour at his bedside and listen to his praises. He knows all that I have written, both prose and music.

On the day of the concert a brilliant audience filled the hall; by their enthusiasm one could see that my music was an old friend. After the *Pilgrim's March* an officer came on to the platform and pinned on my coat the cross of Hohenzollern. The secret had been so well guarded that I had not the slightest idea of such an honour.

But it pleased me so greatly that, just for my own satisfaction, and without thought of the public, I played the orgie from *Harold* in my very own style--furiously--so that it made me grind my teeth.

I might say much more of this charming interlude of my life, but I must only mention the exquisite cordiality of the Prince's circle and particularly of the family of Colonel Broderotti, whose perfect French was a real relief to me, since I dislike to hear my own language badly spoken yet know no German. As I took leave of the Prince he embraced me, saying:

"You are going to Paris, my dear Berlioz, where many love you. Tell them I love them for it."

But I must go back to *Beatrice*.

To my mind it is one of the liveliest and most original things I have ever done, although it is difficult--especially in the men's parts. Unlike *The Trojans* it is inexpensive to mount; but they will take precious care not to have it in Paris; they are right, it is not Parisian music at all. With his usual generosity, M. Benazet paid me four thousand francs for the music and the same for the words--eight thousand in all, and gave me another thousand to conduct it the following year.

The Maidens' duet became very popular in Germany and I remember making the Grand Duke laugh heartily about it one night at supper. He had been catechising me on my life in Paris and my revelations anent our musical world sadly disillusioned him.

"How, when and where did you write that lovely duet?" he asked, "surely by moonlight in some romantic spot----"

"Sir," I replied, "it was one of those scenes that artists mark and store up for future use and which come forth when needed, no matter amid what surroundings. I sketched it in at the Institute during an oration of one of my colleagues."

"Ha! ha!" laughed he, "that speaks well for the orator. His eloquence must have been great."

Later on it was performed at one of our Conservatoire concerts and made an unheard-of sensation. Even my faithful hissers dared not uplift their voices. Mesdames Viardot and Vanderheufel-Duprez sang it deliciously, and the marvellous orchestra was dainty and graceful. It was one of those performances one sometimes hears--in dreams. The Conservatoire Society, directed by my friend, Georges Hainl, was no longer inimical to me and proposed to give excerpts from my scores occasionally. I have now presented it with my whole musical library, with the exception of the operas; it ought some day to be fairly valuable and it could not be in better hands.

I must not forget to mention the Strasburg festival, where I conducted my *Childhood of Christ* in a vast building seating six thousand people. I had five hundred performers, and to my surprise, this work--written almost throughout in a quiet, tender vein--made a tremendous impression, the mystic, unaccompanied chorus, "O my soul!" even causing tears.

Ah! how happy am I when my audience weeps!

I have heard since that many of my works have been given in America, Russia and Germany.

So much the better! Could I but live a hundred and forty years my musical life would become distinctly interesting.

* * * * *

I had married again--*it was my duty*, and after eight years my wife died suddenly of heart disease. Some time after her burial in the great cemetery at Montmartre, my dear friend, Edouard Alexandre (the organ builder, whose goodness to me has been unbounded), thinking her grave too humble, made me a present of a plot of ground *in perpetuity*. There a vault was built and I was obliged to be present at the re-interment. It was a heart-rending scene and quite broke me down; I seemed to have touched the lowest depths of misery, but this was nothing to what followed soon after.

I was officially notified that the small cemetery at Montmartre, where Henriette lay, was to be closed and that I must remove her dear body. I gave the necessary orders and one gloomy morning set out alone for the deserted burial-ground. A municipal officer awaited me and as I came up a sexton jumped down into the open grave. The ten years buried coffin was still intact with the exception of the cover, decayed by damp, and the man, instead of lifting it to the surface, pulled at the rotten boards, which tearing asunder with a hideous noise, left the remains exposed.

Stooping, he took in his hands that fleshless head, discrowned and gaunt, the head of poor Ophelia and placed it in the new coffin lying on the brink of the grave--alas! alas! Again he stooped and raised the headless trunk, a black repulsive mass in its discoloured shroud--it fell with a dull, hopeless sound into its place. The officer a few paces off, stood watching. Seeing me leaning against a cypress tree he cried:

"Come nearer, M. Berlioz, come nearer."

And, to add a grotesque weirdness to this horrible spectacle he added, misusing a word:

"Ah, poor *inhumanity*!"

In a few moments we followed the hearse down the hill to the great cemetery, where the new vault yawned before us. Henriette was laid within and there those dear dead women await me.

* * * * *

I am nearly sixty-one; past hope, past visions, past high thoughts; my son is far away; I am alone; my scorn for the dishonesty and imbecility of men, my hatred of their insane malignity are at their height; and every day I say again to Death:

"When thou wilt!"

Why does he tarry?

XXXVI

ESTELLE ONCE MORE

To M. and Mme MASSART.

"PARIS, *August 1864*.--Yes, really and truly! Marshal Vaillant has written a charming letter to tell me that the Emperor has appointed us officers of the Legion of Honour[30]--yes, madame, both you and me. So arrange about changing your ribbon, *etc.*

"You would not go and dine with the Minister. Sixty of us were there, including His Excellency's dog, who drank coffee out of his master's cup.

"A great author, M. Merimee, said to me:

"'You ought to have been made an officer long ago, which shows that I am not in the Ministry.'

"You see I am a little better to-day and therefore more idiotic than usual; I hope this will find you the same.

"Paris is *en fete* and you are not here! The Villerville beach must be very dismal, how can you stay on there?

"Massart goes shooting--he kills sea-gulls or perhaps an occasional sperm-whale--God only knows how you kill time! You have deserted your piano and I would not mind betting that when you come home you will hardly be able to play that easiest of scales--B natural major!

"Shall I come and see you? You may safely say 'yes' for I shall not come. Forgive me! I am getting serious again, the pain is beginning and I most go to bed. Heartiest greetings to you both."

To A. MOREL.

"*August 1864*.--Thank you for your cordial letter. The officer's cross and Vaillant's letter pleased me--both for my friends' sake and my enemies'. How *can* you keep any illusions about music in France? Everything is dead except stupidity.

"I am almost alone. Louis has gone back to St Nazaire and all my friends are scattered except Heller, whom I see sometimes. We dine together at Asnieres and are about as lively as owls; I read and re-read; in the evenings I stroll past the theatres in order to enjoy the pleasure of not going in. Yesterday I found a comfortable seat on a tomb in Montmartre cemetery and slept for two hours.

"Sometimes I go and see Madame Erard at Passy, where I am welcomed with open arms; I relish having no articles to write and being thoroughly lazy.

"Paris gets daily more beautiful; it is a pleasure to watch her blossoming out.

"I hear there is to be a mighty festival at Carlsruhe; Liszt has gone there from Rome and they are going to discourse ear-splitting music. It is the pow-wow of young Germany presided over by Hans von Bulow."

Rarely have I suffered from *ennui* so terribly as I did during the beginning of September 1864.

My friends were away except Stephen Heller, the delicate wit and learned musician, who has written so much lovely music for the piano and whose gentle melancholy and devotion to the true deities of Art made him to me such a grateful companion. My son was home from Mexico, he, too, was not lively and we often pooled our gloom and dined together.

One day, after dinner at Asnieres, we walked beside the river and discussed Shakespeare and Beethoven, my son taking part in the Shakespeare portion, since, unfortunately, he was then unacquainted with Beethoven. We finally agreed that it was worth while living in order to worship the Beautiful, and if we could not annihilate all that is inimical to it we must be content to despise the commonplace and recognise it as little as possible. The sun was setting; we sat on the river-bank opposite the isle of Neuilly, and, as we watched the wayward wheeling of the swallows over the water, I suddenly remembered where I was.

I looked at my son--I thought of his mother.

Once more, in spirit, I lay half asleep in the snow as I had done in that very spot thirty-six years before, during those frenzied wanderings around Paris.

Once again I recalled Hamlet's cold remark over the Ophelia he loved no longer, "What! the fair Ophelia?"

"Long ago," I said to my companion, "one winter's day, I was nearly drowned here trying to cross the Seine on the ice. I had walked aimlessly since early morning----" Louis sighed.

The following week he left me, and a great yearning for Vienne, Grenoble, above all, Meylan, came over me. I wished to see my nieces and--one other woman, if I could get her address.

I left Paris. My brother-in-law, Suat, and his two daughters met me with joy. But my joy was chastened, for on entering their drawing-room the portrait of my dear Adele--now four years dead--faced me. It was a terrible blow, and my nieces looked on in sorrowful amazement at my grief.

Daily familiarity with the room, its furniture, the portrait, had already softened their loss to them; to me all was fresh.

Dear tender-hearted Adele! my willing slave, my indulgent guardian. How well I remember one day, after I came from Italy, that it rained in torrents, and I said:

"Adele, come for a walk."

"Certainly, dear boy," she said, promptly; "wait till I get my galoshes."

"Really," said my elder sister, "you must be quite crazy to want to paddle about the fields in such weather."

But, despite mockery and jokes, we took a big umbrella and arm-in-arm walked about six miles without speaking a word. We loved each other.

After spending a peaceful fortnight with my brother-in-law, during which he got me Madame F.'s address in Lyons, I could no longer resist a pilgrimage to St Eynard, such as I had made sixteen years before.

There soared the ancient rock, there stood the small white house ... to-day, her old home; to-morrow, perhaps, Estelle herself! Sixteen years had passed as one night, all was unchanged. The little shady path, the old tower, the leafy vines, the glorious view over the valley. Till then I had kept calm, only murmuring, "Estelle! Estelle! Estelle!" but now, overcome with emotion, I fell prone on my face, hearing with each heart-beat the fatal words:

"Past! Past! Gone for ever!"

I arose, and chipping from the tower a morsel of stone that she perchance may have touched, went on my way.

There is the rock whereon I laid my posy of pink peas--but where are the flowers? Gone, or perhaps only past their flowering stage. Here is the cherry tree. How grown!

I break off a fragment of bark and, passing my arms around the trunk, press it passionately to my breast.

Dear tree, you remember her! You understand!

At the avenue gate I resolved to go up to the house; perhaps the new owners would not be too suspicious of me. In the garden I met an old lady who seemed startled at the sight of a stranger.

"Pardon me, madame," I stammered, "might I go through your garden--in memory of--old friends?"

"Certainly, monsieur, go where you will."

Further on a girl was on a ladder gathering pears. I bowed and passed on, pushing my way through the bushes, now so neglected, and cutting a branch of syringa to hide next my heart. As I came to the open door, I paused on the threshold to look in. The maiden of the pear tree, no doubt warned by her mother, came forward and courteously asked me in.

That little room, looking over the wide valley, that *she* had so proudly shown me when I was twelve years old--the same furniture, the same----I tore my handkerchief with my teeth. The girl watched me uneasily.

"Do not mind me, mademoiselle. All is so strange--I have not--been here for forty-nine years!"

And, bursting into tears, I fled.

What could those ladies have thought of that strange scene, to which they never got a key?

Reader, do I repeat myself? In sooth it is always so; remembrance, regret, a weary soul clutching at the past, fighting despairingly to retain the flying present. Always this useless struggle against time, always this wild desire to realise the impossible, always this frantic thirst for perfect love! How can I help repeating myself? The sea repeats itself; are not all its waves akin?

* * * * *

That night I reached Lyons and spent a sleepless night thinking of my meeting with Madame F.

I decided to go at noon, and to send the following letter to prepare her for her visitor:

"MADAME,--I have just come from Meylan, from my second pilgrimage to the hallowed haunts of my childhood's dreams. It has been even more painful than that of sixteen years ago, after which I wrote to you at Vif. This time I ask for more; I dare to beg you to see me. I can control myself; you need fear no transports from a heart out-worn and crushed by the pressure of cruel Fate. Give me but a few moments! Let me see you, I implore.

"*23rd September 1864.* HECTOR BERLIOZ."

I could not wait till noon. At half-past eleven I rang; gave her maid my card and the letter. She was at home. I ought only to have sent up the letter, but I was past knowing what I was doing. Without hesitation she came to meet me. I at once recognised her graceful yet stately air--the step of a goddess. But, ah! how changed her face! Her complexion darkened, her hair silvered.

Yet my heart went out to my idol as though she had been in all the freshness of her youthful beauty.

Holding my note, she led the way to her drawing-room. My emotions choked me, I was dumb; with gentle dignity she began:

"We are old acquaintances, M. Berlioz----" Silence.

"We were but children then----" Still silence.

Feeble as the cry of a drowning man came my halting voice:

"My letter--madame--explains this visit; would you but read it----"

Grenoble

She opened and read it, then laid it on the chimney-piece.

"Then you have been in Meylan; by chance, no doubt?"

"Oh, madame, can you believe it needed chance to take me there? For how long had I not yearned to see it once more?"

Again silence.

"Your life has been a stirring one, M. Berlioz."

"How do you know, madame?"

"I have read your biography--by Mery, I think. I bought it some years ago."

"Pray, do not think that my friend Mery, an artist and a clever man, is guilty of such a tissue of fables and nonsense as that! I believe I can guess the real author. But I shall soon have a true biography ready, one I have written myself."

"And you write so well!"

"Nay, madame, I do not mean to praise the style, but simply to say that at least it will be true. In it, without naming you, I have been able to tell all my feeling for you without restraint."

Silence.

"I have also heard of you," went on Madame F., "from a friend of yours who married my husband's niece."

"Yes, it is he whom I asked to tell me the fate of a letter I wrote you sixteen years ago. I longed to know whether you received it. I never saw him again, and now he is dead."

Silence.

"My life has been very quiet, very sad. I lost some of my children, and my husband died while the others were very young. I did my best alone to bring them up well."

Silence.

"I am indeed grateful, M. Berlioz, for the kind thoughts you have kept of me."

At her gentle words my heart beat yet more violently.

With hungry eyes I gazed and gazed, clothing her once more in the beauty of long past days. At length I said:

"Madame, give me your hand."

Pressing it to my lips, my heart turned to water within me, the world sank away, a long and blessed silence brooded over us.

"Dare I hope," I murmured, "that I may write to you? That, at long distant intervals, I may even see you?"

"Oh, certainly; but I am leaving Lyons soon to live with my son who, after his marriage, is to settle in Geneva."

I rose, not daring to stay longer. She came with me to the door, saying, "Good-bye, M. Berlioz, good-bye. I am more grateful than I can tell you for your long and sweet memory of me."

Once more I bent over her hand, pressing it to my burning forehead, then tore myself away but only to wander, aimlessly and feverishly, near her dwelling.

As I watched the swirling Rhone rush under the Pont Morand, M. Strakosch, brother-in-law of Adelina Patti, came up to me.

"You!" he cried, "Good-luck! Adelina will be so glad to see you. She is singing to-morrow in the *Barbiere*; will you have a box?"

"Many thanks, I may be leaving this evening."

"Well, anyway come to dinner with us to-day. You know how much pleasure it gives us."

"I dare not promise--It depends--I am not very well--Where are you staying?"

"Grand Hotel."

"So am I. Well, if I am not too unsociable this evening I will come. But don't wait."

I suddenly thought of an excuse to see Madame F. once more. If she would go to the theatre I would stay also, if she would allow me the honour of escorting her. If she would not I would leave at once.

I hurried round to her house. She was out but I left a message with her maid and then went off to pass a day of torturing uncertainty. Hour after hour went by and no answer came, time after time I returned to find the house shut up and to get no answer to my ring.

Could it be that she had told her people not to admit me?

What would become of me! Where should I go! What do! There seemed no refuge for me but the Rhone!

Finally in one last despairing attempt I heard ladies' voices above me on the stairs and saw her coming down, a note in her hand.

"Oh, M. Berlioz, I am so sorry I have only just got your message and here is my answer. Unfortunately I shall be away from home to-morrow; a thousand pardons for the inconvenience I have caused you."

She was putting the letter in her pocket when I cried:

"Oh, please let me have it!"

"It is hardly worth while----"

"I beg of you, since it was meant for me."

She gave it me and for the first time I saw her writing.

"Then I shall see you no more?"

"Not if you leave to-night. May your journey be pleasant."

Pressing my hand, she and her two friends passed on, leaving me--can it be believed?--almost happy.

I had seen, had spoken to her again, I had a letter from her in which she sent me her *kindest regards*.

With my unhoped-for treasure I went back to the hotel to dine with Mademoiselle Patti.

As I entered her *salon* the charming diva clapped her hands joyously and danced up to me, holding up her lovely forehead for my accustomed kiss.

During dinner she spoilt me with her dainty coaxing attentions.

"There is something wrong with you," she said, "what are you thinking of? I can't have you miserable."

They came with me to the station, she, with a friend and Strakosch, and they were allowed to go on to the platform. Adelina, dear child, clung to me until the signal was given, then the winsome creature flung both arms round my neck and kissed me, crying gaily:

"Good-bye, good-bye just for a week. We shall be in Paris on Tuesday and you must come and see us on Thursday."

Why could I not claim such affection from Madame F. and mere politeness from Mademoiselle Patti?

Adelina was like a brilliant, diamond-eyed humming-bird fluttering round me; I was enchanted but not touched. Though I liked her greatly, I did not *love* her.

My soul was given to that old, sad, unsought after woman, hers it has always been and will be to my dying day.

Balzac and even Shakespeare--master painters of passions--knew nothing of love like this. Tom Moore alone has imagined and voiced it in--

"Believe me if all those endearing young charms."

How often, through that long night journey, did I repeat:

"Idiot! why did you leave? You might have seen her again to-morrow." True, but the fear of being troublesome restrained me and what could I have done in Lyons during the hours we were apart? it would have been but torture.

After a few miserable days of indecision in Paris I wrote the following letter, which shows my deplorable state and her beautiful calm.

How much worse off am I now that I cannot even write to her! To enjoy that romantic friendship to the end would have been too great a blessing. Wounded, torn, alone, unsatisfied must I totter to my grave!

"PARIS, *27th September 1864*.--Madame! A thousand blessings on you for your gentle reception of me! Few women could have done as much; yet since our meeting, I suffer most cruelly. It is useless to repeat to myself that you could not have done more than you have; my wounded heart bleeds on unstaunched. I ask, why? why? and my only answer is: because I saw you so little; because I said but a tithe of all I wished; because we parted as if for ever.

"Yet I held your hand, I pressed it to my lips--to my forehead and kept back my tears as I had promised.

"And now the inexorable thirst for another word from you has conquered me; in pity grant it!

"Think! for forty-five years I have loved you; you are my childhood's dream that has weathered all the storms of my most stormy life. It *must* be true--this love of a life-time--could it, else, master me as it still does?

"Do not take me for an eccentric, a plaything of my own imagination; I am but a man of intense sensibility, of eternal constancy and of overwhelmingly strong affections. I loved you, I love you still, I shall always love you, although I am sixty-one and for me the world has no more illusions.

"Grant me, I pray you, not as a nurse, from a sense of duty to her sick patient, but as a noble woman stooping to heal wounds she has unwittingly given--grant me those three things that, alone, can give me peace: permission to write sometimes, your undertaking to reply and a promise that once a year, at least, you will allow me to visit you.

"If I called without your permission I might arrive at the wrong time, therefore I shall not venture near you unless you say: 'Come.'

"Surely there is nothing strange or wrong in this? Could there be a purer or more beautiful bond? Who shall say us nay? Still, I must own that it would be painful to meet you only amongst others, therefore if you bid me come it will be that we may talk as we did last Friday when, so deeply was I moved, that I could not savour the sweet sad charm by reason of my terror lest emotion should get beyond control. Oh, madame! madame! I have but one end in life--to gain your affection!

"Give me but leave to try! I will be so humble, so restrained; my letters shall be as infrequent as you wish lest they become a burden to you; five lines only from you will suffice me. My visits will be but rare; yet, if our thoughts may meet, I shall feel that--after these long and dreary years during which I have been nothing to you--I may in time become your friend. Friends with such devotion as mine are not too often found. I will encircle you with love so sweet, so tender, with affection so compounded of all that is simplest in a child and all that is best and grandest in a man that, surely, in time you will feel its charm and turn to me one day, saying:

"I am in very deed your friend."

"Adieu, madame, once more I read your note of the 23rd with its assurance of your *sentiments affectueux*. Surely this is no mere formality? Tell me truly--truly!--Yours to eternity,

HECTOR BERLIOZ."

"*P.S.*--I send you three books; perhaps you will glance at them in your leisure moments. Do you see the author's device to make you take a little interest in him?"

MADAME F.'S *Answer*.

"LYONS, *29th September 1864*.

"MONSIEUR,--I should wrong both you and myself did I not reply at once to your dream of our future friendship; believe me, I speak from my heart.

"I am an old woman (remember I am six years your senior), worn and withered by bodily pain and mental anguish, with all my earthly illusions swept away.

"Since the fatal day, twenty years ago, that I lost my best friend, I have said good-bye to worldly pleasures, and have found my sole consolation in a few old friends and in my children.

"In this absolute calm, alone, can I find rest, and to upset it would be burdensome indeed.

"In your letter of the 27th you say you have but one wish--that I may become your friend. Do you believe, monsieur, that this could possibly be? I hardly know you, I have seen you but once in forty-nine years; how can I understand your tastes, your character, your capacities--all those hundred and one points upon which, alone, friendship can be based?

"With two people of like affinities, sympathy may be born and grow into friendship, but, far apart as we are, no correspondence could bring about what you desire.

"Besides, I must confess that I am most lazy about letters; my mind is as torpid as my fingers. I could not, therefore, promise to write regularly, for the promise would certainly not be kept. Still, if you feel a certain pleasure in writing, I will read your letters, although you must not expect speedy replies.

"Neither can I promise to receive you alone. At Geneva, in the house of my son and his wife, it would be impossible for me to arrange matters as you wish.

"I tell you all this with perfect frankness, for I feel so strongly that, as grey hairs come, dreams must be thrust aside--such friendships belong to the happy days of youth, not to the disenchantments of old age.

"My future is so short; why indulge in a dream that must fade so quickly? Why create these vain regrets?

"In what I say, monsieur, do not think that I wish to wound you, to belittle your remembrance of the past. I respect it, and am greatly touched.

"You are still young at heart, and I am old and good for nothing but to keep a warm place for you in my memory. In your triumphs I shall always take a cordial interest.

"Again, monsieur, I send you my affectionate regards.

ESTELLE F----."

"I have received the books you so kindly sent. A thousand thanks."

Second Letter.

"PARIS, *2nd October 1864.*

"MADAME,--I have not answered sooner, hoping that I might overcome the terrible depression caused by your letter--a masterpiece of sad truth.

"You are right to avoid all that might disturb your calm; but be assured that I should never have done so, and that this friendship, for which I so humbly begged, should never have become *burdensome.* (Is not this rather a cruel word?)

"But you will take an interest in my career, and for that I kiss your hand with deepest gratitude. Yet, with tears, with importunity, I pray for news of you sometimes.

"You talk so bravely of old age that I must e'en be brave too. I pray I may die first that I may send you my last farewell! But if I must hear that you have left this sad earth ... will your son tell it me?--pardon!

"Give me, at least, what you would give to the merest stranger--your address at Geneva.

"I will not go there for a year, I fear to trouble you; but your address! your address! If your silence shows that you refuse even this meagre concession, you will have put a crown on the unhappiness you might have softened.

"Then, madame, may God and your conscience forgive you!

"Lost in the cold dark night wherein you have thrust me, I shall wander--grieving, suffering, alone, but still,--Yours devotedly until death,

HECTOR BERLIOZ."

MADAME F.'S *Second Letter.*

"LYONS, *14th October 1864.*

"MONSIEUR,--I write in haste, that you may believe I have no wish to be unkind. My son is to be married on the 19th, and I shall have much to do.

"Immediately afterwards I must prepare to go to Geneva--no light task for my weak health. Early in November I leave, and, as soon as I am settled in my new home, you shall have my address, which I do not yet know.

"I would have waited to get it from my son, but I feared to pain you by my long silence."

Third Letter.

"15th October 1864.

"MADAME,--Oh, thank you! thank you! I will wait.

"My best wishes for the young couple and for you!

"Dear lady, may this solemn time bring you ineffable joy.

"Ah, how good you are!

"Do not fear that my adoration will become unreasonable.--Your devoted

HECTOR BERLIOZ."

After an impatient fortnight, I received the announcement of M. Charles F.'s marriage, addressed in his mother's writing; which filled me with a joy that few can understand. I was in the seventh heaven, and wrote at once:--

"*28th October 1864.*--Life is beautiful under certain aspects. I have received the notice addressed by you! A thought for the poor exile. May your good angel render fourfold the good you have done! Yes, life is beautiful, but how much more beautiful death. To be at your feet, my head upon your knee, your two hands clasped in mine, and so to end----

HECTOR BERLIOZ."

Days passed into weeks; Madame F. had gone to Geneva. Could she intend to withhold her address? To break her word?

During that anxious time I believed I should write to her no more, and my heart despaired.

But one morning, as I sat drearily musing beside the fire, a card was brought to me:--

"M. ET MME CHARLES F----."

The son and his wife, and *she* had sent them!

Yet how greatly it upset me to find the young man the living image of his mother at eighteen.

The bride seemed quite bewildered at my emotion, although her husband was not; evidently he knew all; Madame F. had shown my letters.

"How beautiful she must have been!" cried the young wife.

"Oh!----"

"Yes," said M. F., "I remember even now how dazzled I was, at five years old, on seeing my mother dressed for a ball."

Gradually I subdued my feelings, and was able to talk sensibly to my visitors. Madame C. F. was a Dutch creole of Java, and knew Rajah Brooke of Sarawak.

How much I should have had to ask her had I been in my usual state of mind.

I saw them pleasantly often during their stay in Paris, and we talked of *her*. As we grew more friendly, the bride scolded me for writing as I had done.

"You frighten her," she said. "Remember she hardly knows you. You must learn to be calm, then your visits to Geneva will be delightful, and we shall be so happy to see you. You will come, will you not?"

"Can you doubt it, if Madame F. gives me permission?"

Schooling myself rigidly, I gave them no letter for their mother when they left; but, as my *Trojans* was to be given, I sent her a copy of the poem, begging her to read the page I had marked with some dead leaves at half-past two on the 18th December, the time at which that passage would be played in Paris. Madame C. F. was to be back in Paris then, and hoped to be present at this concert, which was making some stir in the musical world.

A fortnight went by and she did not come, neither did I have a letter. I was almost at the end of my patience, although I would not write, when, on the 17th, Madame C. F. returned bringing me the following letter:

"GENEVA, *16th December 1864*.

"MONSIEUR,--I ought to have thanked you sooner for your charming welcome of my son and his wife had I not been unwell, and consequently, very idle.

"But I cannot let my daughter-in-law go without my grateful thanks for all the pleasure you have given them.

"Suzanne will tell you all about our life here; I should be as happy as in Lyons, were it not for my separation from my other two sons and from my dear old friends.

"Once more, thank you for the libretto of *The Trojans*, and also for the sweet souvenir of the Meylan leaves--they bring back the bright, happy days of my youth.

"My son and I will read the part of your work that you have marked, and shall think of Suzanne listening to your music on Sunday."

To which I replied:

"PARIS, *19th December 1864*.--Last September, when at Grenoble, I visited one of my cousins, who lives near St Georges, a wretched hamlet niched into the most barren mountains on the left bank of the Drac, inhabited only by a few miserable peasants.

"My cousin's sister-in-law is the sweet providence of this forsaken corner, and on the day of my arrival she heard that one far-away family had had no bread for three weeks.

"She started off at once to see the mother.

"'Why, Jeanne!' she cried, 'how could you be in trouble and not tell me? You know how anxious we are to help.'

"'Oh, mademoiselle, we are not really in want yet; we still have some potatoes and a few cabbages, only the children don't like them. They shout and cry for bread. You know children are so unreasonable.'

"Well, dear lady, you too have done a kind thing in writing. I would not write for fear of boring you, so waited for your daughter's return. She came not! My anxiety choked me. You see, madame, creatures such as I are *unreasonable*.

"Yet surely I--if anyone--hardly need to learn lessons that have been taught me already by so many knife-thrusts in my heart.

"It seems to me that you are sad, and that makes me the more.... From to-day I mean to restrain my language, to talk of outward things only.

"You know what is in my heart--all that I do not say.

"Perhaps you already know that, thanks to the thousand and one annoyances brought upon me by the Conservatoire committee, my *Trojans* was not performed yesterday. Still, I thank you for the time you have spent in thought with us in the concert-room. My son, who has done well in Mexico, has just landed at St Nazaire. He is first lieutenant of his ship, and, as he cannot come to Paris, I am going to Brittany to see him. He is a good boy, but is, unfortunately, too much like his father, and cannot reconcile himself to the commonplaces and troubles of this world.

"We love each other dearly.

"My aged mother-in-law, whom I have promised never to leave, takes the greatest care of me, and accepts unquestioningly my gloomy tempers. I read again and again Shakespeare, Virgil, Homer, *Paul and Virginia*, and travels of all kinds. I am horribly bored and suffer agonies from neuralgia that doctors have tried in vain, for nine years, to cure.

"When the pains of mind, body and estate grow too much for me, I take three drops of laudanum to snatch some sleep.

"If I feel better I go and see my friends, M. and Mme Damcke.

"He is a German composer of rare gifts; his wife is an angel of goodness to me.

"There I do as I like. If I am in the humour we talk or play; if not, they draw up a big sofa to the fire, and there I lie the whole evening without a word--chewing the cud of sweet and bitter fancies. This, madame, is all.

"You know that I neither write nor compose, for the present state of art in Paris makes me both sick and sorry--which proves that I am not dead yet!

"I hope to have the honour of escorting Madame C. F. and a Russian friend of hers to the Theatre Italien to hear Donizetti's *Poliuto*.

"Madame Charton will give me a box.

"Good-bye, madame. May your thoughts be blest, your heart at rest, and your life serene in the assured love of your children and friends. But send a thought sometimes to the *poor child who is unreasonable*.--Your devoted

H. B."

"*P.S.*--It was good of you to send the bride and bridegroom to see me. I was so struck with the likeness of M. Charles to Mademoiselle Estelle that, although such compliments are out of place to a man, I so far forgot myself as to tell him so."

Some time later she wrote:

"Believe me, I am not without sympathy for *unreasonable children*. I have always found the best way to quiet them is to give them pictures to look at.

"I therefore take the liberty of sending you one that I hope, by bringing home the reality of the present, will wipe out the illusion of the past."

She sent me her portrait! My dear lady!

And here I stop.

Now I can live calmly. I shall write, she will reply. I shall see her, shall know where she is, and shall never again be without news of her.

Perhaps, in spite of her dread of new ties, her affection for me may grow slowly and quietly. Already life seems more possible, since the past is not irretrievably over and done with.

No longer is my heaven overcast. My sweet bright star smiles upon me from afar. She does not love me, truly, but why should she? She knows, however, that I love her.

I must find consolation in the thought that she knew me too late, just as I comfort myself for not having known Virgil, Gluck, Beethoven or Shakespeare--who might, perhaps, have loved me too.

(All the same, I am not comforted in the very least!)

* * * * *

Which power raises man the higher? Love or Music? It is a great question. It seems to me that one might say this: "Love cannot give an idea of music, but music can give an idea of love--why separate them?"

They are the twin wings of the soul.

* * * * *

Seeing the conception some people have of Love, and what they look for in Art, makes me liken them to swine rooting in a bed of lovely flowers and among mighty oaks, hoping to turn up with their snouts the truffles for which they are greedy.

I will think no more of Art.... Stella! Stella! I can die now without bitterness or anger.

* * * * *

1st January 1865.

* * * * *

[This is the end of Berlioz' own Memoir. The rest of his life must be gathered from the few remaining letters to his intimate friends and from M. Bernard's short account of his last days.]

XXXVII

THE AFTERGLOW

To HUMBERT FERRAND.

"PARIS, *28th October 1864*.--Dear Humbert,--On returning from my visit to Dauphiny I found your sad letter. You must have had difficulty in writing, yet your young friend, M. Bernard, tells me you are able to go out sometimes, leaning on a friendly arm.

"When first I went into the country my neuralgia was better, but very soon it came back worse than ever, from eight in the morning till four in the afternoon.

"Then, oh! my weariness and troubles of all sorts!

"Nevertheless, there are compensations. Louis is doing well, though our long partings are hard to bear, for we love each other dearly.

"As for the musical world, the corruption in Paris is beyond belief, and I retire more and more into my shell.

"*Beatrice* is to be performed in Stuttgart, and I may go to conduct it. I am also asked to go to St Petersburg in March, but shall not do so unless they offer me a sum tempting enough to make me brave that horrible climate. Then I shall do it for Louis' sake, for of what use are a few thousand francs more to me?

"I cannot imagine why some people have taken to flattering me so grossly. Their compliments are enough to scrape the paint off the walls, and I long to say to them:

"'Monsieur, you forget that I am no longer a critic. I write no more for the papers.'

"The monotony of my life has been broken lately.

"Madame Erard, Madame Spontini and their niece begged me to read *Othello* to them. The door was rigorously closed to all comers, and I read the masterpiece through from beginning to end to my audience of six, who wept gloriously.

"Great heaven! What a revelation of the deepest depths of the human heart! That angel Desdemona, that noble fate-haunted Othello, that devil incarnate Iago! And to think that it was all written by a being like unto ourselves!

"It needs long, close study to put oneself in the point of view of the author, to follow the magnificent sweep of his mighty wings. And translators are such donkeys.

"Laroche is the best--most exact, least ignorant--yet I have to correct ever so many mistakes in my copy.

"Liszt has been here for a week, and we dined together twice.

"As we kept carefully off things musical we had a pleasant time. He has gone back to Rome to play the *Music of the Future* to the Pope, who asks himself what on earth it all means."

* * * * *

"*10th November 1864.*--Can you believe, dear Humbert, that I have a grudge against the past? Why did I not know Virgil.

"I see him dreaming in his Sicilian villa--so hospitable, so gracious.

"And Shakespeare, that mighty Sphinx, impassible as a mirror, reflecting not creating. Yet what ineffable compassion must he not have had for poor, small, human things?

"And Beethoven, rough and scornful, yet blessed with such exquisite tenderness and delicacy that I think I could have forgiven him all his contempt, his rudeness, everything!

"And Gluck, the stately!...

"Last week M. Blanche, the doctor of the Passy lunatic asylum, invited a party of artists and *savants* to celebrate the anniversary of the performance of *The Trojans*.

"I was invited and kept entirely in the dark.

"Gounod was there. In his sweet, weak voice, but with the most perfect expression, he sang '*O nuit d'ivresse*' with Madame Bauderali; then, alone, the song of Hylos.

"A young lady played the dances, and they made me recite without music Dido's scena, '*Va, ma soeur*.'

"It had a fine effect. They all knew my score by heart. I longed to have you there."

* * * * *

"PARIS, *23rd December 1864.*--I have just sent you a copy of *La Nation*, with two columns by Gasperini about *The Trojans* business at the Conservatoire. I did not know of that letter of Gluck. Where the devil did you get it? That is always the way. Beethoven was even more insulted than Gluck. Weber and Spontini share the honour.

"Only people like M. de Flotow, author of *Martha*, have panegyrists. His dull opera is sung in all languages, all theatres.

"I went to hear that delicious little Patti sing *Martha* the other day; when I came out I felt creepy all over, just as if I had come out of a fowlhouse--with consequences!

"I told the little prodigy of a girl that I would *forgive* her for making me listen to platitudes--that was the utmost I could do!

"But that exquisite Irish air, 'The Last Rose of Summer,' is introduced, and she sings it with such poetic simplicity that its perfume is almost enough to disinfect the rest of the score.

"I will send Louis your congratulations; he will be very pleased. He has read your letters and thinks me fortunate in having such a friend as you. Good-bye."

To MADAME ERNST.

"PARIS, *14th December 1864*.--You are really too good to have written to me, dear Madame Ernst, and I ought to reply in a sleek, smooth style, mouth nicely buttoned up, cravat well tied, myself all smiles and amiability. Well, I can't!

"I am ill, miserable, disgusted, bored, idiotic, wearisome, cross, and altogether impossible. It is one of those days when I am in the sort of temper that I wish the earth were a charged bomb, that I might light the fuse for fun.

"The account of your Nice pleasures does not amuse me in the least.

"I should love to see you and your dear invalid, but I could not accept your offer of a room. I would rather live in the cave under the Ponchettes.

"There I could growl comfortably alongside Caliban (I know he lives there, I saw him one day), and the sea does not often come into it; whereas with friends, there are all sorts of unbearable attentions.

"They ask how you pass the night, but not how your *ennui* is getting on;[31] they laugh when you say silly things; are always mutely trying to find out whether you are sad or gay; they talk to you when you are only soliloquising, and then the husband says to the wife, 'Do let him alone, don't bother him,' etc., *etc.* Then you feel a brute and go out, banging the door and feeling you have laid the train of a domestic quarrel.

"Now in Caliban's grotto there is none of this.

"Well, never mind!

"You stroll on the terrace and along the shady walks? And then?

"You admire the sunsets? And then?

"You watch the tunny fishers? And then?

"You envy young English heiresses? And then?

"You envy still more the idiots without ideas or feelings who understand nothing and love nothing? And then?...

"Why, bless you, I can give you all that!

"We have terraces and trees in Paris. There are sunsets, English heiresses, idiots (they are even more plentiful than at Nice for the population is larger), and gudgeon to be caught with a line. One can be quite as extensively bored as at Nice. It is the same thing everywhere.

"Yesterday I had a delightful letter from some unknown man about *The Trojans*. He tells me that the Parisians are used to more *indulgent* music than mine.

"Is not that an admirable epithet?

"The Viennese telegraph that they celebrated my birthday by giving *Faust*, and that the double chorus was an immense success. I did not even know I had a birthday!"

To H. FERRAND.

"PARIS, *8th February 1864*.

"DEAR HUMBERT,--It is six in the evening, and I have only just got up, for I took laudanum yesterday and am quite stupefied. What a life! I would bet a good deal that you too are worse. Nevertheless I mean to go out to-night to hear Beethoven's Septuor; I want it to warm my blood, and my favourite artists are playing it.

"The day after to-morrow I ought to read *Hamlet* at Massart's. Shall I have strength to go through it? It lasts five hours. Of my audience of five only Madame Massart knows anything of the play.

"I feel almost afraid of bringing these artist natures too abruptly face to face with this supreme manifestation of genius. It seems to me like giving sight suddenly to one born blind.

"I believe they will understand it, for I know them well; but to be forty-five or fifty and not know *Hamlet*! One might as well have lived down a coal mine. Shakespeare says:

"Glory is like a circle in the water

Which never ceaseth to enlarge itself

Till, by wide spreading, it disperse to naught."

* * * * *

"*26th April 1865*.--How can I tell you what is cooking in the musical cauldron of Paris? I have got out of it and hardly ever get in again.

"I went to a general rehearsal of Meyerbeer's *Africaine*, which lasted from half-past seven to half-past one.

"I don't think I am likely to go again.

"Joachim, the celebrated German violinist, has been here ten days; he plays nearly every evening at different houses. Thus I heard Beethoven's piano trio in B, the sonata in A, and the quartett in E minor--the music of the starry spheres.

"You will quite understand that after this I am in no mood for listening to commonplace productions praised by the Mayor and Town Council.

"If I possibly can, I will see you this summer. I am going to Geneva and Grenoble.

To LOUIS BERLIOZ.

"PARIS, *28th June 1865*.--I hardly know why I am writing, for I have nothing to say. Your letter troubles me greatly. Now you say you *dread* being captain; you have no confidence in yourself, yet you wish to be appointed.

"You want a home instead of your quiet room; you want to marry--but not an ordinary woman. It is all easy to understand, but you must not shrink from the duties that alone will ensure your gaining your end.

"You are thirty-two, and if you do not realise the responsibility of life now, you never will.

"You need money; I can give you none; I find it difficult to make ends meet as it is. I will leave you what my father left me, perhaps a little more--but I cannot tell you when I shall die.

"In any case it must be ere long.

"So do not speak to me of desires I cannot satisfy.

"I, too, wish I had a fortune. First, that I might share it with you; and next, that I might travel and have my works performed.

"Remember, if you were married you would be a hundred times worse off than you are now. Take warning from me.

"Only a series of miracles--Paganini's gift, my tour in Russia, etc., saved me from the most ghastly privations.

"Miracles are rare, else were they not miracles.

"Your letter has no ending. I feel as if you had suddenly realised the meaning of the world, society, pleasure, and pain.

* * * * *

"*14th July 1865*.--Yes, dear Louis, let us chat whenever we can. Your letter was most welcome, for yesterday life was hideous.

"I went out and wandered up and down the Boulevards des Italiens and des Capucines, until at half-past eight I felt hungry.

"I went into the Cafe Cardinal, and there found Balfe, the Irish composer, who asked me to dinner.

"Afterwards we went to the Grand Hotel, where he is staying, and I smoked an excellent cigar--which, all the same, made me ill this morning.

"We talked and talked of Shakespeare, whom he says he has only really understood during the last ten or twelve years.

"I never read the papers, so tell me where you saw those nice things you quote about me.

"Do you know that Liszt has become an abbe?

"You shall have a stitched copy of my *Memoires* as soon as I get one, but I must have your solemn promise not to let it out of your own hands, and to return it when you have read it."

To M. AND MME DAMCKE.[32]

"HOTEL DE LA METROPOLE, GENEVA, *22nd August 1865*.--Dear Friends,--I only write lest you should think yourselves forgotten. You know I do not easily forget, and, if I did, I could never lose remembrance of such friends as you.

"I am strangely and indescribably agitated here.

"Sometimes quite calm, at others full of uneasiness--even pain. I was most cordially welcomed. They like me to be with them, and chide me when I keep away.

"I stay there sometimes four hours at a time. We go long walks beside the lake. Yesterday we took a drive, but I am never alone with her, so can speak only of outward things, and I feel that the oppression of my heart will kill me.

"What can I do? I am unjust, stupid, unreasonable.

"They have all read the *Memoires*. *She* reproached me mildly for publishing her letters, but her daughter-in-law said I was quite right, and I believe she was not really vexed.

"Already I dread the moment of departure. It is charming country, and the lake is most beautiful, pure and deep; yet I know something deeper, purer, and yet more beautiful....

"Adieu, dear friends."

To MADAME MASSART.

"PARIS, *15th September 1865*.--Good afternoon, madame. How are you, and how is Massart?

"I am quite at sea, not finding you here.

"I have come back from Geneva just as ill as I went.

"At first I was better, but after a little the pain came again worse than ever.

"How lucky you are to be free from such trouble! Having a moment's respite, I use it in writing to you."

"You will either laugh, saying--or say, laughing, 'Why write to me?'

"Probably you would rather that this preposterous idea had not entered my head, but there it is, and, if you find it mistimed, you have the remedy in your own hands--not to answer.

"All the same, the inner meaning of my letter is--to extract one from you. If only you could conceive the frightful impetuosity with which one bores oneself in Paris!

"I am alone, more than alone. I hear never a note of music--nothing but gibberish to right of me, gibberish to left of me. When will you be back? When shall I hear you play a sonata again? I often talked of you in Geneva, where I was petted, spoilt--and scolded a little, too.

"When you come back we will gather together our choice spirits, our good men and true, and read *Coriolanus*. I only really *live* in watching the enthusiasm of fresh sympathetic souls--undeadened by the world.

"I quite enjoyed at Vienne making my nieces cry over it. They are dear girls, impressionable as a photographic plate--which is rather odd, seeing that they have always lived in that most provincial of provinces, among utterly anti-literary people.

"My thick autobiography awaits you, but remember, it is yours only for the time it takes you and Massart to read it. It is very sad, but very true.

"I am quite ashamed that I had not the sense to speak of the many calm, sweet hours I owe to you, and of my deep affection for you both. I have only just noticed that you are not even mentioned.

"Ah, the pain! Madame, forgive me. I can write no more!"

To LOUIS BERLIOZ.

"*13th November 1865.*--Dear Boy,--Your letter has just come, and I want to reply before I go back to bed.

"How I suffer! If I could I would fly off to Palermo or to Nice.

"It is horrible weather. I have to light a lamp at half-past three.

"To-night is our Monday dinner, and as I shall have to get up and go to it, I want to snatch a little sleep first.

"I have had no letter from Geneva, but I did not expect one. When one comes my heart lightens and my spirits rise.

"My poor, dear boy. What should I do without you?

"Can you believe that I always loved you, even when you were tiny? I, who find it so difficult to like little children!

"There was always some attraction that drew me to you.

"It weakened when you got to the stupid stage and were a hobbledehoy. Since then it has come back, has increased, and now, as you know, I love you, and my love grows daily."

To H. FERRAND.

"*17th January 1866.*--I am alone in the chimney corner writing to you.

"I was greatly excited this morning by the manager of the Theatre Lyrique, who has asked me to supervise his intended revival of *Armida.* It will hardly suit his pettifogging world.

"Madame Charton-Demeurs, who undertakes the overpowering role of Armida, comes every day to rehearse with M. Saint-Saens, a great pianist, a great musician, who knows his Gluck almost as well as I do.

"It is curious to see the poor lady floundering blindly in the sublime, and to watch the gradually dawning light.

"This morning, in the Hatred scene, Saint-Saens and I could only grasp hands in silence--we were breathless!

"Never did human being find such expression! And to think that this masterpiece is vilified, blasphemed, insulted, attacked on all sides, even by those who profess to admire it. It belongs to another world. Why are you not here to enjoy it too!

"Will you believe that since I have taken to music again my pains have departed?

"I get up every day just like other people. But I have quite enough to endure with the actors, and, above all, with the conductor. It is coming out in April.

"Madame Fournier writes that a friend she met in Geneva spoke warmly of *The Trojans*. That is good, but I should have done better if I had written one of Offenbach's atrocities.

"What will those toads of Parisians say to *Armida*?"

* * * * *

"*8th March 1866.*--Dear Humbert,--I am answering you this morning simply to tell you what happened yesterday at a great charity concert--with trebled prices--in the Cirque Napoleon, under Pasdeloup.

"They played the great Septuor from *The Trojans,* Madame Charton sang; there was a chorus of a hundred and fifty, and the usual fine orchestra.

"The whole programme was miserably received except the *Lohengrin* March, and the overture to the *Prophet* was so hissed that the police had to turn out the malcontents.

"Then came the Septuor. Endless applause, and an encore.

"The second time it went even better. The audience spied me on my three-franc bench (they had not honoured me with a ticket). There were more calls, shouts, waving of hats and handkerchiefs.

"'*Vive Berlioz!*' they cried. 'Get up; we want to see you.'

"I, the while, trying to hide myself!

"Coming out, a crowd surrounded me on the boulevard. This morning many callers, and a charming letter from Legouve's daughter.

"Liszt was there. I saw him from my perch. He has just come from Rome. Why were you not there too?

"There were at least three thousand people. Once I should have been pleased....

"The effect was grand, particularly the sound of the sea (impossible to give on the piano) at the passage:

'And the sleeping sea

Whispers in dreams her sweet deep chords.'

"It touched me profoundly.

"My gallery neighbours, hearing that I was the author of it, pressed my hands and thanked me.

"Why were you not there?"

* * * * *

"*9th March*.--Just a word added to what I wrote yesterday.

"A few amateurs have written me a round-robin of congratulation. The letter is a slightly altered copy of that which I wrote to Spontini twenty-two years ago about his *Fernando Cortez*.

"Is it not a pretty idea to apply to me what I said to him so long ago?"

To MADAME MASSART.

"*3rd September 1866*.--Such a misfortune, dear madame! This morning--yes, really only this morning--I composed the most clever and complimentary letter to you--a masterpiece of delicate, dainty flattery. Then I went to sleep and--when I awoke it was all gone, and I am reduced to mere commonplaces.

"I will not speak of the boredom you must be suffering in your little card-board bandbox by the sea, lest I should drive you to commit suicide--by no means a suitable way out of the difficulty for a pretty woman!

"Yet, what on earth *are* you to do?

"You have gone the round of Beethoven over and over again; you have read Homer; you know some of Shakespeare's best works; you see the sea every day; you have friends and a husband who worships you.

"Great heavens, what *is* to become of you?

"I do my best to make your sea-side life bearable by not coming near you. Can I do more?

"I ought to be at Geneva, but a cousin of mine is going to be married next week and wants me to be one of his witnesses.

"Could I refuse? One ought to help relations out of difficulties!

"Perrin also wishes me to superintend the rehearsals of *Alcestis*, but he dawdles so, waiting for Society to come back to Paris (as if there were Society for *Alcestis*!), that I am going to leave him stranded and start for Geneva.

"Ah! dear lady, how glorious it is! how grand! The other day at rehearsal we all wept like stags at bay.

"'What a man Gluck was!' cried Perrin.

"'No,' said I, '*we* are the men. Don't get confused.'

"Taylor said yesterday that Gluck had more heart than Homer; truly, he is more thoroughly human.

"And we are going to offer this food for the gods to pure idiots!

"Is Massart shooting, fishing, painting, building, dreaming?

"He has covered himself with glory. His pupils have carried off all the prizes this year; he can wallow in laurels, though he certainly might find a more comfortable bed!

"Here ends my scribble; I press your learned hand."

To HUMBERT FERRAND.

"*10th November 1866*.--Dear Humbert,--I ought to be in Vienna, but the concert is put off. I suppose that *Faust* was not learnt to their satisfaction, and they only wish me to hear it when it is nearly ready.

"It will be a real joy to listen to it again; I have not heard the whole of it since it was performed twelve years ago in Dresden.

"The *Alcestis* rehearsals have done me good; never did it appear so grand, and surely never before was it so finely rendered.

"A whole new generation has arisen to worship.

"The other day a lady near me sobbed so violently that every one around noticed her, and I got crowds of letters thanking me for my devoted care for Gluck.

"Ingres is not the only one of our Institute colleagues who comes constantly; most of the painters and sculptors love the beautiful Antique, of which the very sorrow is not disfiguring.

"I am sending you the pocket-score; you will easily read it and I am sure will enjoy it."

To M. ERNEST REYER.

"VIENNA, *17th December 1866*.--Dear Reyer,--I only got up at four to-day, as yesterday over-did me.

"It would be foolish of me to describe the recalls, encores, tears, and flowers I received after the performance of *Faust* in the *Salle de la Redoute*; I had a chorus of three hundred, an orchestra of a hundred and fifty, and splendid soloists.

"This evening there is to be a grand fete; three hundred artists and amateurs--among them the hundred and fifty lady-amateurs who, with their sweet fresh voices, sang my choruses.

"How well, too, they had been trained by Herbeck, who first thought of giving my work in its entirety, and who would let himself be chopped in pieces for me.

"To-morrow I am invited by the Conservatoire to hear Helmesberger conduct my *Harold*.

"This has been the most perfect musical joy of my life, so forgive me if I say too much!

"Well! this is one score saved at any rate. They can play it now in Vienna under Herbeck, who knows it by heart.

"The Paris Conservatoire may leave me in outer darkness and stick to its antiquated repertoire if it likes.

"You have drawn down this tirade on your own head by asking me to write!

"Good-bye; I have been invited to Breslau to conduct *Romeo and Juliet*, but I must get back to Paris before the end of the month."

To HUMBERT FERRAND.

"PARIS, *11th January 1867*.--It is midnight, dear friend. I write in bed, as usual; you will read my letter in bed--also as usual.

"Your last letter hurt me; I read the suffering between the lines. I wanted to reply at once, but my tortures, medical stupidity, doses of laudanum (all useless and productive only of evil dreams), prevented me.

"I see now how difficult it will be for us to meet. You cannot stir, and for three quarters of the year I cannot either. What are we to do?

"My journey to Vienna nearly made an end of me--even the warmth of their enthusiasm could not protect me from the rigours of their winter. This awful climate will be the death of me.

"Dear Louis writes of his morning rides in the forests of Martinique, and describes the lovely tropical vegetation--the real hot sun. That is what you and I both need.

"Dear friend, the dull rumbling of passing carriages breaks the silence of the night. Paris is damp, cold, and muddy--Parisian Paris!

"Now all is still; it sleeps the sleep of the unrighteous.

"Have you the full score of my *Mass for the Dead*? If I were threatened with the destruction of all that I have ever written, it would be for that Mass that I should beg life.

"Good-bye; I shall lie awake and think of you."

To FERDINAND HILLER.

"PARIS, *8th February 1867*.--Dear Hiller,--You are the best of good friends!

"I will do as you bid me; take my courage in both hands, and on the 23rd start for Cologne.

"I shall be at the Hotel Royal by evening, but do not engage *rooms* for me, one tiny one is enough.

"If I cannot possibly travel, I will send on the orchestral score of the duet from *Beatrice*. It is very effective and not difficult--almost any singers could manage it, provided they were not geese.

"To be sure, we both have an intimate acquaintance with these winged fowl!

"You talk like the doctors. 'It is neuralgia.'

"That is just like Madame Sand and her gardener.

"She told him the garden wall had tumbled down.

"'Oh, it is nothing, madame, the frost did it.'

"'Yes, but it must be rebuilt.'

"'It's only the frost, that's all.'

"'I do not say it is not the frost, but there it is on the ground.'

"'Don't worry about it, madame, the frost did it.'

"I can write no more. I must go to bed."

To H. FERRAND.

"*11th June 1867*.--Thanks for your letter, dear friend, it did me good.

"Yes, I am in Paris, but so ill I can hardly write. Besides, I am worried about Louis, who is in Mexico, and I do not know what those Mexican ruffians may not be up to.

"The Exhibition is turning Paris into an Inferno. I have not been there yet, for I can hardly walk.

"Yesterday there was a great function at Court, but I was too weak to dress and go to it....

"I wrote so far at the Conservatoire, where I was one of the jury in awarding the Exhibition musical prize. We heard a hundred and four cantatas, and I had the very great pleasure of seeing the prize unanimously awarded to my young friend, Camille Saint-Saens, one of the greatest musicians of our time.

"I have been urgently pressed to go to New York where, say the Americans, I am popular. They played *Harold* five times last year with success truly *Viennese*.

"I am quite elated with our jury meeting. How happy Saint-Saens will be! I hurried off to tell him, but he was out with his mother.

"He is an astounding pianist.

"Well! at last our musical world has done something sensible; it makes me feel quite strong, I could not have written you such a long letter were it not for my joy."

XXXVIII

DARKNESS AND LIGHT

To H. FERRAND.

"*30th June 1867.*--A terrible grief has fallen upon me. My poor boy, at thirty-three captain of a fine vessel, has just died at Havana."

* * * * *

"*15th July 1867.*--Just a few words, since you ask for them; but it is wrong of me to sadden you too.

"I am so much worse that I am really hardly alive and have barely sense enough to grasp poor Louis' business affairs; fortunately one of his friends is helping me. Thanks for your letter; forgive my stupidity. I am fit for nothing but sleep.

"Adieu, adieu!"

To MADAME DAMCKE at Montreux.

"PARIS, *24th September 1867.*--Dear Madame Damcke,--I should have written sooner had I known your address, therefore double thanks for your letter.

"My answer is short; I am as ill as usual.

"After my fifth bath at Neris the doctor, hearing me speak, felt my pulse and cried:

"'Be off out of this as fast as you can; the waters are the worst possible for you, you are on the verge of laryngitis. Confound it all, it is really serious.'

"So off I went the same evening and was nearly choked by a fit of coughing in the train.

"My nieces at Vienne nursed me devotedly but, when my throat got better, back came my neuralgia more fiendishly than ever.

"I stayed long enough to see my elder niece married. Thirty-three relations came from all parts to the wedding--but *one,* alas! was missing.

"The one I most rejoiced to see was my old uncle, the colonel. He is eighty-four. We both wept on meeting; he seemed almost ashamed of still being alive--how much more, then, should I!

"I spend most of my time in bed, but the Grand Duchess Helen is coaxing me to get up and go to St Petersburg. She wishes to see me and I have agreed to go on the 15th November and conduct six concerts. Best wishes to you both."

To M. AND MME MASSART.

"PARIS, *4th October 1867*.--Yes, it is quite true. I am going to Russia. The Grand Duchess Helen was here the other day and made me such generous proposals that, after some hesitation, I accepted. I am to conduct six Conservatoire concerts; five of the grandest works of the great masters and the sixth entirely of my own compositions.

"I am to have rooms in her palace and the use of one of her carriages; she pays all my travelling expenses and gives me fifteen thousand francs.

"I shall be tired to death--ill as I am already. Will you not come too? You should play your jovial Bach concerto in D minor and we would enjoy ourselves.

"Three days ago an American,[33] hearing that I had accepted the Russian engagement, came and offered me a hundred thousand francs to go to New York next year. What do you think of that? Meanwhile, he has had a bronze bust of me cast, to place in a splendid hall that he has built over there.

"If I were younger it would please me greatly.

"My mother-in-law thanks you for your kind messages. Are you not ashamed of slaughtering pheasants? It is a noble thing, forsooth, to go out into the poultry yard and kill off the chickens!!! Despite all, my friendship holds good, faithful and warm. Each day I appreciate more thoroughly your loving hearts."

To the Same.

"PARIS, *2nd November 1867*.--How are you, my lord and my lady?

"How is your house?

"Have you forgotten your French?

"Have you forgotten your music?

"Have you forgotten how to write?

"Have you forgotten that you hear of nothing?

"Have you forgotten that we have forgotten you?

"Can you believe that we get on perfectly well without you?

"Can you believe that you are....

"Out of fashion?

"Good-night."

* * * * *

"*2nd November.*--Day of the dead, and, when one is dead, one is dead for a long, long time."

To H. FERRAND.[34]

"*22nd October 1867*.--Dear Humbert,--Here is the letter you asked me to return. Only a line to-day as I took laudanum last night and have not had time yet to sleep it off. I had to get up this morning to do some necessary business.

"So now back to bed. A thousand greetings."

To M. EDOUARD ALEXANDRE.

"ST PETERSBURG, *15th December 1867*.--Dear friends,--How kind of you to send me your news; it seems neglectful of me not to have done the same ere this.

"I am loaded with favour by everyone--from the Grand Duchess down to the least member of the orchestra.

"They found out that the 11th was my birthday and sent me delightful presents. In the evening I was asked to a banquet of a hundred and fifty guests where, as you may imagine, I was well toasted. Both public and press are most eulogistic. At the second concert I was recalled six times after the *Symphonie Fantastique*, which was executed with tremendous spirit and the last part of which was encored.

"What an orchestra! what *ensemble*! what precision! I wonder if Beethoven ever heard anything like it. In spite of my pain, as soon as I reach the conductor's desk and am surrounded by these sympathetic souls, I revive and I believe am conducting now as I never did before.

"Yesterday we did the second act of *Orfeo*, the *C. minor Symphony* and my *Carnaval Romain*. All was grandly done. The girl who sang Orfeo in Russian had an unequalled voice and sang well too.

"These poor Russians only knew Gluck from mutilated fragments, so you may imagine my pleasure in drawing aside the curtain that hid his mighty genius.

"In a fortnight we are to do the first act of *Alcestis*. The Grand Duchess has ordered that I am to be implicitly obeyed; I do not abuse her order, but I use it.

"She has asked me to go some day and read her *Hamlet*, and the other day I happened to speak to her ladies-in-waiting, in her presence, of Saint-Victor's book and now they are all rushing off to buy and admire *Hommes et Dieux*.

"Here they love the beautiful; they live for literature and music; they have within them a constant flame that makes them lose consciousness of the frost and the snow.

"Why am I so old, so worn-out?

"Good-bye all. I love you and press your hands."

To M. AND MME MASSART.

"ST PETERSBURG, *22/10 December 1867*.--Dear Madame Massart,--I am ill with eighteen horse power; I cough like six donkeys with the glanders; yet, before I retire to bed, I want to write to you.

"All goes well here.

"At the fifth concert I want to give Beethoven's *Choral Symphony*, at least the first three parts, I am afraid to risk the vocal part as I am not sufficiently sure of my chorus.

"I have been invited to Moscow and the Grand Duchess permits me to go.

"The gentlemen of the semi-Asiatic capital propound the most irresistible arguments *tace* Wieniawski, who does not wish me to jump at their offer. But I never could haggle and should be ashamed to do so now.

"I have just been interrupted by a message from the Grand Duchess. She has a musical soiree to-night and wishes to hear the duet from *Beatrice*. Her pianist and two singers know it perfectly in French, so I have sent the score, with a message to them not to be nervous as they will get through all right.

"I shall go back to bed. I would tell you a lot more but I am tired out and am not used to being up at such unreasonable hours.

"It is half-past nine. I shall take some laudanum to be sure of sleep.

"You know that you are charming. But why the devil *are* you so charming? Farewell, I am your

H. B."

To the Same.

"18th January 1868.

"DEAR MADAME MASSART,--I found quite a pile of letters on my return from Moscow, among them one that gave me even greater pleasure than yours; you can guess from whom it came.

"Yours, nevertheless, rejoices me too.

"The Michael Square is noiseless under its snowy mantle; crows, pigeons and sparrows stir not; sledges have ceased to run; there is a great funeral--that of Prince Dolgorouki--at which the Emperor and all the Court were present.

"My programme for Saturday is settled.

"Oh! the joy when I lay down my baton at the end of *Harold* and say:

"'In three days I start for Paris.'

"I cannot stand this climate, although I felt better in Moscow. Such enthusiasm there!

"The first concert was in the Riding School and there were ten thousand six hundred people present. And when they applauded the Offertory from my *Requiem,* with its two-note chorus, I must own that the uncommon religious feeling shown by that mighty crowd, went to my heart.

"Do not speak of a concert in Paris.

"If I *gave* one to my friends and spent three thousand francs over it I should only be the more reviled by the press.

"After seeing you I shall go right on to St Symphorien and thence to Monaco to roll in the violets and sleep in the sun.

"I suffer so continually, dear lady; my paroxysms of pain are so frequent that I cannot think what is to become of me.

"I do not want to die now, for I have something to live for."[35]

To WLADIMIR STASSOFF.

"PARIS, *1st March 1868*.--I did not write sooner, I was too ill. And now I want to tell you that I am leaving for Monaco at seven this evening.

"I cannot imagine why I do not die.

"But since I am living, I am going to see my dear Nice, the rocks of Villefranche and the sun of Monaco.

"I hear that the sculptor is having three copies of my New York bust cast; was it you who suggested getting one for the St Petersburg Conservatoire? More can easily be made.

"Address your letters to me to 4 Rue de Calais, Paris, and they will be forwarded.

"Oh! to think that I shall soon be lying on the marble seats of Monaco, in the sun, by the sea!!

"Do not be too severely just to me. Write me long letters in return for my short ones; bethink you that I am ill, that your letters do me good; don't talk nonsense and don't speak of my composing....

"My kindest regards to your charming sister-in-law and daughter and to your brother. I can see them all so vividly before me. Write soon. Your letter and the SUN will give me new life.

"Unfortunate wight that you are! You live in the snow!"

To the Same.

"PARIS, *April 1868*.

"MY DEAR STASSOFF,--You call me *Monsieur* Berlioz, both you and Cui. I forgive you both!

"I was nearly killed the other day. I went to Monaco sun-hunting and, three days after in scrambling down the rocks, I fell head first on to my face and bled so profusely that, for a long time, I was unable to get up and go back to the hotel.

"However, as I had taken my place in the omnibus to Nice, I was bound to get up and go back there next day.

"Hardly arrived there, I wished to see once more the terrace by the sea, of which my recollection was so vivid. I went down and sat there but, in changing my seat, again I fell on my face. Two passers-by lifted me with great difficulty and took me to the Hotel des Etrangers, where I was staying, which was close by. I was put to bed and there I stayed, without a doctor, seeing no one but the servants for a week.

"Feeling a little better after my week's seclusion and damaged as I was, I took the train back to Paris.

"My mother-in-law and servant exclaimed with horror on seeing me; but now I have had a doctor and he has treated me so cleverly that, after more than a month of it, I can barely walk, holding on to the furniture.

"My nose is nearly all right outside.

"Would you kindly find out why my score of the *Trojans* has not been returned. I suppose the copying is finished and that it is no longer needed.

"I can write no more ... if I wait till I am better it may be a long while.... Do write to me. It will be a real charity."

To AUGUSTE MOREL.

"PARIS, *26th May 1868*.--I have been greatly tried and find it still hard to write. My two falls, one at Monaco, the other at Nice, have taken all my strength.

"The traces are almost gone now, but my old trouble has come back and I suffer more than ever.

"I wish I could have seen you and Lecourt when I was near Marseilles; I should have gone round that way had I not been in such a sad state.

"Yet to meet you would have upset me more than to see anyone else. Few of my friends loved Louis as you did. I cannot forget it, so you must forgive me."

To WLADIMIR STASSOFF.

"PARIS, *21st August 1868*.

"DEAR STASSOFF,--You see I leave out the *Monsieur*.

"I have just come from Grenoble, where they had almost forced me to go and preside at a sort of musical festival and to be present at the unveiling of a statue of Napoleon I.

"They ate and drank and did a hundred and fifty other things and I felt so ill....

"They fetched me in a carriage and toasted me, but I could not reply. The Mayor of Grenoble was full of compliments, he presented me with a gilt crown, but I had to sit a whole hour at that banquet.

"Next day I left and arrived home at eleven at night, more dead than alive.

"I feel good for nothing and I get such letters--asking me to do impossibilities. They want me to say nice things of a German artist, which is right enough since I agree thoroughly, but at the expense of a Russian artist of whom I think well also and whom they want to oust in favour of the German.

"I cannot lend myself to it. What a devil of a world this is!

"I feel that I am dying; I believe in nothing; but I long to see you, you might perhaps cheer me up--you and Cui. I am beyond measure bored and weary. All my friends are away in the country or shooting. They ask me to go and visit them, but I have not the spirit.

"Write, I beg; as shortly as you will, but write! I still feel the effects of my Monaco and Nice accidents.

"If you are in St Petersburg write me even *six lines*, I shall be so grateful.

"You are so kind; show it now.

"I press your hands."

Berlioz lived seven months longer.

On returning from Russia he consulted a physician who asked:

"Are you a philosopher?"

"Yes," he replied.

"Then gather all the courage you can from philosophy, for you are incurable."

He was evidently too worn and weak to take the Riviera journey alone.

Although warmly welcomed and cared for at his hotel, his two falls could not but use up his little remaining strength, and that little was cruelly drained by the last journey to Grenoble--a strangely weird and dramatic episode, a worthy conclusion to his stormy, overcast life. The scene is well described by M. Bernard:--

"In a brilliantly lighted hall, hung with magnificent draperies, at a richly spread table a gay crowd awaits the chief guest of the evening.

"The curtains are torn aside, and a phantom appears. The ghost of Banquo? No, the skeleton form of Berlioz, his face pale and thin, his eyes vacant and wandering, his head trembling, his lips drawn in a bitter smile.

"They crowd around him and press his hands--those palsied hands that have so often led the armies of music to victory. A crown is placed upon his silver locks.

"Vacantly he gazes round upon these fellow-citizens, gathered to do him homage--sincere, but how belated!--mechanically he rises to reply to words of which he has hardly grasped the meaning.

"Suddenly a furious Alpine gale dashes down into the hall, tearing at the curtains, extinguishing the lights; outside the squall whistles shrilly, the lightning cuts the blackness of the clouds, casting sinister gleams on the faces of the dumb and startled assembly.

"Alone, amid the howls of the tempest, Berlioz stands, wrapped in flashes of vivid green--the spirit of symphony--colossal musician, whose apotheosis is heralded by Nature with her wildest, grandest music."

That was the end.

On Monday morning, the 8th March 1869, Hector Berlioz died.

His funeral took place on the following Thursday at the Church of the Trinity.

The Institute sent a deputation, the band of the National Guard played selections from his *Funeral Symphony*; on the coffin lay wreaths from the St Cecilia Society, from the youths of Hungary, from the Russian nobles, and from the town of Grenoble.

He was dead--the atonement began.

THE END

Printed in Great Britain
by Amazon

54598633R00142